THE DANUBE AND ITS STRATEGIC LOCATION
SKETCH MAP APRIL 1941, Allied bases Italy 1944 added

USSR

USSR

ROMANIA

The High Carpathians

Odessa

Galati

Braila

Sulina

Ploesti

Iron Gates
Canal

cevo

Craieva

Turnu-
Severin

Bucharest

Constanta

THE BLACK SEA

Brza
Palanka

Giurgiu

Turnu Maqurele

Rustchuk

R. Timok

Vidin

Varna

R. Morava

Nis

BULGARIA

Sofia

Skopje

TURKEY

R. Vardar

GREECE

Istanbul

SEA OF MARMURA

Salonika

TARGET DANUBE

DANUBE AREA FRONTIERS 1938

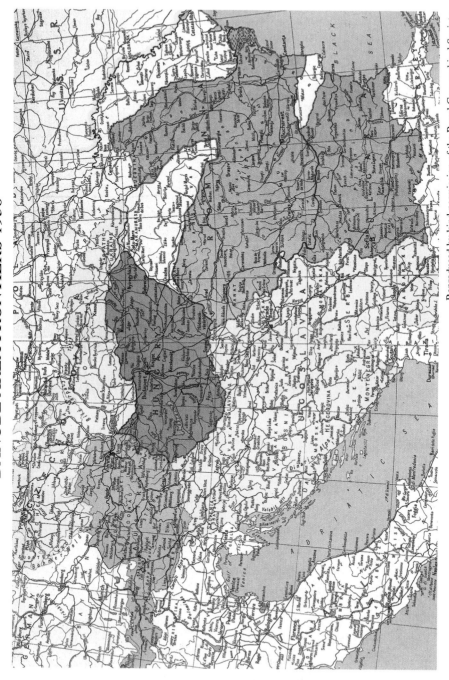

TARGET DANUBE

A River Not Quite Too Far

Alexander Glen
with
Leighton Bowen

The Book Guild Ltd
Sussex, England

First published in Great Britain in 2002 by
The Book Guild Ltd
25 High Street,
Lewes, East Sussex
BN7 2LU

Typesetting in Times by
Keyboard Services, Luton, Bedfordshire

Printed in Great Britain by
Bookcraft (Bath) Ltd, Avon

A catalogue record for this book is available from
The British Library

ISBN 1 85776 643 1

CONTENTS

PREFACE

This book has been a joint effort between Leighton Bowen and myself, a harmonious association which I much appreciated. It is right, however, that the structure is understood and responsibility clear.

Except for Chapter 15, the writing and presentation are mine and if errors have been made, or interpretation of complex events now 60 years ago mistaken, the responsibility is mine. Research of the mass of detailed records at the Public Record Office in Kew and elsewhere has been undertaken by Leighton, a task physically beyond my capacity at 90 with limited mobility, and one he has carried out far better than I ever could.

I must explain something more of the structure of the book. It is necessarily episodic, a good deal consisting of personal reminiscence, and as much or more detailed narrative of events in which I was not directly a party. In the latter part of the book, for instance, my own narrative runs forward in Chapters 10–14, whereas in Chapters 15, 16 and 17 I must ask the reader to step backwards in time.

The subject is one and the same in three aspects: Germany's dependence on Romanian oil products, the Allies' need to cut this supply, and, as war neared its close, the determination of the Soviet Union to control the Balkans and the Danube. Ours is a modest contribution to understanding how events evolved between 1939 and the late 1940s.

Perhaps this may also assist a perspective of the tragic happenings 50 years later in the 1990s. When Britain and the Commonwealth stood alone against the Axis, the Serbian people did not shrink on 27 March 1941. In 1948 Tito was to be the first and only satellite leader to survive a break with Moscow. Yugoslavia gave its people a mainly tolerable life before his death. Fragmentation which then took place was not discouraged by Germany and Austria, and was to produce the fatal combination of Milosovic, overall corruption and Greater Serbian folly. Nor was Croatia innocent under Tudjman and Ustachi fanaticism.

One does not cancel out the other. But, if tomorrow is to be better than yesterday, there must be other objectives than obsession with past wrongs. Indeed there is no lack of immediate problems, moral as well as political, social and economic. Where lies the borderline between legitimate struggle for independence or liberty and terrorism? Can one claim an indefinite extension of human rights for those who planned the attack or destroyed the World Trade Center? Yet attacks of not such a different character in declared wars can be hailed as heroic.

Old age brings no comfort in judgement or in wisdom. The fog of confusion remains as dense, except, perhaps in one clear conclusion. Answers have to be speedy, our civilisations are fragile enough.

Alexander Glen
Stanton, Worcs
May 2002

QUOTES

'To take a brief look back at my career of slaughter on the Danube, the only men I slew with my own hand were, with the exception of those in the German HQ ship, all making violent attempts on my own life.'

— Danube saboteur MICHAEL MASON

'As we went round a long, sweeping bend, there was suddenly no road at all. About 100 metres of it had been demolished and as we came to a sudden stop we saw, ominously at the far end of the gap, a machine gun post. And we were sitting ducks. When we saw three soldiers in long grey coats manning the post suddenly look up startled, we thought our end had come. BUT THEY DIDN'T SHOOT!'

— How Lieutenant-Commander GLEN and Captain FRANKS first met the advancing Red Army

'Statistically, the mining of the Danube became the most effective mining campaign of the entire war. It was also the most economical in terms of aircraft losses.'

— From The History of HMS *Vernon*

AUTHOR'S NOTE

Official documents relating to the war years and the immediate pre-war period show the names of many countries, cities and locales with spellings different from those of today. For instance, Romania will appear, sometimes in the same files, as Rumania, Romania and even Roumania; Yugoslavia as Jugoslavia, with its inhabitants often referred to as Jugs. Similarly, the Romanian oil city of Ploesti became known after the war as Ploiesti.

We have decided to keep the flavour of the war years by retaining contemporary spellings where they appear in official documents etc. Because Ploesti is only referred to in its wartime context, the original version is retained throughout this book.

THE DANUBE

To Johann Strauss, the Danube was a romantic, blue river meandering through eight European countries and three capital cities, Vienna, Budapest and Belgrade.

To his fellow Austrian Adolf Hitler, it was a vital supply artery, carrying, from the Ploesti oilfields in Romania, a third of all his oil and petrol needs to keep his Panzers rolling and his Luftwaffe in the air – plus grain, maize and other vital foodstuffs from the great plains of Romania, Hungary and Bulgaria in cargo ships sailing up from the Black Sea.

The Danube is the largest river in Europe, exceeding the Volga in volume, though not in length. It rises in the Black Forest of south-western Germany and flows 2,850 kilometres (1,770 miles) through central and south-eastern Europe into the Black Sea in Romania.

It passed through eight countries involved in the Second World War – Germany, Austria, Czechoslovakia, Hungary, Yugoslavia, Romania, Bulgaria and Russia – and has long been one of Europe's main water transport arteries, being navigable as far upstream as Ulm in western Germany. It has some 300 tributaries and its delta covers an area of about 2,660 square kilometres (1,000 miles.) The Danube is connected by canals to the Rivers Rhine, Main, Oder and Tisza.

The Allies had managed to block the river for a brief time – and cut off supplies to Germany – during the First World War in 1916. As the Second World War approached, the British and French wanted to do it again. Germany had other ideas...

ACKNOWLEDGEMENTS

To bring together events of some 60 years ago, the small-scale attempts of 1939–41, the period of German control until that was shattered in early 1944 by the Red Army and the Allied Air Assault from Italy, seemed for long an impossible task. To collate with any meaning reports of Special Operations Executive (SOE) missions in the Balkans was unreliable enough; many of us, including myself, lacked knowledge of the peoples concerned or the use of their tongues. Impossible I certainly would have found it, had it not been for the tireless and consistent work of the British Committee for the History of the Second World War. The skill and leadership of Sir William Deakin, the support of Julian Chadwick and Mark Seaman in the admirably-organised Conferences at Cumberland Lodge, St Anthony's, Oxford, and at the Imperial War Museum turned the impossible into a challenge.

I am indebted to so many for the privilege of listening, asking and occasionally questioning. To the likes of David Dilke, the late John Erickson, Maurice Pearton, Michael Foot, Hugh Verity, and to those of many nations who lived and fought under Occupation.

It was the author of *Behind the Battle* and of *Ultra and Mediterranean Strategy 1941/1944*, Dr Ralph Bennett, who persuaded me that the Danube was a story which should be told. My dear friend Joan Bright Astley, with her long first-hand experience and never-flagging enthusiasm, added conviction. Mark Wheeler played his part in revealing much of the Belgrade activities in the early years, as did Julian Amery. But it was an unusual figure in those dire black months, a loner, brave, undefeatable, Michael Mason, who left in me a determination that here was something that must not be forgotten.

Much has been derived from talks with Michael and his son

David years afterwards. Also, I am indebted to Sir Peter Garron and to some personal papers on the political events in Belgrade in Spring 1941 which he entrusted to me. The then Director of Naval Intelligence, Admiral J.H. Godfrey, also played such an influencing role on so many of us, not only in the wartime team he had chosen so brilliantly, but later, too, in the regular meetings of the 36 Club with the likes of Admiral Denning, Pat Beesly, Peter Smithers and Ian Fleming.

With the old and newer Yugoslavia, Fitzroy and Veronica Maclean remain a centre, both in Korcula and Strachur. A careful source has been Vladko Velebit, Foreign Minister of his own country, Deputy Director General in the United Nations and Ambassador in London. We owe much to other friends: the Orecanins, one-time Partisan Commander in Croatia and also Ambassador in London, and his lovely wife, who later had a distinguished career in her own right. To my wife's cousin, Olga Humo and her husband Avdo, to the wisdom and friendship of Vladimir Bakaric when Prime Minister of Croatia, who saw so clearly the dangers ahead, to Tempo, who shared these same fears. Friends with whom there was a trust forged in the earlier bad times and who in no way merited the tragedy which was to destroy their country.

I must add a word of appreciation to others who interpreted in a different sense, wartime events in Yugoslavia. Not only those such as Colonel Bill Bailey, Jasper Rootham and Erik Greenwood, who remained loyal to Mihailovic in the most wearing of circumstances, but also to the Nora Beloffs and Michael Lees who mercilessly pursued their cause. I believe that in their conclusions they were mistaken in the context of their time, but in their sympathy with the predicament in which Mihailovic and his Cetniks were locked, there is much to be pondered and understood. Civil and religious war test loyalties beyond human capacity.

The Allies' effort to reduce or sever Romanian oil supply reached its climax only as late as 1944. The onslaught on the Ploesti Oilfield and the aerial mining of the Danube by MASAF could not be described in any adequate way were it not for Colonel Patrick Macdonald's own research. From his discovery, when Defence Attaché in Bucharest of the small cemetery with its USAAF and RAF graves derived his tireless enquiry into the men and machines engaged in this major campaign by the Western

Allies, coinciding with land operations of the Red Army.

In compiling personal recollections of our time with the Red Army, I wish to emphasise the remarkable kindness and care which as junior officers we experienced from senior commanders with much more important responsibilities. Admiral Sir John Cunningham, Air Marshal Sir John Slessor and Air Vice-Marshal George Baker were inspiring masters to serve. In trying to record accurately these somewhat hectic weeks with the Red Army, I am apprehensive as to my memory of a time when diaries or note-taking was rarely advisable. It has been a great relief on submit-ting my version of events to our then colleague, Captain Dickie Franks (now Sir Richard Franks KCB), to receive back from him not a host of corrections but the contrary.

In the Bibliography are the many books and other publications, official and otherwise, from which Leighton Bowen and I have benefited so greatly. Our thanks go to all, to the Naval Historical Branch, the Imperial War Museum, especially the Public Records Office at Kew, and to the co-authors of the History of HMS *Vernon*. Very sincerely, to my old friends in the Royal Geographical Society for the maps.

Lastly, but certainly not least, to our publishers, the Book Guild at Lewes. Compared with my experience long years ago of London publishers, with friendly parties at the Saville and long lunches, things seem somewhat different these days, unless one is a bimbo or aged under 20. I may be an indifferent writer, cer-tainly an old hack, but a story is a story and should have its merit. So the approach of the Book Guild was all the more re-freshing, the encouragement of Mrs Carol Biss and her colleagues so welcoming. I am all the more grateful to my old friend Leslie Jackson for having made this introduction.

Nor must I forget that had my wife Zorica not produced with the magic of Paul Daniels a replacement car in the small town of Niksic 61 years ago last April, this book would not have been written, more vital, not one of our party would have had much chance of survival.

The authors and publishers wish to thank the following for their kind permission to reproduce extracts in this book: Constable and Robinson Ltd for *Athenee Palace* by Countess Rosie Waldock;

HarperCollins for *Between Silk and Cyanide* by Leo Marks; Patrick Macdonald for *Through Darkness to Light* by Patrick Macdonald (published by Images Publishing Ltd); Macmillan for *The Macmillan Dictionary of the Second World War* by Elizabeth-Anne Wheal and Stephen Pope; David Mason for *One Man's War* by Michael Mason; The Orion Publishing Group for *Canaris* by Andre Brissaud (published by Weidenfeld & Nicolson); Oxford University Press for the *Oxford Illustrated History of the Royal Navy*; The Random House Group Ltd for *Wartime* by Milovan Djilas (published by Martin Secker and Warburg); Sutton Publishing Ltd for *Radar: A Wartime Miracle* by Colin Latham and Anne Stobbs.

1

The Danube: Germany's Achilles Heel

The Second World War was a war of massive, speedy movement on land, at sea and in the air, greedy for fuel, ever dependent on oil for swift deployment, for reinforcement of defences or preparation and build-up of forces, to improvise against the unexpected or to switch attack.

For the western Allies, the Atlantic lifeline was throughout a matter of life or death, as was oil from Abadan for forces in the Middle East. Survival of the Soviet Union would not have been possible had the move of industry across the Urals not been achieved on such a massive scale, for in no way could the hazardous sea route from factories of the West have made up the balance. For Germany, it was a river, the Danube, which provided the principal means of bringing to their forces, and to their industrial heartland, the vital oil products from the Ploesti fields in Romania.

The strategic importance of the Danube to Germany was clear enough to the planning staffs in London and Paris. Even more, it was a priority in Berlin, not only in its direct context, but in that of the political inclination of the Riparian States through which this 1,700-mile waterway flowed.

In the 1920s and 1930s, the Danube was administered by an Allied-controlled Danube Commission and this may have led some to complacency in London and Paris. That is not to say consideration was not given by the British and French to means of impeding Danube supplies to Germany in the event of war. However, the practical means of doing so bore no comparison with the preventative measures established by Germany in the late 1930s.

In September 1939 – when Britain and France declared war on

1

Germany after the invasion of Poland – this Danube story began as a cat-and-mouse scenario in which a vigilant, powerful Nazi cat, which had already devoured Austria and Czechoslovakia, had Hungary and Bulgaria in its claws and was fast extending control in Romania, as described in Chapters 3 and 4.

Yugoslavia, and also Romania, however, were still open to Allied activities. At that time these had something of a mouse-like character, uncertain as to what their masters in London wished, beset as they often were in Whitehall by tribal warfare.

How this situation was to change and develop over the next four years is the subject of this book – to change with many vicissitudes, with failures and triumphs, small and large. Thorough as were the early defensive activities of the Germans, they were to make their mistakes, the enemy is not infallible.

There were strange coincidences, too, in these tangled years of covert and secret operations, of political scheming, of initial enemy success turned into implacable resistance, temporary stale-mate and ultimate defeat.

Usually, there is a key moment of change. In the case of the Danube, the key was the Allied capture of southern Italy during Autumn 1943, when the provision of airfields on the Foggia Plains brought the Balkans and southern Germany within range of over-whelming attack by air. At last the Ploesti fields would be within range of the Allies' heavy bombers and the Danube open to the kind of aerial mining operations that were already proving suc-cessful elsewhere in occupied Europe.

However, this was late in the war. The Allied landing in north-west Europe was planned for Summer 1944 and the Red Army could reach the Balkans at the same time. To weaken Germany's defences by reducing materially her oil supplies from Romania required not only Italian bases but an aerial Armada. Could this be built into an effective striking force speedily enough, remem-bering that the mining operations demanded close Air Force and Naval co-operation both in the design and supply of the mines themselves?

There was a further question of the highest political as well as military significance: cooperation with the Soviet Union to ensure operational compatibility within the region, including their pos-sible need of the Danube as a supply route for their Armies.

How these questions developed is the subject of Chapter 10

and Chapter 13 onwards. Suffice to say at this stage that the 15th United States Army Air Force and 205 Group of the Royal Air Force were consolidated into the Mediterranean Allied Strategic Air Force (MASAF) under the command of General Ira C. Eaker.[1] This was effective by January 1944 when Air Marshal Sir John Slessor[2] became Deputy Air Officer Commander-in-Chief MASAF with Air Vice Marshal George Baker[3] as his senior air staff officer (SASO). Theirs was to be the responsibility for the night mine laying operations by 205 Group and in liaison with the Royal Navy Commander-in-Chief Mediterranean, Admiral Sir John Cunningham.[4]

Such was the speed of planning and the cooperation between all services with HMS *Vernon*,[5] the Torpedo and Mining Establishment in the UK, that this massive operation was in readiness in the first quarter of 1944, two and a half months before D-Day in Normandy. Was this to be enough?

In recounting now these events of around 60 years ago, I feel fortunate in having been involved in the partially abortive sabotage activities in Romania and Yugoslavia in 1940/41 as well as the operations in 1944. The latter provided an opportunity, shared by few, to be with the Red Army in its advance through the Balkans, to witness its speed and tactics, its command structure and its men, as set out in Chapters 13 and 14.

Coincidence certainly had a long arm in what was my somewhat eccentric career in the Royal Navy Volunteer Reserve (RNVR). Its beginning was in 1936 after I led a 14-month Oxford University Expedition to North East Land, which won for each of its members the white-ribboned Polar Medal. The scientific programme included continuous 24-hour research on the ionosphere, successfully completed to the satisfaction of Professor Edward Appleton FRS.[6]

What I did not know then was the relationship between this work and the highly secret development of RADAR, or RDF,[7] as it was then known, by Appleton and Professor Robert Watson Watt.[8] After our return to the UK, Professor Appleton was giving me lunch one day at the Athenaeum when I mentioned, quite casually, that two German naval officers had visited our base just before we left North East Land.

Appleton went very white. 'You didn't show them anything of our work, did you?'

'No,' I replied, 'I tried to but they were not interested, all they wanted to see were our maps.'

'I think we had better go straight to the Admiralty and have a talk with the Assistant Director of Naval Intelligence,' said Appleton. In charge of security was a Colonel Royal Marines, Archie Craig, calm but very shrewd. 'Tell him exactly what happened,' Appleton instructed and, with visions of a life in the Tower of London, I did.

There was a long pause and I counted the minutes. 'Hm,' said Craig at long last, 'I don't think we should worry too much. Agents can be over-concentrated, looking only for what they have been told to and missing the unexpected nugget.'

This led, through Archie Craig, to an acquaintance with the Naval Intelligence Division (NID). I redeemed, maybe, something by helping with information needed on a possible U-boat base on Saseno, that island at the entrance to Valona in Albania. A Balliol friend, Sir Anthony Jenkinson was sailing his boat in the Adriatic and quite simply sailed her into Saseno, was entertained by the Italian commander and given a royal tour of the island.

Not so appreciated was another venture to determine some German activities on the coast of Mexico by another friend, Ivan Sanderson, when a cutting-out party mistook a midnight Mass as their target, the sequel now I hope well forgotten.

I was formally commissioned into the RNVR in 1938 and mobilised in May 1939 for meteorological duties under Admiral Sir John Edgell, whose patience in guiding a brash young man into the Navy I shall never forget. A little later, however, NID intervened and in December 1939 I was summoned by the Director of Naval Intelligence (DNI) Admiral John Godfrey.[9] His orders were simple: 'Cause havoc on the Danube by any means.'

But this first interview with the DNI did not start on a particularly promising note.

'I'm sending you to Belgrade as assistant to Captain Despard,[10] the Naval Attaché there,' said the Admiral.

'Thank you, sir,' I stuttered, racking my brains for some recognition of Balkans territory. 'I am very interested in ... mmm ... Romania, sir.'

'Well, that ought to stand you in good stead in Yugoslavia,' said the Admiral, displaying the slightest suspicion of a smile. 'Captain Despard is Naval Attaché with rather wide duties. Spend a few days in the Section and find out which country is which. The Danube is our interest and both countries may be key.'

There were differences enough between Yugoslavia and Romania, as Chapter 2 recounts, but less known in Whitehall was the scale of protection of their interests by Germany, as set out in Chapters 3 and 4. Nor at that time could I guess the other responsibilities which were to be offloaded onto me by organisations, then unknown to me, over the next 18 months in Belgrade, as described in Chapters 5 to 9.

'Assistant *to the* Naval Attaché' was quickly altered to 'Assistant Naval Attaché', providing diplomatic cover for these additional duties. The months of 1940 until Spring 1941 were to offer in Belgrade an inspiring experience of a people who, at least in Serbia, seemed impervious to disaster. They would reveal rather different impressions in Romania, so in frequent visits to Bucharest, Sofia and Istanbul some understanding of the Balkans and their problems began, slowly, to take shape.

It was the Danube, however, that was our responsibility. If, as the following chapters show, there was to be more frustration then than success, the experience was salutary, at least in the longer term, when the reality of warfare replaced earlier wishful thinking.

2

Yugoslavia and Romania

I arrived in Belgrade station on a cold and frosty morning in January 1940, to find an old Balkan city, with a long history against the Turks, the Austrians and the Germans, a people simple still in their ways, but warm and friendly.

There was still the bustle of horse-drawn peasant carts, the clanging of trams and the occasional traffic policeman, whose concern was more the slow rate of traffic than its speed.

With a population in the whole of Yugoslavia then estimated at around 16,500,000, the Serbs were the largest section, with the Croats well behind but substantially ahead of the Slovenes.[1] Table 2.1 shows how the population was made up. Serbs, Croats and

Table 2.1 Composition of Yugoslav Population, 1940

Serbs	6,600,000
Croats	4,000,000
Slovenes	1,353,000
Macedonians	924,000
Bosnian Muslims	870,000
Volksdeutsch	710,000
Albanians	700,000
Hungarians	500,000
Montenegrans	412,000
Romanians	100,000
Gypsies	100,000
Italians	100,000
Jews	78,000
Bulgarians	50,000

6

Slovenes seem at first glance the constituent elements. However, within these three were causes enough of discord, religious, cultural and historic, the long and bitter enmity between the Catholic and Orthodox Churches and between both of them and the Muslim faith. More, much more, lurked below the surface – dark and dangerous forces.

Montenegrans and many Macedonians might feel themselves as strongly fellow Slavs as the Serbs themselves, but Hungarian and Romanian minorities did not; nor did the Albanians, or Volksdeutsch. Yugoslav in name they might be, but the chance of job or career scarcely existed. It was not that they were deprived – they simply did not belong.

In Bosnia and the south of the country, poverty was extreme. Old women bent double with the firewood they were carrying home were a familiar daily sight; Serbian police bore down heavily on anyone not enjoying full civil rights. And that is not to suggest that Serbs, Croats or Slovenes who disagreed with the regime or its politics were immune themselves.

Formed in 1920 out of the breakup of the Austro-Hungarian Empire, the new Kingdom of the Serbs, Croats and Slovenes was an attempt under the Versailles Treaty to reduce fragmentation by encouraging the three constituents to concentrate a common Slav kinship in a potentially viable Slav state, strongly orientated toward Paris and London. In this, Dalmatia joined with its ancient Venetian traditions, unwilling to accept Italian in place of Austro-Hungarian rule. The new state became Yugoslavia, an independent monarchy under the Serbian Karargeorgevic Dynasty with Belgrade its capital.

In those early years the new kingdom was greeted with some enthusiasm, certainly by the intellectuals in Zagreb, Ljubljana and, not the least, those Serbs who believed their efforts for the Allies in the First World War had been rewarded and their dream of a Greater Serbia achieved.

Factions were to erupt soon enough, encouraged and supported especially by Italy and the Catholic Church. But Yugoslavia developed into the leading Balkan land in the early 1930s, with a powerful army making it a key member of the Little Entente, with which France and Britain hoped to maintain a balance of power in central and southern Europe. This, in turn, made Yugoslavia still more of a target for its enemies in Italy and

Hungary. A result was the assassination of King Alexander in Marseilles by Hungarian-trained Ustachi[2] terrorists in 1934.

Italian policy towards Yugoslavia, their neighbours across the Adriatic, was consistently hostile. In the years after Versailles they did everything short of war to frustrate the new Yugoslavia and used their Italian enclaves in Zara and Fiume, on the Dalmatian coast, to infiltrate propaganda and terrorists. They were aided consistently by the Croat Ustachi Nationalists.

Germany, however, courted Yugoslavia with patience and diplomacy, a policy engaged in through most of the 1930s. By 1939, their commercial and financial influence, while not as great as that of France, the major western player in Belgrade, was nevertheless substantial. The Yugoslavs had justifiable respect for Germany's military capabilities, especially for aerial attack. Despite the restrictions of the Versailles Treaty, by the mid-1930s, Hitler had built up his formidable Luftwaffe. On 18 January 1938 the Yugoslav Prime Minister paid a friendly visit to Juterborg-Damn and was shown the II/JG 132 'Richtofen' squadron of new 'wonder-fighters', the Messerschmitt Bf 109D. The Luftwaffe were ready to fly![3]

The Germans seemed content during most of 1940 to work towards reducing the influence of Paris and London and guiding Yugoslavia towards a degree of neutrality more favourable to Berlin. Britain had been a minor player in Belgrade, almost a traditional role, allowing France the larger initiative and influence. Both London and Paris were equally concerned with maintaining Italian neutrality. This continued until the collapse of France and the entry of Italy into the war in June 1940. From that time, Britain suddenly found a new, unexpected and increasingly responsible role in Belgrade.

With Hitler's occupation of France, many Yugoslavs rediscovered their innate dislike of Germany and intensified their utter contempt for Italy. Support from the people and many political leaders in Serbia, but not in Croatia, swung behind Britain, by then the only western country still defying Hitler.

Members of the proscribed Communist Party, however, were not among Britain's supporters, taking the view that the war was an imperialist struggle of no interest to them.

If in Croatia and parts of Bosnia divergent political aspirations and student involvement were threatening the overall structure of

Yugoslavia, there were strengths elsewhere. Slovenia had a certain commercial good sense of its own. Serbia, however, retained its own robust peasant character, men who never had been serfs, who owned and worked their own land; men and women who did not know an aristocracy, and who never allowed it to be forgotten that they had won their own independence from the Turkish Empire.

As one crosses the Danube from Yugoslavia into Romania, one enters a country totally different in ethnic background, socially and culturally. In the first century AD, the legions held the north banks of the Lower Danube as the frontier of the Eastern Empire. Trajan built the first great bridge over the river at Turnu Severin and it was from Vidin that the Romans concentrated their forces to destroy the Dacians. The Romanesque origin continued in language and in culture, with the growth of powerful families who, when the Turks threatened in the fifteenth and sixteenth centuries showed themselves in no way squeamish in their methods of defence, as they did again later against Tartar bands. As the centuries rolled on, so their estates became greater and their homes more magnificent, especially in Transylvania and Moldova with great good taste reflected in the quality of the architecture as well as in regional art.

It was in the turmoil of the '48' uprisings in central and eastern Europe that the Romanians in Transylvania took action for self-determination and recognition of a Romanian nation, but after an inconclusive struggle, Vienna retained control by the Empire. Although a Greater Romania through the union of Transylvania, Wallachia and Moldova had to await the end of the First World War in 1918, in 1861 an unlikely event took place in the choice of a Hohenzollern Sismaringen as king of the smaller Romania, Carl the First. A dreary and dull character, as was his son and successor Ferdinand, the monarchy was to be enlightened by their consorts, Queen Elizabeth and Queen Marie, respectively – vibrant, beautiful, eccentric certainly, but, especially Marie, with devoted friends the world over.

The make-up of the population (see Table 2.2), taken from the most reliable 1938 figures, showed how the native Romanians dominated.[4] This was indeed a cosmopolitan society. Great names such as the Stirbeys, the Cantacuzino, the Brancoveanu and the Bibescos, to name but four, amassed great wealth and vast possessions.

Table 2.2 Composition of Romania's Population, 1938

Romanians	12,840,000
Hungarians	1,400,000
Volksdeutsch	750,000
Ukrainians	730,000
Jews	728,000
Bulgarians	366,000
Gypsies	260,000
Turks	177,000
Gagaus	100,000

Bucharest itself had long been a centre of Latin culture, language and fashion. Certainly, it was the most beautiful and most civilised city in Eastern Europe; it was also the most wicked, where one never knew who was in bed with whom. As Dudley Heathcote observed: 'the rouge of the women and the Officers would turn the Black Sea red'.

Of those on the land, many were effectively serfs in fact, if not in name, except perhaps in the wilder parts of the High Carpathians, where shepherds had to fare not only against the extremes of climate, but against marauding wolves and bears as well. They were tough folk, indeed, which made it difficult to accept the view that the Romanian army were a sorry lot. It may then have been officered by a flimsy lot of cocktail-party heroes, but there was a reality of courage and tenacity that the years ahead were to reveal at Stalingrad with the Wehrmacht.

In this last year of the 1930s and first half of 1940, the Athenee Palace Hotel in Bucharest, as Countess Waldock aptly described it, combined both theatre and a cast of elegance and high drama. Old worlds and new were the players, spies of every persuasion spied upon, to their confusion, the appeasers for one side or the other, appeased by the lovelies who fed upon them and spilt the lot as their paymaster, whoever he might be, had ordained. To be enjoyed, certainly, we as the others were young enough. To be understood, for all the evidence was there in the lobby of that great and lovely hotel, was more difficult. After all, Romania was our ally, to be protected by treaty from German attack, her oil fields to be destroyed for us, together with the

10

Romanian forces, as planned; the Danube also to be closed to Axis use in other joint operations with our Romanian friends. Of the sincerity of those friends, I do not doubt. For at that time they had much to ponder, with France and Britain far distant. Nor were we showing ourselves particularly effective protecting close neighbours, such as Norway or Denmark, when under attack.

Was Germany inevitably Romania's enemy? After all, a New Order in Germany was not wholly unpalatable, perhaps even to others than the Iron Guard. So where lay the true threat to Romania? From that long northern frontier with the Ukraine, from Soviet Russia, from a Communist menace to all who owned the land and wealth of Romania. This was rational enough and there were not a few in Britain, and more in France, who would have shared these thoughts. But there was a German-Soviet pact. This confused the issue, even if there were those perceptive enough to appreciate its artificiality and certainty that one or other would breach the pact when opportunity was ripe. None the less, would it then be prudent for Romania to play the British along for as long as possible (for France no longer had to be considered), and become amenable to German approaches for safeguarding her interests within Romania?

This is precisely the policy Romania adopted. They probably underestimated the scale and speed of these German measures and, if they did, it was too late; for Germany, as we shall see, was already in control. What is surprising is the extent to which this was missed by both the Secret Intelligence Service (SIS) and the Foreign Office, as the following chapters will describe. It is also strange that, with the personal relations Britain enjoyed with so many influential Romanian families, as well as the large British contingents in the Romanian oil companies, suspicion was not alerted. The latter, after all, had experience of what nearly happened in 1916, but lack of intelligence and a happy innocence prevailed with consequences that were drastic.

The same British connections were nowhere near as pronounced in Belgrade. But I was to learn that the quality of the Legation staff was second to none. It was against this background that I joined forces with the formidable and colourful Captain Max Despard DSC, RN, the British Naval Attaché to Belgrade and Bucharest. I was to discover Despard had his fingers in many pies...

3

British and German Secret Operations in the Balkans

Economy in defence in all its aspects had been British policy until the mid-1930s and even then reluctance to face dangers immediately ahead persisted. Few suffered more than the Secret Services. The close affiliation of the SIS with Naval Intelligence, so outstanding in the First World War, did continue to a reducing but still effective degree. The SIS in 1939 brought off one of the decisive coups of the war, with the help of the Poles and the French: possession of the German Enigma machine. Without it, the speed of success at Bletchley Park[1] could have been very different and the U-boat war against the North Atlantic convoys might not have been thwarted.

Possible subversive operations had been given scant resources, no doubt because enemy control of north-western Europe appeared unthinkable. All the more credit is due accordingly to two officers: Section D of the SIS was formed as a result of the persistence and imagination of Lieutenant-Colonel Lawrence Grand[2] and Military Intelligence (Research) (MI(R)) of the War Office by Colonel Joe Holland.[3] These departments remained separate until July 1940 when they were absorbed into the new Special Operations Executive (SOE).

Interference with the supply of oil and iron ore to Germany was of particular concern to Section D and MI(R). The Danube was key in the Germans' reliance on the Romanian oil fields. Sweden, which is not the subject of this book, supplied its high quality iron ore shipped down the Norway coast from Narvik or across the Baltic from Oxelosund. Destruction of the Ploesti oil fields and disruption of Danube traffic were accordingly priority aims, to be planned in cooperation with executives of the British oil companies in Romania, then deemed a secure ally of Britain and France.

What was overlooked, as already stated, was that Romania's most feared enemy was not Germany but Russia. Britain and France were far distant. As reassurance, Romania had little option but to play a crafty game involving secret and, in the event, far-reaching negotiations with Germany.

The SIS and the Foreign Office either missed or underestimated this. Just as the security of North Atlantic supply was vital to Britain, so to Germany were Romanian oil and the Danube supply route. Each, in its own way, was a life-or-death priority! In Germany's case, this was acted upon with the difference that defence spending, including intelligence, had been an absolute priority with Hitler since he came to power. The Abwehr, the German military intelligence service run by Admiral Wilhelm Canaris,[4] were well equipped to 'protect' the Romanian oil industry and the navigational channels of the River Danube, notably the Iron Gates, the narrow canal link through which river craft had to be guided by experienced pilots. The Abwehr's Section II (sabotage and security) responded with typical German precision and expertise.

On 13 April 1939 Britain and France guaranteed Romania's frontiers against German aggression, an arrangement that suited the Romanians without committing themselves to hostility against Germany. When the crunch came, the Romanians were going to be on the side that would guarantee them against Russia, be it the Allies or Hitler. In August 1939, plans for destroying the Ploesti oil fields by MI(R) and Section D were agreed by the then Major Colin Gubbins[5] with the Romanian General Staff. Liaison in Bucharest was with Romania's Colonel Leonida and the British Military Attaché, Lieutenant Colonel McNab.[6] Operational liaison was given to Romania's Major Radulescu and Major Davidson-Houston, a sapper officer who arrived in Romania in July 1939.

It looked as if the British and French had Ploesti well under control and that, at a stroke, they would be able to deny the Luftwaffe, Kriegsmarine and the Wehrmacht their essential oil supplies. It was not that simple! Firstly, could Romania's King Carol be trusted? Having abolished political parties, he exercised a royal dictatorship, assisted by a Cabinet drawn from the previous leaderships. He took charge of foreign affairs himself and nominated ministers of varying views and interests. Thus, when there was a Cabinet presided over by Armand Calinescu its policy tended towards Britain and France; when under Ion Gigurtu, it could safely reckoned to be pro-German. In the background was the Iron Guard, Romania's own Fascist party, a constant threat to internal stability. King Carol had cracked down on the Iron Guard leadership in November 1938, leaving them waiting for the opportunity to wreak their revenge.

In September 1939 – the month Britain and France declared war on Germany, only a month after Romania had agreed plans with Britain and France to deny Germany oil from Ploesti, and only a few months after publicly proclaiming that in the event of an invasion by Germany or Russia or both they would themselves destroy the oil fields – King Carol announced that Romania was adopting a policy of neutrality. In the same month, King Carol informed the German Air Attaché, Colonel Alfred Gerstenberg[7] that a British plan to sabotage the oil fields had been submitted and he had rejected it. In the same month, too, Admiral Canaris began to take a particular interest in the Abwehr's Romanian operations, establishing a close working relationship with his counterpart in Bucharest, Colonel Michael Morusov, head of the Serviciul Special de Informatii (SSI), in a series of meetings beginning in Venice.[8]

Later in September 1939, Canaris visited Bucharest accompanied by high-ranking Abwehr officers Colonel Erwin Lahousen[9] and Colonel Egbert von Bentivegni[10] to organise the Brandenberg Regiment's special security units in plain clothes to be in key positions along the Danube, especially around the Iron Gates cataracts and the huge Giurgiu terminal and marshalling yards, as well as in the Ploesti oil fields themselves.

This security operation and its deployment of large specialist forces by Germany which so frustrated British plans, was not known to London at the time or, indeed, for some time after the war. Canaris, of course, had the advantage over the British in that he did not have to deal with third-party countries or complicated logistics. All he needed was to bring the Romanians into line. To consolidate this, in October 1939, he despatched Lieutenant Colonel Erich Pruck to Bucharest for talks with Colonel Morusov, aimed at reaching an agreement whereby the Abwehr undertook to 'look after' all supply routes to Germany.[11]

With the ink barely dry on the British-Romanian General Staff plan to deny Ploesti oil to Germany, members of the Abwehr undercover unit, the Brandenburg Regiment, in plain clothes, were positioned in key port and transport activities. As cover, they posed as employees of the Danube Shipping Company. Soldiers, again in plain clothes, policed transport routed through Hungary. The main detachment set up camp near that most vulnerable part of the Danube, the Iron Gates Canal, while 250 Brandenburgers moved to the Bulgarian port of Russe, opposite the main Danube oil terminal at Giurgiu. There they posed as members of a Reichsbund Sports Group and could be seen improving their boating skills up and down the Danube.

Admiral Canaris himself spent four days in Bucharest in November 1939, cementing his personal relationship with Colonel Morusov and clinching an agreement by the Romanian SSI chief to a strict surveillance of refineries and power installations in the oil fields and at river terminals.

In addition, Morusov also agreed to report all foreigners' movements to the Abwehr and remove 'undesirable elements' from oil companies, especially the Shell subsidiary. Canaris then appointed a Major Dr Wagner as his Bucharest link with Morusov and infiltrated an agent into the security section of the Romanian General Staff.

Spreading the Abwehr tentacles even wider, Canaris recruited officers in the upper echelons of the Siguranta, the secret police, whose job at that time was surveillance of Communists, Jews and Hungarians. These officers were the 'Vertrauensmaenner', native Romanians, specifically not including ethnic Germans, on whom the Abwehr relied for its 'illegal' operations, as opposed to those concerted formally with Morusov. Additionally, there was the support of the 'Alarmbereitschaft', an organisation of ethnic Germans and of Reichsdeutsche (German citizens) employed in Romanian industry throughout the country. Their tasks included providing information and assistance to German officials about political developments in their localities and keeping registers of political, military or economic enemies of the Reich.

With its activities in the oil fields also co-ordinated by the German Consul in Ploesti, a Gestapo officer (the British had no consular posts in the oil area), Canaris had in place by 1940 a wide and powerful network of German surveillance in readiness to counter any Allied moves. By then, too, the Romanians themselves had improved their own surveillance of Ploesti. A number of accidental fires in refineries in December 1939 gave the Romanian government the opportunity to station two infantry divisions there, commanding an area of about 40 by 20 miles. The British remained innocently relaxed about this. Romanian troops would pose no problem if the sabotage plan endorsed by the Romanians in August was to be put into place. Only if the Romanian government were to look favourably towards Germany would the Romanian force become a threat to their plans.

The truth was that this decision lay no longer in the hands of Romania but very firmly in those of Germany, as a result of the patient and thorough preparations of the Abwehr and of Canaris personally. Germany had been accepted as the one potential protector of Romania against Russia.

Back in London, that first autumn of the war saw leisurely realisation of the dangers ahead. A Ministry of Economic Warfare was set up under Conservative MP Ronald Cross[12] as its Minister and Treasury mandarin Sir Frederick Leith-Ross[13] as its Director General. No great initiative was apparent from the top but its membership was in time to show the mettle of younger men such as Hugh Gaitskell[14] while in the wings, hungry for office, was the patrician Labour member, Dr Hugh Dalton (see notes, Chapter 5).

Section D and MI(R), however, were already at work, both in carrying through with the Romanians the plans for Ploesti, and with the Admiralty in regard to the Danube. In all, three major operations were intended and were, in fact, attempted. However, the joint agreement between the British and the Romanians to deny Ploesti production to Germany, finalised in August 1939, was quickly shown as it went into operational planning to be a logistics nightmare. Physical occupation of the vast production areas by a British field force, even with supportive Romanian forces, would be essential, and was a virtual impossibility, as the Military Attaché, Colonel McNab, correctly assessed.

Nonetheless, Commander R.D. Watson, RN, arrived a few weeks later to take command in Bucharest itself and Major G.A. Young, of the Royal Engineers, proceeded to Egypt to form the field force and its onward transport to Romania, if and when ordered. An advance party of four RAF officers and radio operators (to receive and transmit intelligence) would present little difficulty. They could – and, indeed, eventually did – travel in civilian clothes by train, through Palestine, Lebanon and neutral Turkey to Istanbul. Moving the field force and its equipment, in terms of transport, at that time was quite another matter. They could go by sea or air, or a combination of both. Three routes were possible: the first by sea to Istanbul, with transfer to airfields in Thrace from which RAF 'Bombay' troop carriers would fly to Ploesti, arriving three days after leaving Alexandria. Secondly, the troops could be ferried by air, with stopovers in Greece or, preferably, Turkey, effectively two days in each case. The third proposed route would be by ship from Alexandria to Constanta or Galati and then by motor transport to Ploesti.

Greece excepted, the routes required the acquiescence, if not the positive cooperation, of the Turkish Government. Aircraft would need to land and refuel; a ship would have to go through the Straits, or at least into the Sea of Marmara. Both courses of action had to comply with international treaties, interpretation of which gave Turkish negotiators ample room for manoeuvre. The Turkish government proved willing to turn a blind eye to flights in Turkish air space, provided they looked suitably civilian, and was even prepared to allow refuelling on Turkish soil. But they maintained that the number of flights required to move the company in the aircraft then available would be impossible to conceal and would allow the Germans to intervene or claim political compensation for breach of neutrality. Because of this, the air route was dropped in favour of travelling by sea.

Two merchant ships were chartered, one bringing some of the equipment that was required. By then events within Romania had already frustrated any prospect of success and events outside were having an even more devastating impact. Britain's failure in Norway in March, April and May 1940, on land, in the air and, even more despairingly, at sea, to combat German aggression against a friendly neighbour convinced even the most loyal that it was time for reflection. Any thoughts of a field force introduced from Egypt had evaporated!

In short, Britain failed in political intelligence to assess Romanian priorities and in military intelligence to perceive the comprehensive protective measures that the Abwehr, in conjunction with the same Romanian agencies with whom the British believed they were working, had established. The Germans had made a clean sweep! As for the hapless British field force training in Egypt, at least some of its equipment did get through to Romania in the SS *Fouadieh*, ending up in a mountain artillery depot between Ploesti and Brasov. That this included an army Bible, a darts board, three hockey sticks, some Arabic grammars and packets of toilet paper, and that for a whole day the trucks had stood unguarded in the market-place at Ploesti, must have hoisted local bewilderment, if not Britain's reputation. As the memoirs of the unfortunate officer in charge, Major Davidson-Houston revealed: 'The toilet paper at least was seized and put to use as office stationery'.

In those dire days of Spring 1940, a major naval venture against the Danube was perhaps the last thing one might expect. Despard, however, had certainly not forgotten the years of the First World War when British gunboats, such as HMS *Ladybird* and HMS *Gnat*, ruled the Danube and even snatched to safety the last empress of the Austro-Hungarian Empire from the Red forces of Bela Kun. Whether Section D remembered those great days is not known, but they shared Despard's determination for a Hornblower-style exploit.

On 29 March the SS *Mardinian*, out of Liverpool, berthed at Sulina. She carried 68 Royal Navy officers and ratings, with Commander A.P. Gibson, RN, in overall command, and cargo, including 65 cases invoiced as Chrysler spares and addressed to their agent in Bucharest. The Royal Navy personnel were immediately dispersed, contrary to Romanian regulations, into river craft. Customs cleared the cargo, encouraged by the £1,500 'sweetener' provided by Despard, which was then handed on to a group with a distinctly non-Romanian but rather an RN look, including a certain Michael Mason, of whom much more will be heard later.

So far, so good, with 30 tons of arms loaded onto a lighter, the *Termode*, including three Vickers machine-guns, limpet mines and a selection of explosives. Other craft, all flying the Red Ensign, joined in to sail in convoy as a commercial enterprise. By then, not unexpectedly, they had come under the scrutiny of the Brandenburgers.

From the Black Sea to Braila, the Danube was under the jurisdiction of the Romanians and Commander Gibson's first objective was to negotiate this initial 110 miles of waterway without raising the suspicions of Romanian officials – and certainly not giving the local German presence cause to put pressure on the Romanians to investigate anything suspicious.

Above Braila, the river was under the regime of the International Danube Commission, on which British and French representatives continued to sit, offering some hope of protection. The flotilla of lighters, barges and tugs left Sulina on 1 April 1940. They were not alone; shadowing them astern was a river steamer hastily chartered by the Abwehr. The flotilla arrived at Giurgiu, where the tugs had to refuel, on 3 April, still not alone. By this time, Giurgiu already had a strong German military and security presence, with enough influence over the port captain, Drencianu. In Romanian maritime administration, these port captains were key officials, whose power to interpret regulations, not only those of the port administration and Customs authorities but also those of the National Bank, effectively controlled all shipping operations.

They were political nominees (as Maurice Pearton says, 'disinterested bureaucracy was unknown in the Balkans'), they were not well paid and, within broad limits, they were able to set their own agenda. The agenda of Giurgiu's port captain, Drencianu, was decidedly pro-German.

Unexpectedly, Gibson's flotilla was ordered to be searched, this at the instigation of the port captain, urged on by Major Dr Wagner, Admiral Canaris' link with the Romanian Secret Service, on the grounds that it had not been cleared through Customs. Drencianu, who was related to Admiral Pais, the Romanian Minister of Marine, also delayed giving permission for the British tugs to go to the oiling berth, about four miles from the port, for 36 hours. This gave time for the Giurgiu officers to carry out a thorough inspection of the main tug, where they found uniforms, arms and the equivalent of £500 in the local currency, lei. The arms and money were impounded.

The British Legation immediately made representations to the Romanian authorities in Bucharest, and orders came through to the Giurgiu officials to desist. They returned the impounded items and Commander Gibson thought the incident closed. It was not! Another sudden inspection on 5 April revealed the nature of the cargo on the *Termonde*. It did not help that one of the cases still had attached the official label, 'Demolition explosives'.

There followed a complex struggle between sympathetic

officials in Bucharest and their pro-German subordinate officers in Giurgiu. This only ended when Fabricius, the German Minister in Bucharest, overcame the helpful obstinacy of Gafencu, Romania's Foreign Minister, by threatening to stop further delivery of arms from Germany to Romania if the flotilla was allowed to proceed. This argument was referred to King Carol and, not surprisingly, the King decided in favour of Germany.

The flotilla was ordered to return to Braila and their cargo to remain in Giurgiu, though with the promise that, Romania being neutral, the British could have access to their property later. No legal charges were levelled.

The ships arrived at Braila on 10 and 11 April and were then directed to Sulina for repairs and strengthening for a sea voyage to Istanbul. This was protracted by bureaucratic delays and the need for Admiral Pais' permission to sail, which had to be negotiated separately for each vessel.

In the second week of May, events in Europe were exploding. Hitler's armies moved against France and the Low Countries and Britain was suddenly alone. Romanian sympathies switched decisively towards the Germans.

So, by the time the flotilla, though still unprepared for a sea voyage, left Sulina by individual units at the end of May, not only had the overall strategic situation altered but the local backdrop too. Romanian and Yugoslav delegates, under pressure from Germany, had persuaded the International Danube Commission to rule that the only armed vessels allowed on the Danube were to be those of the Riparian States (those whose banks bordered on the river) and then only in their own sectors of the river. Further, that the Commission's permission was required for every transit of arms and explosives. In consequence, the Romanian authorities blocked the Danube at Sulina, controlling entrance to and exit from the river. German forces took over at Constanta. As far as Britain was concerned, the Danube was shut!

The SS *Mardinian* was too late, the planning, without appreciation of the thoroughness of enemy control in Romania, was a failure. But in it was something redeeming, too. Michael Mason and others involved were to play their parts, minor perhaps, but not to be discounted. And in the time and circumstances of planning SS *Mardinian*, there is another element which should not be overlooked. This was the even more hazardous Operation Rubble, planned by the Admiralty, the Ministry of Economic Warfare and the MI(R) in Sweden – the successful cutting out in Gothenburg, by Commander Sir George Binney, DSO, RNVR,[15] and the sailing to the UK of four fast Norwegian cargo liners loaded with precious ball bearings.

Operation Rubble succeeded, SS *Mardinian* failed; one wins some, one loses others!

4

Canaris Shapes Romania to his Design

By July 1940, Germany had occupied France and the Low Countries, as well as Norway and Denmark, while her control of the Danubian States of Austria, Czechoslovakia and Hungary had been extended to Romania, in fact if not in name.

On 28 June, Russian tanks entered Bessarabia, an event that incurred as great alarm in Germany as it did in London. At his daily conference at the Berghof the following day, Hitler took General Jodl[1] aside to express his fears that the Russians might attack the Romanian oil fields which the Führer described as 'vital to the German war effort'.

German reaction was immediate and substantial: two armoured and ten infantry divisions were deployed protectively in south-west Poland against this eventuality. This proof of German intent and ability to protect Romania against Russian aggression further enhanced the influence of Admiral Canaris. At a security conference in Vienna later, on 3 September, this led to important talks between Canaris and Colonel Michael Morusov, head of Romania's SSI, when they stayed at the Hotel Danieli in Venice.

The account of that meeting, as given by André Brissaud[2] is of unusual significance in explaining the internal political developments within Romania between Spring and September 1940. These culminated, on 6 September 1940, in the abdication of King Carol in favour of Prince Michael and the appointment, two days earlier, of General Ion Antonescu as Prime Minister.

Their meeting-place was 100 yards from the Doge's palace, looking out on the island of San Giorgio, on 3 September – the first anniversary of the British and French declaration of war on Germany.

As Brissaud describes it:

They discussed the serious discontent that was evident in Rumania after the Vienna tribunal had awarded a large part of Transylvania to Hungary. King Carol knew that his throne was insecure and on 4 September he dismissed Gigurtu and named General Ion Antonescu as Prime Minister.

On hearing this Canaris asked Morusov what he thought of General Antonescu and he replied: 'The King may think he has saved the situation. I cannot think of a more unhappy choice. Antonescu represents nobody, neither a party nor a political idea. The army refer to him as the red dog. He was no more than a bandit chief in 1919. He hates the King and holds him responsible for everything that has gone wrong in Rumania. The King asked me to arrest him early this year and shut him up. I would have liked to have eliminated him altogether.'

'Can there be a compromise between the generals and the Iron Guard?' asked Canaris.

'King Carol is making use of the Iron Guard with the idea that the compromise cannot last for long and that he will emerge as the arbiter of power.'

Events went even more swiftly than Morusov had predicted. Antonescu held a conference with the three main parties: Juliu Maniu of the National Peasant Party, Dinu Bratiano of the Liberal Party and Horia Sima of the Iron Guard. The three Party leaders refused him their cooperation as long as King Carol retained power. The walls of Bucharest were plastered with posters accusing King Carol of murder and every imaginable crime against his country. When Antonescu informed the King of their views, Carol realised that he must abdicate. The terms that he made included safe passage to the West for himself and his mistress Magda Lupescu, and permission to take with him the collection of pictures in Sinaia Palace as well as the royal treasure. Fearing a *coup* by the Iron Guard, Antonescu accepted all these conditions and the King declared in favour of his heir Prince Michael, aged nineteen.

The royal train loaded with treasure left Bucharest on 6 September and arrived in Yugoslavia scarred by the parting shots of the Iron Guard.

On the evening of 7 September Canaris and Morusov emerged from the Hotel Danieli and walked along the St Mark canal, pondering over the dramatic events in Rumania. They made their way along the crowded pavements, sunset colouring the domes and spires of Venice, and sat down for a drink at the Cafe Florian. Morusov was still talking about Antonescu.

'He's not what you would call a Germanophile. He was a military cadet at St Cyr, don't forget. He was one of the group of Rumanians who worked with General Berthelot and the French mission in Bucharest. He was Military Attaché in London for years and a close friend of Nicolas Titulescu when Titulescu was ambassador there. He is no friend of Germany, but he will have to work within the framework that King Carol left behind him.'

Canaris came out of his reverie and asked: 'Do you believe that the arrival of the German military mission can upset him?'

'We are dealing with a man whose power has no basis and who imagines that his own will-power can suffice to keep the country on the path that he has chosen. This is one reason why I am going back tomorrow to Bucharest.'

'From what you tell me, I have some fears for your personal safety.'

'Do not worry. Antonescu needs me. I am the only one who knows what precautionary measures you and I have taken for the oilfields. I am the only one who knows how to run the Security Service and works in collaboration with the Abwehr. No, I must go home.'

Canaris, who did not find Morusov entirely congenial, hesitated and then said: 'Well, Morusov, if you change your mind and decide not to go home you may be assured of my protection.'

'My sincere thanks, Admiral. I will go home tomorrow as I have already decided. We have a lot to do together in Bucharest.'

They walked back towards the Hotel Danieli and dined at the Taverna dei Dogi on seafood with a Verona wine that Canaris especially liked, their last dinner together. On his return to Berlin, Canaris found a message awaiting him from the Abwehr in Bucharest. Morusov had been arrested on his return to Rumania by the Chief of the Gendarmerie, Aurel Tobescu. He was in Jiliva prison, and Colonel Eugene Christescu had been appointed as his successor. The Admiral reacted in a characteristic way: he set out at once for Bucharest with the idea of speaking to Antonescu on Morusov's behalf. He felt under an obligation to the prisoner, who had worked closely with the Abwehr, though Canaris knew that he had also worked closely with the Soviet Intelligence Service.

Canaris was received by General Antonescu and explained to him Germany's interest in Morusov as a man who could help further foil British sabotage attempts in Rumania. He even added that Hitler had shown an interest in his welfare. Antonescu assured Canaris that nothing disagreeable would happen to Morusov, whose arrest had been an exceptional measure, and that he would soon be released. Canaris was reassured, and after some routine work at the Abwehr office in Bucharest and with the Germany military aid mission, he returned home.

Shortly after this visit, Canaris heard that Morusov had been brutally murdered in Jilava prison with a score of other prisoners, apparently by legionaries of the Iron Guard. He expressed a harsh opinion to his staff of Antonescu, whose assurances he had accepted in good faith, saying: 'I wish to have nothing further to do with a man of that sort.'

The first six months of 1940 had seen the collapse of the original agreement between the Romanian and British governments for collaboration in destroying, or at least reducing, the output of oil from the Ploesti oil fields, as a result of Romania's deliberate decision to renege. The scale of German security throughout the country, including the Danube, had also resulted in the failure of the SS *Mardinian* operation.

London had not given up, however, even in these direst of circumstances, and in June 1940 a third major operation was planned – the capping of the oil wells with cement and steel, to be undertaken by the companies themselves, aided by a number of demolition experts posing as oil technicians. This joint project between the companies themselves and MI(R) agents, was to be authorised at a final meeting on 26 June – for action the next day – in the guesthouse owned by one of the biggest companies, Astra Romana, in the Transylvanian hills not far from Ploesti. Every step, however, had been under observation by the Abwehr and it would be difficult indeed to set out what transpired more accurately than in Canaris' own description. He is very understanding of the British predicament which, as a professional, he understood so well:[3]

To the Russian threat [Bessarabia], Hitler reacted quickly by a direct proposition to Stalin defining their respective limits of interest in Rumania, after which he demanded 90 per cent of Rumanian petroleum production for Germany. The Rumanian Government accepted this ultimatum.

The British took the only possible decision, that this 90 per cent flow of oil to Germany must be stopped. The oil companies brought new personnel from Britain and Rumanian officials were astonished at the numbers that these reached. The Head of the Abwehr in Bucharest was not hoodwinked; he thought that the new arrivals looked more like British officers in plain clothes than oil technicians. Their free use of money in Bucharest gave him the impression that these men belonged to the Secret Service.

A German lieutenant of the Brandenburg Regiment, seconded to the Ploesti oilfields, reported in July 1940 to his Abwehr Chief in Bucharest that the British were sending to their Middle East headquarters plans of all the oil installations in Rumania. On the following day, the heads of the oil companies were asked to take part in a secret conference organised by the British Intelligence Service. A code word had been agreed for action in which the wells would be blocked with quick-setting concrete and steel plates.

The Abwehr passed on this information to the Rumanian Security Service. On the following morning, on board a steamer in the port of Constanza, Colonel Morusov's men seized the Astra Romana Company's consignment of maps and plans for the oilfields consigned to Alexandria. Lahousen and the Head of the Abwehr Group in Bucharest meanwhile mustered and armed their agents from the Brandenburg Regiment and infiltrated them into the oilfields. They were carrying explosives bearing British marks of manufacture.

The British secret conference was being held [probably on 26 July 1940] in the Transylvanian foothills not far from Ploesti, at the guest-house of the Astra Romana company. The British Intelligence Service had taken every precaution and had brought in men specially from London, co-opting the managers and technical directors of the oil companies on the spot. The plan was to increase deliveries of petrol in the immediate future, so that the suspicions of the Abwehr and the Rumanians would be allayed. The sabotage operation itself would be synchronised to the minute, but about three days would be needed before the concrete set hard in the wells. Businessmen who had worked for twenty years in Rumania on oil production found themselves in the sad position of planning to destroy their life's work. There was a tense atmosphere in the oil company guesthouse.

The British Colonel in charge of the operation told the meeting that ships were ready to embark all British personnel, but that evacuation orders were only to be issued at the last minute. He added: 'The operation begins at 9am tomorrow.' At this moment a watchman entered, breathless, and said: 'The Rumanians are here.'

For the first time the Rumanian police were taking action inside the Astra Romana concession. Captain Stefanescu and half a dozen Rumanian officers burst in on the bewildered British. Stefanescu bowed and said: 'I am sorry but Colonel Morusov orders me to make a search here.'

'Here?' exclaimed Page, the Technical Director of Astra Romana. 'What for?'

'We are looking for contraband explosives.'

The British burst out laughing but Stefanescu and his men remained serious and began a room-by-room search of the guesthouse. In every room there were packages of explosives and crates of revolvers, rifles and sub-machine guns of British manufacture.

'Those damned Germans!' exclaimed Miller, the Director-General of Astra Romana, who had guessed at the conspiracy between the Abwehr and the Rumanian Security Service. Despite an energetic protest from Sir Reginald Hoare [in fact Sir *Rex* Hoare], the British Minister in Bucharest, the Rumanians did not relent, expelling all British oil personnel from the country. The Abwehr men occupied the oilfields to await the arrival of German technicians.

On 26 July Ion Gigurtu, the Rumanian Prime Minister, discussed with Hitler at the Berghof the future of the Rumanian oil industry and the possibility that Rumania would nationalise it. Germany would succeed to the British and French shareholding in the oil companies and precautions would be taken to ensure against sabotage of the wells. Germany would provide a military mission to assist in training and equipping the Rumanian army. As to Hungary's claims on Transylvania, Hitler decided that these would best be submitted to arbitration, which took place on 30 August when a German-Italian tribunal decided in favour of Hungary.

This signalled the end of British operations against Ploesti, and in much of Romania, although one move, initiated in June, should not be forgotten. It was an order by Admiral Sir Andrew B. Cunningham, Commander-in-Chief, Mediterranean Fleet,[4] to study the possibility of mining the Danube using naval aircraft. It was found to be impractical then because of the limited range of available aircraft and the lack of suitable mines, but the Admiral insisted that the possibility be kept under review.

It was to be three and a half more years before that situation would be ripe...

5

Summer 1940: Europe and London

When the war began, Britain's defences, lean enough in themselves, were spread worldwide, from Singapore to the western hemisphere, the entire Mediterranean from Suez to Gibraltar, with responsibility also for the defence of India and Australasia. Germany's defences, on the other hand, were more concentrated within Europe, her essential supplies, particularly from Romania and Sweden, within close range.

Less than a year later, in mid-1940, Germany was in control (more accurately in occupation of) most of Europe, from Norway to Czechoslovakia, from Poland to France. With the rail and road facilities this provided, she could move forces speedily and efficiently from east to west or north to south in what, effectively, was one operational theatre. In contrast, Britain had to contend with movement by sea, long enough when the Mediterranean was open, but grievously more consuming of shipping when routing was around South Africa, with the further compounded danger of U-boat attack.

Was this German military triumph all that it appeared to be – effective control of most of Europe? Were other elements of Nazi policy capable of eroding this success? Administration of occupied territories represented a huge challenge in civil government, if civil is a word that can be applied to a country already set on ethnic cleansing of Jews and others deemed inferior by their Aryan masters.

In short, neither the SS nor the Gestapo were likely to win support or sympathy, nor did they do so in conjunction with local collaborators. Resistance, passive at first but active also, especially in Poland and Czechoslovakia, quickly took root. In those countries it was part of life over long centuries of oppression. In

Norway and France, it was to be something new and all the more inspiring for that reason.

This resistance would demand a source of supply and direction, guidance and encouragement. Without Britain, it would have perished. But Britain survived the appalling disasters of the Spring and Summer of 1940 to continue as the heart and source of resistance elsewhere.

Dunkirk, unquestionably, had been a turning point: the saving of more than 300,000 British and French fighting men had galvanised a nation and victory, despite huge cost, by the Royal Air Force over the Luftwaffe in the Battle of Britain, secured the essential base for ultimate victory.

If in the early months of the war lethargy had been the character of the government's handling of affairs, Winston Churchill changed that speedily. Especially important were decisions on policy concerning active operations, of any and every kind, into enemy-occupied Europe. Not only in individual sorties or specific sabotage, but in the understanding that in the occupied lands were men and women capable of providing, when the moment was propitious, forces strong enough to wreak havoc on the enemy.

The flow of those escaping, first from France and Norway, always including, somehow, Poles and Czechs, gave the first evidence of how men's minds were moving, how powerful human courage and determination could be in the blackest of circumstances. They were listened to!

Structurally, Section D, still a part of SIS, and MI(R) were already in action. They had a record of some successes and some failures, too. But they lacked status; engaged on sabotage or subversion, they were a threat to the intelligence responsibilities of the SIS. The solution was their amalgamation into the new Special Operations Executive (SOE) in June 1940, designed to be independent of traditional military thinking, but with full paramilitary powers, a civilian director-general its own government minister with senior status and, crucially, its own Budget.

That this was not welcomed in several quarters was soon evident. The Foreign Office, as sponsoring department for the SIS, had its reservations; the Treasury, too. The Admiralty was supportive. As Ralph Bennett in his excellent work *Behind the Battle* pointed out, the Naval Intelligence Division, in its highly imaginative selection of staff, was one Whitehall department ready and capable of a wider vision, including turning material from Bletchley Park into operational use immediately it began to flow. The War Office seemed relieved to be rid of a responsibility while the Air Ministry was disinterested except when aircraft were required.

The new coalition government – with Clement Attlee[1] as Deputy to Winston Churchill and Lord Halifax[2] and Ernest Bevin[3] as respectively Foreign Secretary and Minister of Labour – included Hugh Dalton,[4] a Socialist Old Etonian, hungry for action but too often dismissive of those who worked with him. Particularly determined that interference with oil supplies to Germany should be a first priority, and well informed on the subject after making it his business while an Opposition front bench spokesman, Dalton was SOE's first minister. It was he whom Churchill exhorted to 'set Europe ablaze'. Dalton was to prove a bonny fighter for the SOE and its independence over this next delicate 12 months against what was excessive interference from the SIS and a sceptical Foreign Office.

Sir Alexander Cadogan[5] was said by some to express the view of not a few of his Foreign Office colleagues in his comment: 'Set Europe ablaze, more bloody likely to set London ablaze'. However, other figures were emerging who had no illusions as to the military might of Germany or the need to discard old habits of war and speedily apply new ones. Foremost among these was General (later Field Marshal) Sir Alan Brooke,[6] at that time in command of home defences but six months later to be appointed Chief of the Imperial General Staff (CIGS) and, in June 1942, Chairman of the Chiefs of Staff Committee.

He was vividly clear about the importance of operations within occupied Europe and of the potential that they contained. He knew and had a high opinion of Gubbins who had organised and commanded the Independent Companies.[7] In General Brooke, the SOE had certainly an influential supporter. He was a soldier whose contribution to victory in the Second World War was second to none.

The SOE's first head, known as D, was Sir Frank Nelson,[8] to be joined shortly by a deputy, Harry Sporborg[9] who was to serve Nelson and his successors, Sir Charles Hambro[10] and the future Major-General Sir Colin Gubbins with quiet skill and utter dependability. Sporborg had been a partner in the well-known and appropriately-named firm of City solicitors, Slaughter and May, and as such was responsible for bringing into the SOE a number of distinguished colleagues from the world of law who were to prove themselves just as formidable in the world of secret warfare.

From MI(R), the SOE inherited officers as experienced as Peter Wilkinson,[11] already distinguished by his work in Poland and with the Polish underground, and the then Major Gubbins previously responsible for liaison with the Czech army in exile.

It was Colonel Hutnik, the Czech Chief of Staff who, as early as January 1940,[12] brought an early project of sabotage against Danube shipping to the attention of Gubbins and Wilkinson. If this operation did not proceed with the speed which Wilkinson intended, it may be that there was some conflict in those early days with Section D's activities directed by the somewhat sinister but Balkan streetwise Julius Hanau (codenamed Caesar)[13] in Belgrade.

Those early weeks were not easy for Dalton. He had fallen out with Lawrence Grand, who had hoped to be director of the new subversive organisation, a job for which he was indeed well qualified. It proved an ill-mannered dispute, the damage reduced by the diplomatic skill of Gladwyn Jebb[14] who had been released by the Foreign Office to act as special adviser to Dalton.

Viscount Halifax's subsequent appointment as Ambassador to the United States in Washington DC was also a blow to Dalton, as the Viscount, rather surprisingly, had been supportive of the Minister of Economic Warfare and the latter's future relations with the new Foreign Secretary, Anthony Eden[15] were to be distinctly fraught.

An essential change, however, had been secured in the overall conduct of the war. The SOE was now formally in existence with the authority to undertake operations of a subversive and covert character in enemy-occupied territory, whether those operations be short, sharp exercises or of long-term duration. The SOE was charged with the responsibility for the design and supply of equipment and there was to be growing independence in the sensitive and important area of communications. Indeed, the SOE was to make a fundamental contribution in the security of codes, largely due to the relentless concern to the integrity of existing and new systems by their young coding officer Leo Marks[16] and his chief, Brigadier F.W. Nicholls.[17] Perhaps as important as anything, SOE had its own budget, its own money to spend.

As Autumn 1940 approached, it was clear that little, if anything, could now be achieved in Romania. Yugoslavia was still neutral, however, as were Greece and Turkey, while in the north, Sweden had maintained its neutrality. However, work into the occupied countries of Europe was intensified and high dividends were to result in due course, especially from Norway, France and Denmark.

6

Yugoslavia, 1940: That Brave, Unlucky Land

When Glen arrived in Belgrade in January 1940, it was still three months before war in Europe erupted with the German invasion of Norway and Denmark. An atmosphere of phoney war still prevailed and the natural warmth and welcome of the Serbs made those early months deceptively enjoyable and reassuring.

French and British were held as the natural allies and friends of Yugoslavia and, to a newly-arrived young Scot, the complexities which the country might conceal were unknown. Particularly moving was the continuing regard for all that the Scots and English nursing missions had done in the 1917 typhus epidemic. As a naval officer, it was also good to be told of Admiral Troubridge and his exploits from the bitter days of the 1916 retreat of the Serbian armies through Albania.

The team in the British Legation were welcoming and not patronising, in the way professional diplomats could be at that time. Ronnie Campbell, the minister, known as Little Ronnie to distinguish him from his immediate predecessor of the same name, was another Scot, a bachelor, quiet and determined but approachable by the likes of us, still young and brash. Terence Shone was then councillor, to be succeeded by Armine Dew, later killed in the York crash on the way to Yalta. A young Australian, Peter Garron, was Second Secretary, with a distinguished career ahead of him. He brooked no nonsense but was always constructive; one learned much from him and he became a lifelong friend.

Those first weeks I saw little of Captain Max Despard, the Naval Attaché, who was mostly in Bucharest on activities of which I then knew nothing. Hugh Macdonald, the Air Attaché,

34

made me welcome and invited me to share his office; Charlie Clark, the Military Attaché and yet another Scot, was equally hospitable but had his own office which was rather carefully guarded. Both Macdonald and Clarke had built close links with the Yugoslav Air Staff and General Staff respectively.

Accordingly, I was left rather to my own resources, partying most nights with the Americans, Belgians and Greeks, and with new Yugoslav friends. It was a bit bewildering as to what my own duties were, and all rather heady stuff. It was only when a still younger Balliol undergraduate, Julian Amery[1] more or less appointed himself Assistant Press Attaché and we decided to set up in a flat together that I began to guess that there was far more complexity and potential pitfalls in the affairs of Yugoslavia than I had been told in Whitehall.

Yes, one knew that the Kingdom of the Serbs, Croats and Slovenes had been created less than 20 years before at Versailles, embracing major parts of the former Austro-Hungarian Empire; yes, one knew this had later been changed to Yugoslavia, the land of the South Slavs under King Peter and then his son King Alexander, murdered in Marseille in 1934 by the Ustachi; yes, one knew that the Serbs had been the first to win freedom from the Ottoman Empire in the first Balkan war and that centuries back there had been a great battle at a place called Kosova with consequences, not unlike Bannockburn, of lasting emotional impact.

But no, I knew nothing of the Fracture Zone, that northwest/south-east divide from the Krajina that had separated western from eastern culture over the centuries; of the bitter tension and hate between the Church of Rome and the Orthodox faiths. Nor was I aware of the complexity within Bosnia and Herzogovina – not essentially ethnic, for a Muslim could be as Slav as his Orthodox Serb or Catholic Croat neighbour, but division just as bitter and the oppressed as heartless as the oppressor.

In the Sanjakas, over the border in Montenegro, old memories of Turkish rule tangled with more recent ones of no less harsh Austrian administration. Sadly, Ivo Andric had not then written his brilliant and enlightening *Bridge over the Drina*, or one might have sensed the proud legacies of the Ottoman Empire, of exquisite taste in architecture and the arts, still cherished in precious memory by Muslim families.

35

If only an Andric or a Steven Runciman had been there, so much would have been clearer then and later. True, Rebecca West had not failed in giving a hint of darker forces (Albanians conveniently known as Arnauti) and of Greater Serbian aspirations. Enlightenment was to be a slow process, not least in understanding that the wrongs of the past transcended most matters of the present or of tomorrow.

Then I met Julius Hanau, it must have been in late January. Lean, sallow with a pronounced South African accent, he certainly had something of a John Buchan character, if not of his near namesake in *Greenmantle*. His questioning was skilled, but he made it clear that I was intended for duties other than I had thought. It was also clear that here was a professional, highly disciplined with no illusions and Balkans-wise after his long years as a Vickers agent in Yugoslavia.

Section D was to be my second boss in London, agreed with the Director of Naval Intelligence and accepted by Despard so that I had a formal D identification.

The Danube was a priority target and already work was underway on two major operations to block the river, which Hanau did not then detail. Important, too, was the sabotage of rail traffic to Germany, already undertaken in Slovenia and Romania. Hanau had more than the nucleus of a skilled team already, including several mining engineers made available by London friends from the mines in South Serbia.

Meanwhile, confusion in London did tend to complicate operational impact. Was the objective of subversive action overseas immediate military success at the cost of longer-term diplomatic danger or disadvantage? There is no easy answer and, if in those early days, the Foreign Office and, on occasions, the Treasury also, were to behave like an uninvited guest at a wedding in withholding assent for projects they thought 'ungentlemanly', today we can be more understanding of the hard decisions war demands. In fact, 1940 and 1941 were learning curves for us all.

The use of Diplomatic Bags was a case in point, one interestingly enough circumvented as happened in Belgrade in February 1940. When a courier was expected it was our habit to meet him off the Orient Express, arriving at about 7am local time at Belgrade Station; rather dramatic on a cold morning, with the steam roaring out over the platforms and the general hustle and bustle of a busy station. This particular morning, we were waiting when Bill Bailey[2] suddenly said: 'Sandy, look, he can't be!' For there was this highly-suspicious figure, one-eyed with a black patch over the other, lugging two large suitcases. It was! We greeted him but were waved aside. 'These have to be delivered immediately and directly to Major Hanau,' he said. Our car was there but, no again. Into a taxi he jumped and off to Hanau's house which, predictably, took him an hour to find.

Hanau had gone to an early meeting of the Franco Serb Bank of which he was a director. The meeting was in progress in the boardroom on the first floor. Again pushing off any opposition, our single-minded friend charged upstairs, burst open the double doors, caught his toe in the door-rail and the King's Messenger with his two suitcases went skating across the parquet floor.

That was not the end, as Julius Hanau told me later. Within minutes, his Serb colleagues were on the floor, opening the suit-cases and examining and identifying the contents, enjoying them-selves hugely as one seized this and another that, exclaiming at the time: 'No, not that way, detonators go here,' and 'That's wrong, come on let me do it.' Serbs love bangs!

A routine of Diplomatic Bags from London was now a regular early-morning affair with the Belgrade porters. 'Never mind the big ones,' they said, slinging them onto a pile, 'it's the small ones that have the detonators, the ones you have to watch for.' In those early days, some of us were amateurish beyond belief!

It was about the same time that Despard returned from Bucharest and, with his secretary, Charles Everett, set up his office with Hugh Macdonald. But in fact, most of the work we did together was at his comfortable villa in Dedigne.

The impact of Max Despard was dramatic! He was huge, with a massive head, dominant in every way, incisive and cutting. Anglo-Irish in family, his brilliant First World War career was ter-minated by a delayed explosion of a 4.7 inch shell which took away part of his hip, but only after he had won his Distinguished Service Cross as First Lieutenant on HMS *Broke*, in Captain E.R.G. Evans[3] epic attack on seven German destroyers.

Despard could relax and enjoy; alternatively, he could withdraw into himself. He was in constant pain but rarely showed it. Some of his views were totally unreal, such as that we had no need of any outside help to defeat Germany. But when the going for

Britain turned bad, as it did in the Spring of 1940, his courage stood out like a beacon. To Yugoslavs and others alike, Max Despard never faltered in his conviction that both the British and the Yugoslavs would eventually turn adversity into victory!

Of what was planned in Romania, Despard told me little except that a Commander Gibson was shortly to be engaged in something important. Of German countermeasures, he made no mention, except to confirm what Hanau had told me that one scheme to block the Kazan Gorge by blowing up the high cliffs overlooking the Danube had run into difficulties with both the Romanian and Yugoslav authorities.

However, one or two small green shoots were appearing that early Spring. An attempt to pre-empt German operations on the Danube by purchasing and chartering as much tonnage as possible had been prepared by the Ministry of Economic Warfare (MEW) and MI(R), and approved by the Treasury and the Foreign Office. The vehicle was the Goeland Transport and Trading Company Ltd, which held its first meeting in Treasury Chambers, Whitehall, on 1 February 1940[4] when the Hon. Maurice Bridgeman,[5] then with the MEW and a future Chairman of British Petroleum, was elected Chairman. Captain William Harris-Burland, a peacetime chartered accountant, was appointed Managing Director and given full powers of attorney to act for the Company in Romania, later extended to include the USSR, Yugoslavia, Turkey, Greece and Cyprus, Bulgaria, Egypt and Palestine.

This move in that period of the 'phoney war' was typical of the thrust of Maurice Bridgeman and his colleagues, including another MEW high-flyer Mark Turner. Equally inspired was the choice of Harris-Burland, a real professional, quiet, discreet and always in command. He travelled the Danube from Sulina to the Hungarian ports, his eyes ever open for any opportunity, working in cooperation with the experienced and wise Bischoff, owner of the Anglo Danubian Shipping Company. Together, they were a formidable alliance and, trusted as they were by the Danube pilots, able to provide valuable intelligence to the Admiralty.

Harris-Burland's first act was to purchase the Simon Schultz fleet of tugs, tankers and barges, based at Pancevo, which brought into his team its owner, Deutsch, who detested the Germans and never hesitated to show it. He next bought up two more companies, the Compagnie Continentale d'Importation and the Anglo

Danubian Transport Co. Ltd, both further fruitful sources of commercial intelligence. Previous responsibility for the Anglo Danubian had been with the old established Galatz ships' chandlers Watson and Youell, who for many years had provided operational cover for agents working for Britain's Naval Intelligence Division and the SIS.

With Watson and Youell at the time were two young British employees, Dennis Wright[6] and G.B. Marshall.[7] Downriver as they were, in Sulina and the estuary, they were very exposed indeed but their contribution to Harris-Burland's success was greater than anyone then realised. As Germany and Britain locked horns in Romania, what had been known and prepared by the one or the other increasingly determined subsequent events. As Dr Ralph Bennett stresses: 'It is not only the quality of Intelligence received that is essential, but the ability of the receiver and end user to interpret and apply'.

The scale of the German protective measures, the Brandenburgers and the skill of the Abwehr penetration of the Romanian establishment were not known. The Abwehr were far ahead in the spying game and Britain was left at the starting gate. That certain operations did succeed is due to the Harris-Burlands and the Hanaus, despite the odds against them.

Reaction in Belgrade, and no doubt elsewhere in Serbia, to that 1940 summer of Allied disaster was remarkably muted. Sympathy for Britain did not seem to falter. That Italy had entered the war was described as the jackal picking up the scraps, but in Croatia its effects were very different in terms of the prospects they encouraged.

One moment had particular humour, ten days or so before Italy entered hostilities, when the rather nervy French Naval Attaché burst into the British Legation to say that the Italians had attacked Nice. The Councillor at the Italian Legation, Gastone Guidotti, had become a good friend, so I telephoned to ask him if this was true. 'Hold on,' he said, 'I will find out.' Some moments elapsed and then he replied: 'No, but we might have dinner together next week.' And we did – two days before Italy's entry. What neither of us could have guessed then was that three years later we would have dinner again in London, when he reopened the Italian embassy after the Armistice.

Serbian faces certainly did not turn away if you were British in that bleak summer of 1940; they did if you were Italian and went positively cold if you were German. What did begin to change, however, was the tolerance shown by the Yugoslav government, no doubt because of German pressure against the SOE presence. In fairly rapid succession, both Julius Hanau and Bill Bailey, who had taken over from him, were ordered to leave the country. The outcome was my taking up their duties.

Julian Amery had already left, to my deep regret; not because of German pressure but because of a private and audacious plan of his own for Bulgaria that would have left Frederick Forsyth and the Jackal nowhere!

The SOE's work nevertheless jogged on. The action had largely moved from Romania and Harris-Burland was extending his shipping activities on the Danube into what proved an imaginative and successful ploy to bribe the key Danube pilots from their essential jobs, as is described in Chapter 7.

A good team had by then been formed. Work against rail transport in the north to Germany was on an effective regular scale, helped by the skill of the Consul General in Ljubljana, Lawrenson, and his colleague in Zagreb, Cecil Rapp. Both had far from friendly locals to fend off and evade, but both succeeded in outwitting them.

Trepca Mines and the mining companies provided the nucleus: Bill Bailey was later to be senior Liaison Officer with Draza Mihailovic's Cetniks; Bill Hudson,[8] the first man to be landed back in Yugoslavia in September 1941, five months after the Axis invasion and occupation of the country, was also the first British representative to make contact with both Marshal Tito and Mihailovic. There were the Morgan brothers; R.G. Head, so active in the crucial Iron Gates area; and, from London, John Bennett,[9] a loveable lumbering buccaneer, despite his father being a judge, with Archie Dunlop Mackenzie, an old Arctic colleague and Peter Boughey, joining a few days later.

British policy in Yugoslavia in 1940 was very clear: to help and maintain Yugoslav neutrality and to encourage Yugoslavia against sliding into any association with the Axis powers. Yet at the same time, Britain was undertaking covert operations against the Axis on Yugoslav territory. A careful and difficult balance was required, lest those activities called down Axis reaction which could be irresistible.

40

Within the Yugoslav constitution, established as a quasi-dictatorship by King Alexander before his death, power held by the so-called Parliament was truncated and that of ministers and the Cabinet more in name than in fact. It was the Prince Regent, Prince Paul, who exercised authority until Alexander's son, Peter, came of age.

Changing governments had their influence, nonetheless. The previous government of Stoyadinovic[10] certainly had leanings towards Germany and Italy, in the case of the latter for reasons other than political, if Ciano,[11] then Italy's Foreign Minister, is to be believed. Cvetkovic, his successor, was more neutral, although doubts were held as to the Minister of Foreign Affairs, Cinzar Markovic.

The key in major decision-making lay with Prince Paul. His own personal preference was strongly with the British; he enjoyed our culture, our history and his friends were British, including several politicians. He abhorred Communism, for so many of his relatives had found death in the Soviet Union during and after the 1917 Revolution. He feared Germany and had few illusions over Italy, although several entries in Count Ciano's diary[12] show how carefully he trod the thin line between friendliness and collusion.

There were those who found Prince Paul vacillating and weak. His failing was to be too cultured and too intellectual for his Serbian people. Homespun King Alexander had been at home with the peasants in Shumadia, where they would talk straight to him in the familiar way: 'Alexander you listen to me, I have the word'. Prince Paul could not do this, but it was not his fault. He did his best but it was not good enough in that complex time.

Despite the dictatorship, the political parties remained alive if not active. The Communists were proscribed; the Serbian Radicals extreme right-wing with a Greater Serb obsession; the Serbian Democrats moderate and of a Yugoslav conviction; the Serbian Peasant Party similar and also anxious to forge close links with Matic's Croatian Agrarians in Zagreb. And here lay an enigma: did Matic favour a continued Yugoslavia, perhaps even a federal Yugoslavia, or was there just a hint that he might prefer an independent Croatia, probably not an Ustachi version, but one not necessarily independent of Italy?

This was the backcloth against which the British had to work. The Serbian Peasant Party, felt by the British Legation to be the most likely long-term supporters of resistance, should German occupation occur, and it was they, under Milan Gavrilovic, and later Tupanjanin, whom we British supported with arms and finance, although we also maintained relations with the Democrats.

This was, of course, in parallel with work by the Service Attachés with the Yugoslav General Staff and Air Staff. Curiously, the Naval Attachés had little real contact with the Yugoslav naval authorities in the Adriatic HQ, although over the Danube cooperation was quite good. Senior officers of the three services tended to be ambivalent and out of date; middle ranks much more to the point.

The situation differed from that in Romania. There was little German penetration, as compared with Bucharest, and the Legation staff's 'unofficial activities' were tolerated to a surprising extent.

The Abwehr were not absent, but their activities had less impact than in Romania. Yes, the Yugoslavs did cause the Kazan Gorge operation to be terminated, and they did undertake that both the Kazan and the Greben Narrows (in which cement-filled barges would be scuttled to block the river) schemes would be activated if Yugoslavia was ever attacked by Germany.

As 1940 neared its end, the SOE's activities were showing results in rail and road sabotage, with results, too, on the coast. But more and more of the effort was being aimed at the future, at a post-occupation resistance and in public relations throughout the country, designed to show people as a whole that Britain was far from defeated. London gave good support. George Taylor[13] was very much the spokesman for the SOE's efforts and when Colonel Tom Masterson arrived to take over, from me, control of the SOE team, it served as a real confidence booster.

So that late summer and autumn of 1940 we mixed with a wide range of politicians and army officers, including the then Colonel Draza Mihailovic,[14] who had been charged with preparing post-occupation operations. These were the establishment, those running the country, almost all Serb. There was another Yugoslavia we also knew. Proscribed as a party, the Communists were of unknown strength, many in prison, and it was exceedingly difficult to make contact with them. To them the war was still a Capitalist affair, to be shunned and not participated in until, in June 1941, their policy was shaken apart by the attack on their beloved Soviet Union.

Contact had been established by Julian Amery, with a few young Party members in Belgrade University, specifically with Olga Nincic and her brother Djura, unlikely Communist Party children of Momcilo Nincic, veteran politician of the extreme right. In Zagreb, too, there were contacts with whom Clissold and Jim Glanville trod carefully and well. In my own case, it was the Serbian Peasant Party that enabled me to enter local village life, at Party meetings, local marriages and funerals. Old days would be talked over, new days too. The village priest would point out a Party member saying: 'He will cut my throat one day, but I may do him first,' as he proceeded up the church aisle, often dropping a hand grenade as he fumbled for a missive. There were proud Cetnik tales to be heard, of the Turkish Wars, when the raids would stop as the leaf came onto the trees, so the fruit and harvest could be brought in.

Visiting much of Serbia in my Packard saloon, an impressive one-time palace car, helped me to form my perceptions of the country. I was accompanied often by Shems Mardin, secretary of the Turkish Legation, who had wide historic knowledge, and sometimes by the Greek minister, Rosetti, with whom at first light we would hunt wildfowl on the Danube, fortified with sacher tortes, their caramelised exteriors hiding the most delectable centres, washed down with the good local wines as the sun rose slowly.

Unlike Bosnia, the valleys of Serbia are rich, lavish with fields of maize and grain, the blue plums and fat apricots weighing down the trees along the lanes and tracks. Village occasions revolved around the suckling pigs and baby lambs turning slowly on the spits outside, basted with good beer. Afterwards, the *kola* was danced in long weaving lines over the fields and hills.

In the smallest tavernas you ate well, the local dishes with a wealth of character as in Leskovac, while in the towns and cities, restaurants like the Dva Ribara or Magestic in Belgrade gave the best of Hungarian and old Turkish cooking, none of the nonsense of some television chefs of today.

Life was good for those in the country and those with means in the towns. Yet there was another side, a darker side, of the many with either menial jobs or no jobs at all and for young and not-so-young intellectuals struggling for a living.

Yugoslavia was a dictatorship, its political parties effective in name only. Here, Slav kinship with Russia clashed with the regime's abhorrence of Bolshevism, and the police operated with a heavy hand. True, future leaders found prison an opportunity for study, as did Tito himself, and the likes of Moshe Pijade and Milovan Djilas. But this did not mean that oppression was anything but hard.

These perceptions were much limited to Serbia with a growing sense of affiliation, indeed deep affection, for the stalwart peasant folk with whom, I as a Scot, found myself so much at home. In my own life, a crossroads had opened. I had been married to Nina for four years. Our son, Adrian, had been born in 1939. But Yugoslavia had opened horizons of life and emotion very different from anything I had ever known before and I fell violently in love with a Yugoslav girl. She, though, was married, to a Belgian diplomat, Baron George Cartuyvels de Collaert. After the fall of Belgium, she had made her way through Spain back to Belgrade, where her stepfather, Ago Bukovac, son of the great Dalmatia painter Vladko Bukovac, was *Chef de Protocol* at the Foreign Office.

Tall, very Slavonic and with Byzantine looks, Zorica looked the immaculate product of a Paris *salon*. This hid a willingness to embark on the most hazardous enterprise with a total disregard of danger or hardship. With command of almost every European language, she also had the gift of being at home immediately with those of any and every background or nationality.

That Zorica and I have had 60 years of great happiness is an enormous blessing but deserting – and that is the word – my first wife in the circumstances of that time weighs heavily. That she found a happy marriage with my friend Peter Boughey is a consolation. It is not, however, an alibi and I can only leave it like that.

Of the many gifts that Zorica brought was an entry into the lives and confidences of other political parties. The Serbian Democratic Party were widely orientated, working especially hard to forge lasting links with Zagreb, with Matic's Croat Peasant Party. That they were to fail was no fault of their leader, Grol, or her uncle, Bozidar Vlaich, who spent endless effort on this essential key if Yugoslavia was to remain one country.

From this I began to guess that if the Serbs regarded the Croats as polished softies, the Croats, not without reason, thought of the Serbs as tough hicks without culture. In this case, each was a bit off centre. Serbs forgot that the old martial skills of the Croat regiments might still survive and that, as an important part of the Austro-Hungarian Empire, they had administrative talents rare in Serbia. But the real divide, the hatred of Catholic for Orthodox and vice-versa, rarely came through and it was only early one morning in April 1941 in Mostar that I discovered its fury, as Chapter 9 will testify.

Of the complexity of Bosnia, I was still blithely unaware; of the impact of poverty, history and religious hate, of mixed Muslim, Serb and Croat villages, of the explosive forces that lay ahead with fuses of infinite timing.

Autumn came and the effects of the long summer heat of 1940 on Max Despard's old wounds were all too obvious. His pain was excruciating and stoical as he was, a limit had been reached. His was a serious loss. Few matched his understanding of the complexity of our friends, devious and cunning, coupled with utter loyalty for a past which could be more compelling than the present. No replacement was appointed, but Captain Denis Larking CMG, RN, then *en poste* as Naval Attaché in Budapest took over as Naval Attaché, Balkans, a wise pseudonym. In the First World War he had been Naval Attaché, Rome, serving with great distinction and with responsibility at the end of the war for handing over the Austro-Hungarian fleet to Italy. Small and tubby, he was the most generous of hosts, fun to work with always, but with the lightest touch of leadership.

Then, on Monday, 10 October 1940, Mussolini made the crass mistake of attacking Greece through Albania. In the bitter cold of an Epirus winter, the tenacity of the Greek defence astounded the world and confounded the Italians. Attack too often turned to rout, in which Albanian leaders like Abas Kupi, who two years before had defended Durazzo so well, gave the Greeks such help as they could.

The SOE had responsibility to do what we could to assist from Belgrade. Two members of the old Gendarmerie, who had held the peace under General Percy in Albania in the early 1920s, volunteered: the much-decorated Colonel Frank Stirling, who had also served with Lawrence, and Major Oakley Hill. It was too late. Overwhelming force was to negate their efforts and those of the Greeks, as Germany reluctantly but decisively intervened to save their Axis partner.

The consequences were unmistakeable. A German Balkan Front could best be undertaken through Yugoslavia, by the Morava Valley, by sea down the Adriatic. This did not in itself imply an attack on Yugoslavia. It could be achieved more cheaply and more effectively with the compliance of the Yugoslav government, as a new member of the Tripartite Pact,[15] on terms which could appear not as an affront but acceptable to those in Croatia, and even those in Bosnia and Slovenia, which Berlin and Rome knew were not over-enamoured with Belgrade.

Already Bletchley Park was revealing a change in Berlin's attitude to Yugoslavia, with evidence, too, of pending troop movements all pointing to the same conclusion. 1941 was to bring another world to all of us!

Colonel William Harris-Burland (left) and Ralf Navratil (right), who were key figures in the only successful sabotage operations on the Danube in the early years of the war. See Chapters 6 and 15.   Photographs courtesy of Mrs H. Harris-Burland and Mrs Ludmilla Loughran

Colonel D.T. 'Bill' Hudson, the first British officer to be landed back in Yugoslavia after the April 1941 invasion by Axis forces. He linked up as liaison officer with the Cetniks and Partisans only five months after the invasion and survived one of the most cruel winters the country had experienced.
Photo: Imperial War Museum, HU68050. By permission of the SFC

Michael Mason, Commodore of the Royal Ocean Racing Club, pictured in his yacht *Latifa*, one-time winner of the Fastnet race. His extraordinary exploits as a Danube saboteur are related in Chapter 7.   Photo: David Mason

The young King Peter of Yugoslavia, who had to flee his country when Hitler mounted the invasion codenamed Operation Punishment, pictured with his Prime Minister General Simovic (left) and Court Minister Radoje Knezevic. See Chapter 8.

Photo: Imperial War Museum HU55654

Comrades in arms: Marshal Tito (right), who led the four-year Partisan struggle against the occupying Axis forces, pictured with Brigadier Fitzroy Maclean (centre), Winston Churchill's personal envoy to Tito and who became close friends with the Yugoslav leader, and American Mission chief, General Thayer.   Photo: Imperial War Museum NA22902

Worlds apart: Yugoslav Partisans load much-needed supplies, dropped from four-engine Handley Page Halifax bombers of the RAF's Balkan Air Force, on to their primitive oxen-drawn carts. This picture was taken by one of the Partisans.

Photo: Imperial War Museum CNA3240

Tea and sympathy: Leading Aircraftman W.H. Gorry, of Liverpool and Aircraftman G.A. Bumphrey, of Hull, serve food, tea and a little cheer to four stretcher-case Partisans, two of them female fighters. In the biggest operation of its kind, more than 900 wounded Partisans were air-lifted out of Yugoslavia and flown to Italy in RAF Dakotas of the Balkan Air Force across hundreds of miles of enemy-held territory, sometimes escorted by Spitfires and Mustangs. Incredibly, no planes were lost.

Photo:Imperial War Museum CNA3078

Balkan serenade: Male and female Partisan fighters form a chorus to celebrate the inauguration of the Yugoslav National Liberation Constitutional Assembly at Jajce in November 1943.

Photo: Imperial War Museum K7041

Little Big Man: Deputies and Officers line up to be photographed with little Colonel Canica Opacic, the legendary Partisan hero, at Jajce in November 1943.

Photo: Imperial War Museum K7043

7

Belgrade, Winter 1940/41

Britain had survived a near-disastrous 1940 with control of most of Europe in German hands and, despite Dunkirk and the Battle of Britain, a war at sea still critically in the balance. Nor did prospects for 1941 look any brighter, certainly not for us in Yugoslavia, with the near certainty of a German move to bolster Italian failure against Greece by military reinforcement which could scarcely fail to involve Yugoslavia.

Yet that Christmas and New Year of 1940/41 – or rather the two of each, as in an Orthodox country such as Serbia there are two calendars – remain in my memory as the time when a tiny, niggling confidence began to emerge. It may have been simply the amazing Slav ability to cast off tomorrow's problems and enjoy today; but no, for it revealed itself at one of the many parties to see in the New Year, whether the Catholic or Orthodox, I no longer remember.

We were in the American Legation, in the wee small hours, relaxing over the last brandy or bourbon. A long silence was broken by the normally canny Belgian minister, Alain Obert: 'You know,' he said, 'I am just beginning to believe the day is coming when I will stalk again in Scotland.'

There was no immediate response. Then our American host, Bliss Lane, rose, topped up our glasses and said: 'Alain, that's strangely prophetic, for I've been thinking that we will be in this with you before '41 is out.'

Call it the small hours or a good whisky, for there was little enough to justify wishful thinking. Yet despite the many failures and frustrations, especially in Romania, and the bleak prospects ahead, the fact was that Britain *had* survived. In our own small way, too, there had been successes. Despite the effective German control over the Danube, Harris-Burland had extended his preemptive Goeland operations by suborning from their duties a good number of Danube pilots: 22 of the 45 at the Iron Gates and 50 on the lower reaches of the river. Employed by the International Danube Commission, these were skilled men who could take long years to master their duties and understand the shifting channels and powerful currents. For ceasing to work for the Germans they received a lump sum and monthly payments for two years in Swiss francs, together with the option, if they wished, of being evacuated with their families to Britain.

Two Czechs played a huge part in making this possible: Ralf Navratil, a Danube pilot himself, and Jaroslav Vrana, a ship's engineer. Recruited by Harris-Burland, they were ringleaders in this operation but it was not to be their sole contribution to the Allied war effort in the Balkans. Later, they were to play a part that, if anything, was even more distinguished. In the immediate sense, their efforts were great enough, for the river traffic very soon slowed down. Trained replacements for the defecting pilots did not exist, so the Germans introduced temporaries, causing barges to collide and run aground. In some of the more treacherous areas there was panic and confusion. The one plus factor for the Germans was that in the late autumn of 1940 the water levels were considerably higher than normal, otherwise much more damage and confusion would have ensued.

These were, in truth, small successes, trivial even in comparison with the overall dangers Britain, still standing alone, was facing. Our principal responsibility remained unaltered: to help maintain Yugoslavia's neutrality, to prevent her being drawn into association with the Axis, partially or completely, by blandishment or threat. Britain was in no position to provide weapons or physical aid, that was as clear to our enemies as our friends. After all, our record as an ally in Norway, as in western Europe, was pretty damning.

Looking back, it is difficult to believe that even in those dire days the Serbs did not cease to believe that Britain would win the war. I recall a talk with Colonel Draza Mihailovic who was quite certain it would take time but felt the outcome was sure. This confidence around us nurtured our own. No doubt we were still either on or near the edge of a precipice, but such confidence was stimulating and every straw that floated by was grasped.

My own work nurturing the Serbian Peasant Party went ahead, again mutually reassuring, with this down-to-earth solid lot who had often seen defeat turned into victory. With the middle-ranking officers in the air force and the army, our Service Attachés found the same attitude; older generations of generals were more ambiguous but few even of these were defeatist.

Of the straws I mentioned, a few were drifting in from Romania, mostly about what a certain Michael Mason, operating under the pseudonym of David Field had achieved 9 or 12 months before. Despard had never revealed much, if anything, of what had gone wrong in Romania, something which may well have contributed to his growing indisposition when he left; a realisation, perhaps, that this was a new type of warfare which he did not understand. The rumours were there, all right, of a Superman character who, in a schoolboy way, was quite inspiring. In circumstances such as these, snippets of good news can have a disproportionate effect. Some of the rumours were apocryphal and, indeed, fictional. These have been discarded and from his own book and from conversations after the war, I believe the extracts that now follow to be a fair record of Michael Mason's doings in the first half of 1940.

A nephew of the author of the *Tales of the North West Frontier*, and of films including *The Four Feathers*, A.E.W. Mason, Michael had been first recommended to Admiral Godfrey by his predecessor as Director of Naval Intelligence during the First World War, Admiral Sir Reginald Hall, under whom A.E.W. Mason had served. 'Blinker' Hall was the archetypal Intelligence Chief and Godfrey respected him as such.

Michael Mason was a large landowner in Oxfordshire. An Etonian, he travelled the Badlands of Canada, a wildlife expert and self-sufficient; he also had been a good enough boxer to be a sparring partner of Jack Sharkey when he was cruiserweight champion of the world. As alert mentally as he was tough physically, he carried out special pre-war duties for the Director of Naval Intelligence, not least in his RYS yacht *Latifa* and a converted Brixham trawler, searching out suspected or potential U-boat bases on the west coast of Ireland.

Admiral Godfrey, on the outbreak of war, charged Mason with overall sabotage in Romania. As a Lieutenant Commander RNVR, he was notionally responsible to the Naval Attaché in Bucharest,

Captain Despard, but in fact went his own way under the cover name of David Field, sometimes as one of the Legation drivers, sometimes as a vice-consul. His remit: direct action against Danube traffic, against the railways and, if possible, against Black Sea shipping.

Before leaving for Bucharest, Mason had been told he would be accompanied by an assistant, an RNVR Lieutenant Merlin Minshall, forced on him without his blessing. In his book of his wartime experiences[1] Mason referred to Minshall as having:

his good points and his bad ones. He was good company, talkative and clever. He spoke good French, German and Italian. He was about 34 and had been about a bit. Well-made and bodily fit by nature. No notion of discipline but capable of deep attachment. There was a reckless streak in him that was bravado rather than boldness. In a hard battle he might have earned a VC or he might have run away. I think he was the child of an unhappy marriage and seemed to have no solid ideals beyond having a good time. However I found him good company and really liked him, though I realised I could not trust him far out of my sight. He would suddenly start violent quarrels, quite senselessly, with perfectly harmless people. If we sat down to dinner together, peacefully, in a good-class restaurant he always had to have a row with the *maitre d'hotel* about the dinner and with the wine-steward about the wine. Such a bore! Still a little boy showing off.

Mason's description later proved prophetic. It was Minshall's behaviour which frustrated one major scheme planned for the Danube. His quarrelsome nature soon came to light. Minshall was assigned as a vice-consul in Galatz. That lasted only a few days, then Minshall was sent back to Bucharest after being involved in a mighty, and unnecessary, row with his nominal boss.

Mason first set his sights on wrecking lub-oil laden trains going into Germany from Constanta. He wrote:[2]

Naturally we chose places where they had to stop just before the steep pull over the Carpathian Mountains. All we did (Blackley[3] and I) was run about in the dark, pouring acid into the axle-boxes of the trucks. Then various forms of wreckage happened. At the least degree the truck seized up or caught fire on the way up-hill and the line was jammed. At the best, the whole train dived in ruin down a mountainside as it rocked its way down on the far slope. It wasn't very much but it irritated the Germans because they lost trainloads of lub-oil from Russia or of petrol from Ploesti. What it meant to the Romanians was of no matter to us. Fortunately, they are people to take other people's troubles lightly.

In Mason's early days in Romania at the beginning of 1940, the Danube was thick with ice in many parts. But Russian ships were still arriving at Constanta with lub-oil destined for Germany and they were targeted. Mason takes up the story.[4]

There was a little Sapper Major[5] who helped me load gelig-nite into limpet-bombs, to attach to ships. He was an expert, but the cavalier way in which he punched and manhandled that gelignite made me feel my last hour had come. All in my office, which had been a housemaid's bedroom, attached to the British Consulate. The sweat used to drop off my nose to the tune of melted castanets, as this sapper frightened me to death. Such a nice young man! The time-bomb explosion-switch I put in myself, or the Doctor did.

One of the Greek skippers of the British river-tugs had a little daughter, living in Constanta, who used to deliver my limpet-bombs in her school satchel to the Doctor. She was 15 years old, a nice little girl; about the most inconspicuous and unsuspicious person to be found in the whole of that filthy city.[6]

The Doctor I call him because he actually was one. He dropped everything and became one of my best men simply because he hated the Germans. He was a Romanian. Instead of being a doctor with a modest but good practice, he became a common bum-boat man in the harbour. It is a big harbour. This bum-boat man became a familiar figure whom nobody questioned. He would row men ashore, bring them off drunk and pile them back on board, sell cigarettes, oranges, any-thing. Probably pimp for them, too.

Nobody noticed, as his bum-boat came alongside, that

when he heard my limpet-magnet-bomb clank dully against the ship's side, alongside the engine room, he quietly lifted the thole-pin (to which the bomb had been attached) and quietly put it back again. He'd keep these bombs in his place for more than a night at most. The Greek girl could do no more than carry them to him. He was the man who most easily learned the ship's sailing time, so he himself adjusted the time-fuse for the explosion. Set it to go off in the middle of the Black Sea. Several we never saw again. Very satisfactory. I never liked Bolshy Russians. My middle-aged, plump, paunchy, dull little doctor was a very devoted and clever man.

Mason and his colleagues were staying at the Athenee Palace Hotel in Bucharest, so they got to see their opposite numbers on the German side on a daily basis, as several of them were also billeted there. And Mason could never resist baiting them. So much so that several attempts were made on his life. He dealt with a couple of would-be assassins in the dark streets of Bucharest by simply shooting them and when two attempts to kill him were made by trying to run him down in cars, he again turned the tables on his attackers:[7]

The first time I shot the rear tyre and wrecked the car. The driver was badly hurt. Next time the driver had a man sitting by him, shooting at me. This was a bit thick! I had jumped backwards into a doorway to avoid the car, and only did it by inches. I shot the driver and the gunman, and everybody was so busy admiring the crash I walked quietly away unnoticed.

Soon afterwards, he was called in by the Chief of Police to explain some of his activities and was told the Germans were making complaints to the Romanian police about his behaviour. The Chief particularly wanted to know why he went to Turnu Severin so often. Mason said it was because he was having an affair with a married woman. The Chief, who seemed happy to accept this explanation, said he would pass the information on to the Germans. In reality, these trips were tied up with the enticement of pilots scheme, in which Mason played a large part with

William Harris-Burland. The story about the married woman had no chance of succeeding with the Germans.

Mason picks up the sequel in his rather quaint and picturesque style:[8]

Next time I came down from Turnu Severin, on the late night train, two German agents got on with Blackley and me. This train is the Orient Express. It is different from our trains inasmuch as that you can open the outer door, at the end of the carriage, while the train is in motion. This is convenient for murder. One man holds the door open while the other pushes the victim through. Money for old rope! These two Apostles of '*Freude durch Arbeit*' were typical of their kind, though of different types. I knew them well by sight, which proved Little Audrey's[9] stupidity. One was short and thick-set, bull-necked and powerful, dark-eyed and with a bullet-shaped head. He was just a simple brute. The other was the far more dangerous type: fair-haired, lean, with pale-grey eyes, pink-rimmed eyelids, and that curious pink tinge round the edges of his thin lips. This man would use a gun but never his muscles, and would do all the planning, especially of the torturing. No viler form of creature alive on earth!

I knew what they were up to, but when it comes to that sort of 'funny business' I am something of a humorist myself. Blackley was lying asleep in a First Class compartment we had to ourselves. I peeled off my jacket and went to spring the trap. A half-arm blow with my right, just under his heart, put 'paid' to the short chap. The thin fellow was holding the door open, but in his astonishment at developments got in front of the opening himself. A long left to the chin sent him flying backwards and the door shut behind him. The short chap was groaning on the floor. I opened the door and flung him through. The train was roaring through the dark at sixty miles per hour. All without noise, bloodshed or marks of any kind. 'Two drunk Germans fell out of the train.'

Blackley was snoring along his seat when I got back. Two minutes later, I was snoring along the other.

Little Audrey was not one bit pleased. He rang me up and was quite truculent. Explained in detail how he and his

53

college chums would torture me to death. But 'first catch your hare,' I told him.

I first heard about the train incident from the minister in Bucharest, Sir Rex Hoare. Later, the Romanian Minister of Foreign Affairs, Gafencu, telephoned and said that while they understood Michael was under a great deal of pressure, would we ask him next time to dispose of the bodies more carefully because the Germans were being awkward about it. It was at one of Lady Hoare's last receptions, still full fig, decorations and tiaras, that Michael had to leave early, excusing himself to his hostess with the words, 'Forgive me, Lady Hoare, but I must leave as I strangled someone in a snowdrift.' His hostess, it is said, was understanding.

Another operation, one that led to the Germans putting a price of 5 million lei (around £5,000) on Mason's head, was the single-handed destruction of a German boat on the Danube, used as a headquarters for the Abwehr and Brandenburgers employed in the Danube surveillance operations. This is how Mason recalled what happened:[10]

Many of the top planners lived together on this boat. To get the whole lot in one bang was a fairly obvious move, so three limpet bombs, one loaded with highly incendiary matter, were got ready and synchronised.

On the general principle that the fewer the stalkers, the better the sport, I did the job alone. It involved a good deal of swimming and wading, for at that time the limpets were of strong magnets and too heavy to swim with more than one at a time. But I got them well planted, the incendiary against the engine room. Then I waited, shivering in the sandy-muddy water under the bank. The water was beastly cold. The bangs went off nicely; ten seconds would have covered the three. I was waiting to make sure no-one came out alive. Blackley, who was no great swimmer, was keeping guard above, against shore interference.

Only three men swam ashore, for the vessel was a sinking furnace within a few moments. I shot the first man through the head; then my Luger pistol jammed, from mud and sand, and I used it as a club to brain Chappie No. 2. He sank, too,

54

but the sharp, claw-like foresight (of the Luger) gouged a chunk of flesh clean out of the palm of my right hand. With a muted curse, I flung the pistol aside and Chappie No. 3 got the full force of my ill-temper. I grabbed him by the neck and strangled him under the water. I had no way of knowing who or what he was, for in the dark night and with the blazing ship behind them I could not see any of their faces, but even in my weariness and fury of the time, I remember hoping very much he was an important swine of a Nazi, and not some harmless servant. Thirty men were written off at that time, of which probably ten were harmless but the other twenty sheer poison.

Mason's reaction to the price on his head was that 'it was the highest compliment I had ever been paid'. But it increased the pressure on him, as it spurred local people to help the Abwehr in trying to hunt him down. Mason summed up his five months of frenzied activity in the Balkans thus:[11]

To take a brief look back at my career of slaughter on the Danube, the only men I slew with my own hand were, with the exception of those in the German H.Q. ship, all making violent attempts upon my own life. I don't count the Russian ships or the oil-trains. Bearing in mind the old saying 'Least said, soonest mended' I never saw any need to acquaint Despard or anyone else with my casual pastimes among the homicidalists. He was a secretive and brilliantly-clever man. I was not so clever but I chose to be secretive about little things like just having killed a couple of murderers in a dark street. It was entirely a matter between me and them. They were dead. I was alive. Why tell anybody? If those Gestapo swine I killed are not frying in Hell, then there is no such place.

It was only fragments of Mason's activities that filtered through to us in Belgrade at the end of 1940 but at the time they certainly helped to enhance morale. In fact, Mason may have played down his greatest achievement, his sinkings in Constanta of ships outward-bound to Russia. How many reached their destination? How many lie at the bottom of the Black Sea?

Mason was a friend of Ian Fleming, who at the time of these events was personal assistant to Admiral Godfrey. If there was a model for the later exploits of Fleming's 007 hero James Bond, Mason's fit was good enough, better than any other.

In Yugoslavia, we had another contender for Bond role model, Bill Hudson, for his later exploits in 1941 and 1942 and for one in 1940 which I have good reason not to forget. I did a very silly thing. I had sent Bill down to Split to see what mischief he could get up to and when nothing seemed to happen, I sent him a coded signal saying: 'I expect you are enjoying the sunshine and the girls and drink'. Unfortunately, the signal arrived just after he blew up this rather large German ship in Split Harbour. He returned to Belgrade that weekend and sent a message to say he would like to have a drink with me in the bar of the Serbski Kralj Hotel. I walked up to greet him at the bar and he knocked me out. Just like that! Well deserved! I woke up a few minutes later and he said as far as he was concerned everything was all right now. It was a very, very good lesson for me not to be silly.

8

Belgrade Makes Its Stand: 27 March 1941

In the early months of 1941, Britain and the Commonwealth, still alone in opposition to the Axis forces, were going through hard and dangerous times. Shipping losses were high with the critical trade routes under intense U-boat attacks. While initial success had been won against the Italians in North Africa, this was endangered as German troops were deployed to reinforce their Axis ally.

This scenario looked as if it would be repeated in the Balkans, as Bletchley Park indicated increasing evidence of a major Wehrmacht move through Yugoslavia in support of the flagging Italian operations against Greece. This prompted Prime Minister Winston Churchill to urge SOE chief Dr Hugh Dalton at MEW to take some positive action against the 'pro-Axis government in Belgrade'.

For Dalton, this was manna from heaven! After the first difficult six months of the SOE's existence, the organisation had been notching up evidence of its potential, especially in Norway and France, despite, in the latter case, endless wrangling with the supporters of General Charles de Gaulle in their own London organisation.

The SOE's enemies at home, particularly the SIS, made the most of any lapses or failures by Baker Street while Dalton himself was by no means skilled at making friends out of enemies. At the Foreign Office the replacement of Viscount Halifax by Anthony Eden was in no sense as favourable to SOE as Clement Atlee had forecast, in fact the opposite. So one can imagine the relief for Dalton in January 1941 when Churchill, acting on the by then positive evidence of German movements against Greece, charged him to respond. This was reinforced by similar instruction from Eden. Whether or not Churchill's description of the government in Belgrade as 'pro-Axis' was correct, this was the opportunity for the SOE to show its mettle and Dalton grasped the chance!

George Taylor, now in the rank of full colonel, was sent to Belgrade via Athens, where he was to spend rather a longer time than intended in discussions with the British Military Mission and with Ian Pirie[1] and the Greek SOE team.

Admiral Sir Andrew Cunningham, Commander-in-Chief of the Mediterranean Fleet, sent his Senior Staff Officer, the rather frightening Captain 'Lofty' Power and, among others from Cairo, Brigadier Bob Laycock,[2] reassuring as ever and still wearing the same Shetland jersey he used in his days in one of Sven Ericksen's sailing ships in the grain race from Australia. That the visitors included American Colonel 'Wild Bill' Donovan[3] on a 24-hour visit was to have a key influence on the SOE's future 18 months later – providential indeed.

Underneath all these visits, however, remained the stark truth that Britain was in no position to offer material supply or effective support to any Yugoslav government. Britain simply did not have the resources! Formal talks between the German authorities and the Yugoslavs began in February and went on in a series of meetings, some attended by Prime Minister Cvetkovic and his Foreign Minister Cinzar Markovic, but later by Prince Paul as Regent, with Hitler. It was certainly Germany's intention that war should be avoided through concession by Yugoslavia, permitting full transit rights for the Wehrmacht, formalised by the adhesion of Yugoslavia to the Tripartite Pact.

In our later knowledge of the preparation for Operation Barbarossa, to be launched on a massive scale against the Soviet Union in early June, military diversion by German forces south and possible action against Yugoslavia cannot have been welcome in Berlin. Whether that is the reason the talks seem to have been allowed by the Germans to go on unresolved for quite a time, or whether Prince Paul showed himself a more skilled negotiator than was believed, is not clear; but the outcome was inevitable and on 25 March 1941, the Pact was accepted.

In Belgrade, as in Serbia, there was public uproar. 'Nema Pakt, ima Rat': 'No Pact, better war' was the chant around the solidly-packed streets and squares of Belgrade with young and old, men and women, clamouring that national honour and Serb integrity came first, that death was preferable to dishonour. In Croatia, it was certainly different; here was an opportunity to change sides many awaited, while in Slovenia, reaction both ways was muted. For us, it was quite simple: there was more work to be done. Air Attaché Hugh Macdonald and his assistant Tom Mapplebeck[4] virtually disappeared; Charlie Clark scarcely left the Yugoslav General Staff; while the rest of what were now 24-hour working days were spent with Tupanjanin and his friends.

It was near midnight on 26 March when I got to bed, to be awakened at around 4am by a call from Zorica. 'Tanks are moving here in Dedinje, things are happening,' she said urgently. They certainly were! Troops were out on the streets and by early morning a *coup d'état* had taken over the government, Prince Paul had been arrested and the young King Peter installed on the throne. It was a strange *coup*, perhaps unique, instigated neither by senior politicians nor by army generals. An air force general, Bora Mierkovic, was one of the leaders, the much-respected Radoje Knezjevic another. His younger brother Zivka, of the Royal Guards, brought in a tank battalion. But however unusual the leadership, the reaction was explosive in its relief that the honour of Yugoslavia had been restored and saved. Rejoicing and celebrations continued that day and night.

In London, Churchill declared: 'Yugoslavia has found its soul' and the Chiefs of Staff sent their congratulations to Dalton on the SOE's achievement in sowing the seeds of the *coup*. Dalton found this gracious on the part of the Chiefs of Staff and acknowledged that the SOE had done well and that their considerable investment in the Serbian Peasant Party had been 'thoroughly justified'. Unquestionably, the status of the SOE was strengthened, rightly as later events in the war were to show, but the immediate compliments over the events in Belgrade may have been less convincing than thought at the time.

The 'lobbying' efforts of Macdonald and Mapplebeck with the Yugoslav air force had been consistent and effective; so too was the sowing of seeds among younger officers of the General Staff, although the Yugoslav High Command was cautious and non-committal. In Serbia, however, the *coup* certainly represented politically the will of most, and I believe the pertinent question is rather: 'Would the *coup* have taken place without British encouragement?' My view is yes, it would have. It was a Yugoslav – more accurately, a Serbian – occasion, a brave if reckless move, in the tradition of a people who place honour above anything else, one which should be remembered as such and not forgotten.

The new government which followed under General Simovic was bewildered and rudderless. This was not surprising. It was a makeshift combination of the former discredited parties; it lacked infusion of the new and Simovic himself had played no decisive role in the events of the previous days. Whether any government could have made effective deployments against the earthquake that they had inherited is doubtful. Hitler had decided immediately that Yugoslavia's action was unforgivable; that they, and especially Serbia, must be punished mercilessly. Nine days later, on 6 April, Belgrade was bombed and the country invaded, a day Zorica and I will never forget, as we moved suitcases of plastic explosives and 'other toys' from burning houses to the greater safety of a villa outside the city.

Quite recently, the then Croatian Ambassador to London spent an evening trying to persuade me that these events had been a disaster for Serbia and the whole of Yugoslavia. 'Irresponsible and crazy,' were his words. 'For the whole of Yugoslavia, surely not,' was my reply. 'Croatia was speedy enough to ally herself with the Axis and Pavelic [the Ustachi leader] saw to it that the Ustachi did their full share for them of the dirty work. And as for us British,' I added, 'we had a war not to lose.'

Almost all in the country faced appalling years ahead, endless suffering, under an occupying regime comparable with that in Poland or Czecho-Slovakia. The toll on those active in Resistance or the innocents was equally harsh, 100 hostages shot for a single German casualty, over 2,000 young people in Kraguevac alone. 'I ask for no mercy, but none will be given you,' as Rade Koncar shouted from the scaffold, and none was shown, just as little was to be offered later. But the efforts of Tito's Partisans and Mihailovic's Cetniks did tie down Axis forces and diverted them from other theatres of war. And it is just possible that in launching Operation Punishment against the Yugoslavs on 6 April, Hitler delayed the opening of Operation Barbarossa, the German offensive in Russia.

The Croatian Ambassador was right, of course, that the Yugoslav forces in 1941, whether ready or not, were no more capable of resisting the Wehrmacht and Luftwaffe than were the French or ourselves a year earlier. On military facts, the *coup* and its consequences were foolhardy. Its preparation and execution were Serb, essentially so because of its blatant disregard of military reality. But in its maddening obstinacy and courage, the *coup* was heroic, in true Serb tradition.

9

Hitler's 'Operation Punishment' and the Yugoslav Collapse, April 1941

It was the beginning of the end, an end which culminated in Hitler's response to the *coup* in Belgrade. Non-combatants, wives and children were being evacuated to Salonica, together with a good number of all nationalities: Poles, Czechs and many Jewish families from the Ukraine, Poland and Romania. With tragically reducing items of value they had managed to slip through and survive previous assaults, now again having to seek yet another refuge.

My mind went back often to an evening in Hamburg in September 1936. I was on my way from that wonderful year in the Arctic, very much at peace with its memories. I had a quick supper, went out and suddenly saw an angry crowd ahead. They had smashed the windows of some Jewish shops and, on the pavement, were forcing half a dozen old Jewish men and women to clear up the mess. My first reaction was to do something to help. But to intervene was to invite a certain beating-up. Then I had a thought: go down on my knees too and help clean up. At least they would have had one friend. But I chickened out!

Fear, those pitiful eyes, helplessness, these were all there again in those first days of April 1941. Yet among the people of Belgrade, there seemed little panic. Perhaps they had been through all this too often before.

For us, like those in other Embassies and Legations in Europe at that time, routine held good. Confidential documents were burned, anything sensitive was disposed of (and we had a lot), evacuation plans were finalised (who with whom, in which car), some to Greece, others to follow the government or General Staff wherever they might go.

I must not forget Ronnie Campbell's constant advice: 'Look after yourselves, but first must come those Poles, Czechs and Yugoslavs, whose heads are at special risk.' My job was to take the Serbian Peasant Party leader, Tupanjanin, his son, Alexi Gavrilovic, the son of the Yugoslav Minister in Moscow, Hugh Seton Watson, Tupanjanin's Peasant Party driver and Zorica in the Packard, with John Bennett's old brown Cadillac in company, and strike westwards towards Zvornik, where it was believed GHQ was to be established.

We knew the German attack was timed for 6am on 6 April and at that minute the Luftwaffe attack on Zemun airfield began, destroying most of the Hurricanes which, with great difficulty, the Assistant Air Attaché, Tom Mapplebeck, had secured for the Yugoslav Air Force. At that moment I was picking up Hugh Seton-Watson[1] at his flat. Unperturbed as ever, he was in no hurry. They were carpet-bombing the city but he had lost his trousers and no other pair would do. But all was finally well as he retrieved them from under the mattress where they were being pressed, the first and only time he had done this. Then, and by this time the bombing was vicious, he decided he had to go back for *War and Peace* in Russian. 'I must have something to read,' he said.

As it turned out, delay didn't matter. A message from Tupanjanin reached us that his party would not be ready to leave until late evening. We had already picked up Zorica and looked in on a deserted Legation. Our flat had been hit, so what were we to do? Hugh then thought of the many suitcases of explosives in safe houses. I would have preferred not to have thought of them, but there it was, so we did.

This brought one memorable scene in a small square in which stood the Egyptian Legation, all four corners on fire. As we lunged out with the last suitcase, the Egyptian *Chargé d'Affaires*, a dear friend but rather less dusky than usual, emerged, took Zorica's hand and kissed it with the words: 'Chère Baroness, my humble regards to your charming mother.'

We beat it, the car filled with plastic explosives, out of town to beyond Dedigne. We had been lucky: The three or four hours' bombing had been continuous in a crossover pattern and damage was everywhere. Our objective, unknown to him, was Tom Mapplebeck's country house, which had a massive swimming pool, the only safe place for our precious suitcases and their explosive contents. We did not know then that the future tenant would be the German Commandant of Belgrade, or we might have arranged something special.

The next days and nights remain pretty chaotic in my memory. I know I did most of the driving, with the weather deteriorating as we passed through Zvornik, the Gorge and the Drina a still half-dream image, with snippets of news, all bad, of shattered defences.

Our orders had been to maintain contact either with the Yugoslav Government or the General Staff. We knew their intentions but early losses combined into effective rout and total confusion. Some units, mostly Serb, were holding, others were close to mutiny. Effective contact was no longer possible and the only option escape to the west, Kotor preferably. Sarajevo was the only route, involving for us a winter journey in snow and ice over the mountain mass, a tough track at the best of times but in darkness, with slit headlights, a nightmare. Whether I fell asleep or the car hit ice near the top, I do not know, but she slithered sideways out of control, coming to rest with the front wheels jammed on top of a tree and some thousand feet below us.

I climbed out and so did the others, but not quite so quickly. Hugh simply remained where he was, taking out *War and Peace* to read. Then followed an odd event. Half conscious, I staggered back to the track and there approaching us was a Bosnian peasant with an ox. In English I asked: 'Can you help us? The car is over the precipice.' The reply came back in English: 'How strange, I have been living in Manchester and have just come home.'

Years later, Hugh maintained that the Bosnian from Manchester had a bicycle not an ox. I am certain it wasn't a bicycle that hauled the Packard from the treetop. Not that it mattered anyway. The car was broken in two, a write-off. So we all piled into the accompanying Cadillac and I remember nothing more until waking up in Sarajevo. A brief meeting confirmed collapse on all fronts so it was straight on to Mostar and the coast.

Again this involved an overnight drive, coming down to Mostar about 6am on a perfect morning. A strange quiet, no noise of aircraft and at the barracks on the left of the road, two Yugoslav army officers standing alone. We stopped. Both were Serbs, both majors, fine looking men in their forties. 'What news?' we asked. There was no reply but one looked at the other. A moment's silence. Then he said: 'Our dear friends the Croats.'

We thought we knew, and drove on. There was no way back, but we were not fast enough to miss seeing in the mirror both Serb majors seized and their throats slit. Some 200 yards ahead, a road block was being set up by the mutinying Croat troops. We came to a halt, we had to. Under the rug behind us on each side we hid a Tommy-gun. The door was opened by a middle-aged officer wearing the yellow Croat shoulder flash. He cannot have failed to recognise Tupanjanin as the Serbian Peasant Party leader, while I was in RNVR uniform and the car had a CD Belgrade number plate. He paused, then said very quietly in Serbo-Croat: 'There is some trouble here. A little way ahead you will find a rough track up to the hills, take it quickly, it will be better.' He then closed the door and saluted. We did as he said, without interference, passing hundreds of yellow-flashed troops taking up defensive positions near Mostar.

He saved our lives, but why? For this was the time I realised how little I had learned of the real black hatred between Catholic and Orthodox, the timeless relentlessness of that hate. Yet, at that moment, a Croat officer had risked his life for us.

It was a good half-hour before we left the mutinying troops behind, a long half-hour, silent and very tense. It was then I began to grow up, dimly to see that this was not just cloak and daggers; to understand that this was not only the defeat of a Yugoslav army, but the breakup of a country, treachery and betrayal alongside earlier heroism and great courage.

If we had some chance of escape, others had none – the lives of millions were inevitably to suffer and, if at that time the scale of barbarity to be wrought by the Ustachi on the Serbs in the months ahead was still unthinkable, Mostar had given an early warning.

We passed over that lunar landscape through Nevesinghi and Gatsko, silent and sore in heart. Then we ran out of petrol, but chance was kind. A Yugoslav air force bowser caught us up, filled our tank and sped off with the warning to lose no time in reaching Kotor. It was high octane they had given us and the Cadillac did not like it at all. She grunted and stopped but we forced her on over the last pass and down the long decline to

Niksic. Then she finally gave up, black smoke streaming from her bonnet. We were by a small farm, and we settled by the roadside. Tupanjanin was in despair. This strong, powerful man whose hopes and beliefs all had been shattered, broke down completely, in tears and hopelessness that this was the end.

Zorica it was who thought there was still a chance to get a car in Niksic. 'A car in Niksic, don't be a bloody fool,' we said, but off she set at a fast trot in her red fox coat. If she was going to be such an ass, I thought, I had better be with her. The two of us, travelling at a fair pace, reached the town in a couple of hours, found the Town Major, a good Serb, from whom Zorica demanded a car. Apparently, I was the First Lord of the Admiralty, if I understood the conversation correctly. She got the car, and we went back to pick up the party at the farm and headed on, without incident, to Kotor, arriving about midnight. There, already, were most of the British Mission, Ronnie Campbell and the Rolls, some Poles and Czechs, Belgians and other Allied colleagues and a number of nannies and governesses who had reached Kotor, a haven. But for how long?

There was talk of a destroyer from Malta but I knew how heavy our naval losses had been and surely we were not worth that risk. A submarine perhaps, despite the minefields of the Straits of Otranto. Rumour intensified and the next night we all boarded a tug to rendezvous with a destroyer. An hour or two later we disembarked and moved from Kotor to Herzognovi, near the entrance to the Gulf.

There, drama did develop, for early that morning the first Wehrmacht column swept into and through the town. Mighty impressive the young men looked. I gave Zorica a cyanide pill, keeping one for myself. Hers she put down the loo, with astounding foresight, for at that moment the Germans moved on as it was the Italians, not they, who were to occupy this part of Dalmatia. With the Italians, we thought, some kind of *combazione* might be possible. With the Germans it would have been the Gestapo. Relief surged through and even more as a British submarine did, in fact, surface off Herzognovi. The Italian colonel immediately signalled: 'Welcome. Come ashore and lunch.' The British replied: 'As visitors it is only polite if we invite your officers to join us.' Whereupon two Italian officers went out to the submarine and boarded her just as a German bomber came in to attack. The submarine dived and her two guests enjoyed her hospitality for rather longer than they expected.

'Bloody Germans, they interfere with everything we do,' said the Italian colonel, who by then was becoming quite a friend. The drama of that day was not yet over. Hugh Macdonald, the Air Attaché, had a signal from Athens that a Sunderland flying boat, flown by Group Captain Francis, would attempt a landing off Herzognovi to take to safety those Yugoslavs and Allied personnel in greatest danger. This meant moving 40 or 50 by boat from Herzognovi across the bay to the small cruise liner moored below the cliffs on the west side of the Gulf, from where, if the Sunderland succeeded, they could be transferred. No easy exercise, but with Denis Larking's and the Belgian minister, Alain Obert de Theuisse's, quiet and determined leadership and control, all was accomplished.

The Sunderland was on time, the transfer brief and speedy. Her takeoff, with the numbers packed, seemed to take an eternity, but there was then a moment of exultation as she broke from the water, with so many good people like Tupanjanin on board. It was a great piece of flying by a great flying boat skipper!

For us, there was an incredible sense of relief as our Allied friends had good prospects of safety. For ourselves, about a 100 in number, at least we were in an Italian, not a German, zone of occupation and many had diplomatic status, for what it was worth.

We were to be more than fortunate. We were taken by army truck and bus to Tirana in Albania, then flown by Savoia-Marchettis to Foggia, where I had an amiable conversation with some of the Afrika Korps, passing through to Tunis. They seemed pleased I was British and not Italian. We ended up in Tuscany and there in Cianciano we were lodged in a pleasant hotel. We played cricket until, unexpectedly, we were evacuated through France to Spain in a sleeper train and fed beer, bacon and eggs all night.

They say Count Ciano, Italy's Foreign Minister and son-in-law of Mussolini, had decided Italy would not win the war and we were convenient pawns. I do not know. It is another story. But my love of Tuscany and of the Italians has never lessened.

But neither had Yugoslavia seen the last of me...

10

Intermission Elsewhere, but in 1944 Back to the Danube

We British at Kotor were to be indeed fortunate. Deemed eligible by Rome for repatriation, we travelled by luxury train through unoccupied France to Madrid. Here we went our different ways, in my case with Zorica to Lisbon and then by Clipper back to the UK.

Germany was in total control of the Balkans and of the Danube. Traffic by the river had become even greater with the new task of meeting ever growing demands from the Wehrmacht and Luftwaffe as they drove farther east and south towards the Caucasus.

There was no scope for Allied interference. However a new sector of warfare was emerging, one in which I had some experience of life, the Arctic. To supply our new ally the Soviet Union, the one possible route was through the Northern Seas to Murmansk or Archangel, long and hazardous, exposed as it was in the 24-hour daylight of summer to unremitting air and U-boat attack from north Norway.

These operations do not belong to this book. However a brief sketch of my own minor part may not be out of place. It included the mistaken British decision in August 1941 to leave unoccupied the pivotal island of Spitsbergen by evacuating its Norwegian and Russian coal miners. Within 24 hours the Germans were there, establishing weather stations and an air strip. To dislodge them a Norwegian commando was formed and sailed in April 1942, when on arrival we were sunk while ice breaking by four Focke-Wulf bombers.

These Arctic operations demanded aircraft with a range previously thought impossible. The USA had them, amongst the first the Catalinas with 24-hour-plus endurance. They made continuing major contributions to the convoys not least in their surveys of the polar sea ice, and in Spitsbergen turned initial disaster into success.

For me most of 1942 accordingly passed in the combined role of flying in the Catalinas of 210 Squadron and in Spitsbergen with the Norwegians, a determined and stimulating lot led by Captain Ernst Ullring, DSO, RNN. It was no accident that Hitler later was to choose this garrison of 100 men as the target on the one occasion he risked his heavy ships together at sea in September 1943.

Two other operations I would prefer to forget might none the less be mentioned. One to sabotage the torpedo bombers at Banak I thought up myself. It was foolhardy, logistically impossible, beyond any capacity of mine to lead and would have cost ten men their lives. Duke Hussey has written 'Chance Governs All'. Chance was kind for the Germans moved the aircraft elsewhere and the operation was cancelled.

The other, a raid in January 1942 by two slow Armed Merchant Cruisers, was different. The target was Harstad. When in sight of Lofoten in perfect visibility we were sighted by a HE 111. Convinced no doubt that no Allied force would be so foolish to be there, he concluded we could only be German blockade runners from the Far East and escorted us maintaining radio silence. Meanwhile we hoisted German colours and gave Nazi salutes. Then, as he left us, in came the signal 'Return Scapa, *Tirpitz* reported northbound'.

We did so flat out at 10 knots, unscathed, dropping anchor some 60 hours later. A fruitless impossible mission, 400 men's lives needlessly at risk. No official report has so far been found bar one stating our two ships were at Scapa throughout that period.

It was with some relief that in Spring 1943 DNI ordered me back to the Mediterranean to report to SO(I) Alexandria. As summer moved on Sicily was liberated in 38 days in July making possible the early invasion of mainland Italy. Action against the Danube and the Romanian oil fields no longer was remote. Once the Allies had secured Brindisi and Bari, the air fields of the Foggia plain would open a new dimension of attack on the Balkans and south Germany.

In fact return to Yugoslavia did occur surprisingly soon, to the island Korcula where, despite its being reported under German control, we were to rendezvous with Fitzroy Maclean and give him a new radio transmitter. David Satho and I were landed by an ML in darkness on a long muddy beach. Hampered by the radio and a square tin of peanut butter which I knew Fitzroy craved, we crawled on gallantly until challenged by a Detroit-born Partisan guard. 'Are you guys doin' this for dooty? There ain't a German on the island.'

Much slivovitz followed, a taxi driven by a drunk White Russian, and then the rendezvous. The peanut butter cemented a life-long family friendship with consequences which still steer our life today.

Some months in Albania followed as a small part of an overall deception plan. Our role was limited to beach surveys and checking enemy coastal batteries. Quite fun but it could seem rather pointless as life in a cave with millions of fleas in the dust floor and black scorpions in the ceiling. What made it memorable was the company of Anthony Quayle,[1] his kindness, inimitable humour and the reckless courage of one of the bravest men I have ever known Munsitti, previously Intelligence Officer in the Italian Army who had come over to join us. Later he was to be the very distinguished Mayor of Genoa who outfaced the Communist efforts to take over the city.

Last days in Albania were made rather special however by the arrival of a group of exceedingly attractive American nurses whose aircraft had made a slight navigational error. Instead of landing them in Sicily, they crashed several hundred miles off course in eastern Albania. Saved by a British Military Mission they showed the greatest courage and endurance in being moved from Mission to Mission across that harsh mountain country, evading German capture and reaching our sea base. Their lipstick and nails were as immaculate as if they had been on Fifth Avenue. Their legs, however, were torn by the thorns and the undergrowth through which they had scrambled, morale intact and triumphant in spirit.

An MTB (motor torpedo boat) from Bari collected them at first light the following morning. Naturally, they had to have an escort and as the only naval officer in Albania, it was my privilege. It was a glorious dawn and a speedy passage with all the girls on deck. As we approached the swept channel to Bari, Admiral Carlill's flotilla of destroyers was just sailing for action further

70

north. They sighted us and their bow waves exploded as they passed the signal 'What the devil do you think you are doing?' With the authority of the President of the United States behind us we replied: 'Proceeding on Most Secret Duties'.

It was difficult in Bari to find out what, if anything, was afoot in regard to the Danube. All I could glean at the SOE were mutterings about possible sabotage, as in the old days. So those first days in the region left me with little hope of playing any further part in Yugoslavia. SOE Bari clearly had no time for me; anyway, I was an Admiralty interloper, not one of theirs, and worse, a friend of Fitzroy Maclean,[2] from whom they, or rather their Cairo HQ, had received such a drubbing. And, it seemed, I was out of touch!

All the greater then was my surprise at a signal from the DNI: 'Top secret and personal, return London forthwith, report to me. Immediate priority air travel confirmed'. I lost no time. Best of all was confirmation on arrival at Naval Intelligence Division (NID) that mine laying of the Danube was *on*.

At NID, I joined an old Danube hand, Commander Dillon RN, to prepare a report on mine laying operations and also on the consequences of the arrival of Soviet forces on the river. The Chiefs of Staff had already approved the first and also agreed that assistance be given to subsequent clearance of the mines to enable Soviet forces to use the river as they moved westwards and northwards.

To crystallise the operations, the DNI held a final meeting at which Commander Vladimir Wolfson, RNVR,[3] the experienced Assistant Naval Attaché in Turkey, was also present. Wolfson's responsibilities were made clear: to form a Royal Navy minesweeping unit, skilled in shallow-water operations, which he would command and hold in readiness to assist the Soviet forces as soon as they reached the Lower Danube. Whether the Soviet High Command would accept such assistance was unpredictable. The unit, however, would be prepared and ready.

My own role was left unspecified. I was to fly back to Naples for orders from the Commander-in-Chief Mediterranean, Admiral Sir John Cunningham himself!

Wolfson, an old friend, and I flew to Italy in mid-April via Algiers. I was uneasy and anxious; I hate uncertainty and patience has never been one of my virtues. Wolfson continued on to

Istanbul and I to Naples, reporting to Admiral Cunningham at the lovely Villa Emma,[4] his formal residence.

'Sit down,' he said, in his warm, quiet way. 'This is a tricky and dangerous one. The Danube mining is of the highest importance and we want as much on-the-spot intelligence on it as we can get. That will be your job, but there is more to it. Soviet armies will need the use of the river and as you know, Wolfson's mine-sweeping force will be waiting to help them.

'This cannot be done, out of the blue, you can understand what I mean, so we are counting on you to make early contact with the Red Army, get through to their High Command, inform them of the mines, of our wish to help and, of course, find out if they will accept that help.'

I was pretty stunned and doubt if I made an audible reply.

The Admiral continued: 'We are asking both Moscow and the Soviet Liaison Officer with Fitzroy (Maclean) at Tito's HQ to have you accredited as my personal representative, authorised to act on my behalf at all levels of command. You will, of course, be working closely with Mediterranean Air Forces, but that should not be difficult, as Jack Slessor and Baker seem to know you, some Arctic antics with Catalinas!'[5] He got up from his chair, put his hand on my shoulder and added: 'It's a tough one. I am right behind you and ask for anything. Good luck, you will need it.'

I took some days to think things through. Meet the Red Army! Simple enough if one wanted to be shot at once or end up in Lubianka prison. These fears were eased somewhat when I learned I was to be dropped to the Partisan force nearest the Danube and they would do the meeting. What about language, however? I was not a Russian speaker, after all, but that too solved itself. The Red Army bit, anyway, was months away so I turned to more immediate problems.

Thorough was the cooperation at Mediterranean Allied Air Forces at Caserta. The personal welcome from Air Marshal Sir John Slessor, Deputy Commander-in-Chief MAAF renewed a friendship in London in the early months of the war when he was Director of Plans at the Air Ministry. His SASO was Air Vice-Marshal George Baker. They arranged that I was fully informed of the mining operations already underway and those planned for the rest of that summer and autumn, as well as the raids on the

72

Ploesti oil fields. I was put in contact with the Torpedo Officer, Captain Roger Lewis,[6] and his first-class team at Taranto, which was building up the essential mine stocks.

The Commander-in-Chief's letter of appointment was circulated as follows:[7]

> Lieutenant Commander A.R. Glen, DSC, RNVR, of my Staff, has been appointed British Naval Liaison Officer Middle Danube. In addition to other duties with Partisans, he is to act in liaison with such Soviet Forces as may penetrate the river. Please inform Soviet Mission accordingly. Brigadier Maclean concurs. Soviet Mission in Cairo and Algiers also being informed.

He signed his letter on 28 April. Already in SOE's Cairo HQ feathers were flying. In a sense it was understandable. After the frustrations of 1939/40, they were hoping that their old sabotage plans for the Danube could now be achieved. What they overlooked was that the days when small-scale operations were the only options – and difficult at that – had gone and the present was one of massive air assault. They were also inept in failing to appreciate the logistic importance of the Danube to our allies, the Red Army.

This was a strange contrast with the imaginative success of the SOE London in support of Operation Overlord, on and after D-Day with the Jedburgh Missions[8] and the French Resistance. Indeed, with the vital role Douglas Dodds Parker and Massingham[9] had already played in the Italian Armistice and the SOE's continuing operations in Italy, especially as the Wehrmacht withdrew northwards, in easing the transfer of power and the reduction of civilian casualties.

SOE Cairo's attitude was not easy to understand except they were an odd bunch anyway. Perhaps it was that the Admiralty was my master and not the SOE; quite simply, they may not have trusted me. A few extracts from the records should be quoted, the first a reasonable memo from D/HT (Lieutenant Colonel Talbot Rice, MBE) to Director/Navy on 4 April 1944:[10]

> There is one point which I think might perhaps be taken up with advantage at this stage with the Admiralty, namely that

Glen stresses in his report (a) the necessity of intelligence and (b) the necessity for re-opening the Danube. Intelligence is, of course, extremely important but I understand that the JIC[11] gave a ruling a short time ago that the Danube was not likely to be of great importance to us when once the Germans had moved out of the Balkans, whereas the denial of it to the Germans as an arterial route was of major importance to the war effort. I feel, therefore, that the emphasis has perhaps been put by Glen on the wrong aspect of the matter and that we should press for stress being put on the importance of sabotage, not only because that is SOE's task but because it has been stressed by JIC as of major importance.

This led to several exchanges involving differences of opinion which lasted some weeks and underlined the uneasy relationship between myself and the SOE. They seemed to have forgotten that at one time in 1941 I was their main link in the Balkans, after their own operatives had been expelled. Or perhaps they remembered it only too well! The tension obviously struck a particularly sour note with a certain Major J.A. Dolbey,[12] based in SOE Cairo. In his reply to SOE HQ London, on the possibility of my being dropped to the Partisans, he made out a nine-point case[13] *against* this happening, including:

6. It is not, repeat not, clear who Glenn [*sic*] is working for and what the purpose of his Mission would be.
9. Request that you clarify Glenn's position before sponsoring his efforts. It seems to us that he is trying to play off one branch against another.

He was probably right in that. I knew there was a vital job to be done and I was determined to do it by whatever means I had. After all, *nine* reasons against were sporting odds!

In the choice of a wireless operator, however, SOE Bari turned up trumps with Sergeant Turner of the Royal Corps of Signals (RCOS). He was skilled, with a calm courage that was to see him through every panic and crisis; a reassuring companion and friend, we were extremely fortunate.

In fact, relations with SOE Bari were thawing; I was not their body and maybe they were realising that this was for the best.

Certainly, now that they had their orders, our flight and comfort lacked nothing.

Perhaps I had been told too much of the mining operations and future plans, considering the possibility that I might be captured. The SOE were less forthcoming for that very reason about reports from their own agents in the field and future plans. Perhaps correctly!

Bari in those months was a hive of activity, arms being shipped by the little boats and schooners to the Yugoslav coast, the Royal Navy, with the likes of Admirals Carlill and Morgan-Giles, raiding almost every day enemy targets in the northern Adriatic, and Tom Churchill's Commandos, not unduly welcomed by Tito's Communist followers.

In our own context were the meetings of the Danube Committee, a coordinating body whose minutes, reread these long years since, fail to convince me of the value of these meetings which they record my attending. No doubt useful work was done, but with hindsight much, too, was not anticipated or allowed for, responsibility for which I share.

Important was the question whether the Red Army would permit us to use our own wireless telegraph (W/T) communications. There was a legitimate question of security. In any event, it would have been prudent to ensure a mutual signals plan with them. So, what details of the mining, the sectors in which mines were 'sewn', should be in our possession, or that of any other mission, in the event of capture by the enemy?

Most important was the passage of time since the mine laying and the bombing of Ploesti, both of which had begun in April. If the clearing of the river for its use by the Red Army was to be of maximum benefit, then it would be to the Red Army that our mission should be dropped and not to a Partisan unit, with the prospect of infinite delay. Whether, politically, this was practicable was another matter, but at least it should have been examined.

As D-Day came and the initial landings succeeded, I began increasingly to fret. Unnecessarily, I was told, as Partisan forces were still too far from the river. By the third week in June, however, progress had been made and a well-chosen dropping point agreed: Citluk, some 30 miles north-north-east of Nis. Best of all we had a date: 28 June.

Sergeant Turner and I dined well in the Navy mess and reported in good time at Brindisi. We were thrilled to learn that one of the great Polish Halifax squadrons was to take us; we knew that no hitch or setback would stop *them*. Their welcome was, as always, warm and friendly, yet we both sensed something – a restraint, not quite Polish. It was only much later that we realised their fears for those in Warsaw under immediate attack by the Germans, heightened by doubt as to any help being likely from the advancing Red Army.

This had no impact, however, on the competence and kindness of our aircrew, who dropped us precisely on target and on time. As their aircraft flew on, the prospect that it, together with the entire Polish squadron, was to perish in the final heroic but impossible attempt to bring aid to Warsaw, was unthinkable.

11

Chintz and Scrambled Eggs

'Dwi minuty!' The Polish pilot's voice crackled into the earphones and the dispatcher tapped first Sergeant Turner and then myself on the shoulder. The warning light flashed red, two fingers indicating it was only a couple of minutes to the drop zone.

I went first, a bit slowly, crouching with the weight of parachute and accoutrements under limited headroom, then arranging myself comfortably on the edge of the hatch, legs dangling. Red to green and, with a hefty Polish push from the dispatcher, out into the slipstream, with that exhilarating silence – and the comforting view of Sergeant Turner, not far above.

As a return to Yugoslavia some three years after leaving as a prisoner of the Italians, memories stirred as prospects posed their questions.

However, there was not much time for either as both Turner and I landed right on target, between the guiding fires laid by the Partisans.[1] Our reception was prompt and speedy. Rounds of embraces from roughish faces, raki too, a welcome far preferable to the chilly procedures today at Heathrow and Gatwick and, of course, no Customs or Immigration!

'Give me travel by parachute any day,' said Turner, quite unaffected by it all, or by the Breughel-like activity in the dim light of the dwindling fires, as figures shuffled into view and disappeared again with supply containers being loaded into peasant carts.

Within an hour we were on our way. Where to? Yes, we knew, presumably Citluk village, but to a comfortable and well-kept little house? That we could never have guessed. More was to come: a warm bedroom with a couple of beds, chintz curtains and a tough but loveable old bird, anxious to pamper us.

Turner and I looked at each other in amazement before falling into our beds. We were asleep within minutes. Next morning was every bit as good: breakfast with coffee and scrambled eggs, served with a smile which waned only as gunfire broke the silence outside. 'Bulgars,' she said dismissively, 'we'll see them off!'

'Give me Citluk any day rather than army quarters in Bari,' said Sergeant Turner. 'I thought we were coming to an occupied country.'

We were, of course, unbelievably lucky. Most missions with both Partisans and Cetniks experienced very different circumstances from the moment of landing, some facing immediate attack by Axis troops and imminent danger. Cooperation with resistance forces could be knife-edged, suspicion turning into outright hostility and patience and understanding tested to the limit.

What Fitzroy Maclean and Bill Deakin[2] achieved on their visits to Marshal Tito[3] was indeed remarkable. But one should not forget the other side, the Cetniks.[4] Jasper Rootham,[5] Erik Greenwood[6] and Bill Bailey had huge problems to confront and every credit is due them. Of all, however, it must be Bill Hudson, the first British officer landed back after the German invasion, who faced the worst in surviving, mostly alone, that terrible first winter of 1941/42.

In our early good fortune, there was enough reality to make us remember and ponder.

As we were assembling our weapons and belongings, Turner checking his wireless set, the door opened. A Partisan officer came in, looked at us quite carefully, and said quietly: 'Welcome!'

12

Tito's Partisans

He was middle-aged, rather tubby and wore an unmarked battle-dress, hardly the role model for a resistance commander. But he was, introducing himself modestly, commanding officer of the 23rd Partisan Brigade, the first, he explained, to operate in eastern Serbia.

Partisan operations had hitherto been concentrated farther west and south, in Bosnia and Montenegro, as well as in South Serbia, as has been described by Fitzroy Maclean and Bill Deakin. Serbia itself had been subject to harsh German oppression as well as that of the Bulgars and Hungarians. In addition, the Ljotic and Nedic[1] auxiliaries had played their part, making Serbia more difficult and dangerous for the Partisans to penetrate.

'Anyway, we are here now, and on our way north,' said the Partisan leader. 'I know you want to reach the Danube, it may take time, but I will keep you informed on what we hear about the Danube. We have a lot of friends, you know. You will have a liaison officer who speaks your language, let him know what you need.'

Our own understanding of the precise situation near the river was fragmentary. Tito and his Partisans had been accepted, much on the advice of Maclean and Deakin, as the goodies, the Cetniks, under Mihailovic, as the baddies, no longer to receive British support.

On immediate military grounds, this was certainly a correct decision. It was the Partisans who were diverting Axis troops from other more important theatres, even if many were non-German units. Yet the abandoned Cetniks were still conducting to safety Allied airmen who had been shot down. Generalisations are dangerous things, and I cannot forget that during the German attack on Yugoslavia on 6 April 1941 the Communists lent no support and it was Mihailovic who first began resistance in the hills.

Tito certainly initiated and developed active war against the occupiers on a scale that won German respect and without restraint as to the human cost involved. Mihailovic did not; with the memory of 1914/18 when Serbia lost nearly a quarter of its people, he was determined not to allow this to happen again and we British should not have believed he would falter in this conviction.

I remembered Mostar too, and the slaughter that followed that bloody summer. Was it a quarter of a million Serbs killed by the Croat Ustachi, men, women and children? Was it half a million? Figures matter, as does the enormity of the evil perpetrated by Ustachi leader Pavelic and too many in the Catholic hierarchy. In truth, those years of 1941 to 1945 witnessed such tragedy and horror as to make confusion total. Religious wars between Orthodox, Catholic and Muslim; war against the occupiers, be they German, Italian, Bulgar or Hungarian; civil war between Left and Right; the war of greed for a neighbour's piece of land; and, just as bitter, to settle old scores, and new ones as well.

What alone seemed clear was that revenge would come; that a torch of hate would smoulder and remain alight for decades, for generations. I felt for these people in this unhappy, cursed land, with humanity both at its worst and most gallant, a product of ruthless extermination and astounding survival.

As we set off in this eastern sector of Serbia, the Brigade, then numbering 250, proceeded with caution. Skirmishing with Bulgarian forces was not infrequent and involved hard fighting, although deserters were coming over. There were Cetniks in this part of Homolje, but conflict was rare. I recall only two encounters and was sad to see two young officers dead, both wearing the sky-blue tunics of the Royal Guard, which I had last seen on 27 March 1941, when they mounted the *coup*.

Only later did we meet Wehrmacht forces, as their withdrawal from Greece, by the Morava Valley, was interrupted by Allied air attacks, thus forcing them to Nis and the Timok Valley to Negotin.

In the villages, as we bivouacked, we saw little of anti-Partisan sentiments, rather the opposite. Receipts were given for food or shelter provided, and on Turner and myself there were no restraints at all as to where we went or with whom we talked. Particularly interesting were the recruits coming in – most days perhaps 10 or 15 – men and women of every type and age: a banker, doctors, peasants, women young and not-so-young. There was a lovely Jewish girl in her last, elegant black dress, the only survivor of a rich Sephardic Sarajevo family, speaking English and French. One of the many students who joined, from Dubrovnik, knew Zorica's mother and stepfather.

It was a continuous circular route we took, edging gradually further north. Much of the landscape was parkland, with great meadows and woodlands, offering cover from the very occasional enemy aircraft. I have perhaps understated the amount of action for, inevitably, we had casualties and serious ones, too, whom we had to bring with us in the farm wagons, jolted and bumped over rough tracks, heart-breaking in their stoicism.

Fortunately, by that stage in the war the recently-formed Balkan Air Force were flying Dakotas from Italian bases and their British and American pilots engaged in these missions of care were landing on unprepared strips in Yugoslavia – usually maize fields, lit by flares. There were few moments of exultation greater than seeing a fully-laden aircraft stagger into the night sky with its cargo of men and women who, in a couple of hours, would be safely in hospital.[2]

I was given a regular flow of information as to what was happening on the Danube. They were invariably second- and third-hand reports and, initially, I was sceptical about their integrity, but the theme was consistent as to the positive impact the aerial mining of the river was having, both on the interruption of craft carrying oil to Germany and on the morale of the barge crews. When later these reports could be compared with operational records, they proved surprisingly accurate.

By August, there was consistent evidence of Yugoslav crews and pilots deserting from German barges and of the limited success German countermeasures were having against the low-flying Wellingtons and Liberators laying their mines.

During July and August, life with the Partisans was surprisingly relaxed. Long marches, much by night, but gentle sleeping in the shade, often enough by day. Plenty of fresh fruit to be plucked, strawberries, apricots and the ubiquitous blue plum, of which I once ate about 60 and then couldn't climb down from the tree.

Daily life followed a pattern: breakfast at first light of a hunk of bread, a whole garlic and a drop of slivovica; supper at any time, either afternoon or early evening, depending on how much ground we had to cover. It was worth waiting for with either a full plate of scrambled eggs, or an omelette, with lots of bread and the hard, Serbian cheese, with onion and garlic.

There were dangers, sure. There was the pig which, while I was shaving in a farmyard, ate my toothpaste and spectacles with frothy enjoyment; the hornet that kept us submerged in an icy pool for what seemed hours. But of the Germans at that time there was little sign.

Losing my glasses meant the following two days were a nightmare of stumbling up and down hill paths, almost sightless. But on the third night we were told to meet a drop of supplies from a Halifax. The drop was right on time but all we could find was one parachute container with, inside, Chinese box within Chinese box. Finally, one pair of spectacles compliments of Admiral Sir John Cunningham, to whom I had signalled my predicament. I must say, I had been more popular with the Partisans than I was that night.

This quiet life changed in mid-August! The retreat of the Wehrmacht from Greece was in full flood, 'highly impressive' as Djilas[3] wrote about the quality and discipline of an army in retreat. In Romania, Marshal Tolbukhin's[4] Third Ukrainian Army was moving swiftly towards the Danube, already near enough for a Partisan mission under Major Djuich to be sent to them. I asked to accompany them but was refused on the grounds of danger. I suspect they felt this great Communist event would be spoilt by the inclusion of a Capitalist lackey! Their refusal was just as well. All the Russians did was to lock up the Partisan mission.

We were still moving fast, capturing in turn Zajecar and Negotin, but from the latter having to move out again as German armour counterattacked.

Now heading for the Iron Gates Canal on the Danube, we moved past the great copper mines of Bor and then headed back again towards the open country east of Negotin. It was here that we made our first contact with the Russians on 2 September, with a small but high-level meeting in a remote farm. Again, I was not allowed to sit in with the morning session, but the sequel was illuminating.

In our farmhouse, I had a room to myself. At about 2pm, the door opened and the Partisan Brigade's Political Commissar, a tiresome young man, came in and sat down, looking thoroughly dejected. 'The Russians are worse than you,' he snorted. 'We have fought this war for them and now they treat us like dogs.' He left without any sympathy from me. I felt rather good about it. No sooner had he left than a NKVD[5] officer, a good-looking man in his forties, entered. He sat down, looking very weary and asked: 'You are a professional?' I felt I should be and nodded, 'Yes.' He went on: 'You will understand what it is like being told by these tin-pot amateurs how to fight a war. Rather than spend a morning with them, I would rather do the Dniester and Dnieper[6] crossings again.' And with a wry smile, he left.

A few days later, on 14 September, a new mission codenamed Dolphin, parachuted in. Led by Captain Dickie Franks, it had a specialist Danube role. Dickie himself, young and fresh-faced, combined a vivid mind with exquisite manners, not so common in those days. It did not take long to assess that he was destined for high places.

What was a special pleasure was reacquaintance with two old Czech friends from the Michael Mason days in 1940: Ralf Navratil and Jaroslav Vrana, who had helped so much in enticing the Danube pilots from their jobs. Navratil had not changed at all. Lean and alert, he was now a convincing RNVR Sub-Lieutenant using the name Ralph Turpin. Vrana, however, still tubby with his innocent baby face, looked less the part of Pilot Officer Peter Bing, of the RAFVR, but I knew enough of his exploits to recall that this was a most formidable chap, whose path I would not choose to cross. I shall never forget the occasion, later, when we first met up with the Russians. Our party had strayed into the forest behind Klokosevac, for no good reason. Bing was suddenly taken short and went into the trees. Moments later there was a burst of gunfire and Bing re-emerged, trousers still half-down to declare: 'I am a little upset.'

In the fourth member of the mission, Dolphin was equally fortunate. Their wireless operator, Sergeant Roberts, of the RCOS, was a good linguist, robust and already experienced behind the lines in Yugoslavia, having accompanied a previous mission to Mihailovic's Cetniks.

They were all welcome for many reasons, then and later. Some of their objectives had already been overtaken by the Red Army's advance, but in the field of intelligence, especially with Turpin and Bing's knowledge of the river and of so many pilots and other crews, the mission was invaluable. Equally, in contact with the Red Army, their command of the Slav tongues and Dickie's sharp eye for detail, surpassed anything we possessed. Years later, it was no surprise when Dickie Franks rose to the very top of British Intelligence in MI6.

Dolphin's brief included that of providing intelligence on the Danube, a task which, as described in Chapter 15, they were to fulfil brilliantly within a few brief weeks. Their other duties of scorch and sabotage had been overtaken by the mammoth scale of the aerial mining of the Danube and the advance of the Russians. So, in effect, we, the Twilfit and Dolphin missions, settled down to work as a combined team.

The Wehrmacht retreating from Greece northwards had been largely diverted, by Allied air attacks, from their preferred escape route via the Morava Valley farther east to the Timok, past Negotin. Somewhere they had to cross the Danube, although the use of the river was closed to them, as they were well aware, by the mines. They were on an inevitable collision course with the Red Army, already established in battalion strength on the west bank of the Danube Bulge around the Iron Gates.

The Red Army had the initiative, fanning out in increasing strength to prevent a Wehrmacht escape towards Orsova, and gaining control of the west bank between Turnu Severin and Vidin. In this, Partisan units played an effective part, resulting in German forces being steadily concentrated in a reducing pocket. That this was effectively surrounded and finally liquidated in early October did not mean there was no fight left in the Wehrmacht. There was plenty before that fateful time in October, determined and hard, as we ourselves were to find out.

By then Sergeant Turner and I had finally broken away from the SOE Twilfit mission and, together with the four-man Dolphin party, transferred to the 25th Partisan Brigade, which was moving closer to where we wanted to be. Just before this, I had a tricky few days with a touch of pleurisy, slung over a mule with little awareness of where we were, except that it was cold, wet and bloody uncomfortable. But it cleared up, after, if it is not a dream, being cupped in some peasant hut.

It was imperative that Red Army HQ were informed without further delay of the mined areas of the Danube and the availability of minesweeping assistance from Commander Wolfson's team. German counter-attacks spoilt two efforts to break through but on the third, on 26 September, we succeeded in reaching an advance Red Army HQ in the little village of Klokosevac.

13

West Meets East: September 1944

The 26 September 1944 began as a calm sunny morning. We were on one of the many timbered ridges, with steep valleys plunging below. Confused fighting was taking place not that far away but, comfortingly, not too near either. This was to be the day when we made contact with the Red Army, through the Partisans, as we had hoped, but not in a manner so theatrically improbable!

Early that morning we had come across a discarded German motor-bike and sidecar. For once, too, we were on a road, not a mountain track. The tank had petrol and there were no apparent booby traps. Too good a chance to miss so five, yes five, of us piled on. We went for half a mile or so, and then round a long bend, with the ground falling away on the left and then, suddenly, no road at all, for it had been blown up. Beyond, ominously, was a machine-gun post manned not by Germans but by Russians. And they didn't open fire! Three of them, wearing long grey coats, slowly stood up and, to our surprise, waved us to come forward. When we did so, there were bear hugs and mutual embraces.

We seemed incredibly lucky, running as we did into the usually trigger-happy Russians manning a machine-gun post while we were riding a swastika-marked German motor-bike. And not getting shot on sight! The truth was that contact had been made between the Red Army Battalion Command and the Partisans late the previous night. I can only assume, and it is only an assumption, that the Russians had been given orders not to open fire on any stray Partisan units or lunatic Brits.

That assumption seemed all the stronger when our new Russian friends knew exactly what we had to do. Battalion HQ was a few miles down the valley, in the hamlet of Klokosevac, where we would find their commanding officer, Colonel Sucharnikov, and our Partisan comrades as well. One of them would accompany us and on we went, finding, incredibly, a carnival in full swing.

The small taverna was packed and *raki* flowing freely, but within a matter of minutes Dickie and I were with the Colonel, a slim, blond man, alert but looking far too young for the two 'Hero of the Soviet Union' insignia he was wearing. Later, we learned he had survived Stalingrad. No time was lost by him ascertaining the urgency that our responsibilities concerning the Danube must reach the appropriate Soviet High Command.

Thank heavens for Turpin and Bing, our two interpreters. 'I will arrange all this for you at once,' the Colonel confirmed but now, he stressed, we had to celebrate this first meeting between the forces of the East and the West. Who was my commanding officer?

'Admiral Sir John Cunningham, Commander-in-Chief, Mediterranean,' I told him. Would we send the Admiral his compliments? We did! Sergeant Turner got the signal off at once and within three hours the reply came with Cunningham's compliments to the Colonel and the Red Army. This was the signal for more celebrations that continued most of the day. We met some of Sucharnikov's fellow officers, all veterans of the eastern campaigns, tested, tough and immensely friendly, each with little gifts for us, such as battered tin cigarette cases. Little they may have been but they became treasured memories of great fighting men.

Even now, almost 60 years later, I remember the exultation we shared that day. The Red Army, we knew, had turned almost inevitable defeat first into dogged resistance in holding Moscow and then, after Stalingrad, into defeat of the Wehrmacht, perhaps the most deadly war machine the world had then known.

To be with them, a key assault unit, the officers and men who had achieved this, was a privilege, as was the welcome that they gave us. On a lesser note, the relief that at least part of our mission had been accomplished was not small.

A few days later, arrangements were complete for us to proceed with a Soviet escort of a sergeant and eight men to Division HQ at Brza Palanka. Three troikas, each with two horses, were provided and, early on a perfect morning, we set off.

As the sun rose and we reached the treeless open country, life seemed good, all the more so as we noticed the number of Soviet troops over a nearby hillside. Suddenly, two of our horses fell dead. 'They're bloody Germans, not Russians,' shouted Dickie Franks, 'get the hell out, quick.' As I dived out of the troika, the lanyard attached to my Luger pistol caught on one of the spokes of the cart, but broke as if it were thread.

Several members of the escort in the front troika were killed but not their sergeant, a bull of a man. Following him, we slid down a ravine under heavy fire, twisting and turning and, in our minds at least, becoming the first men to run a mile in under four minutes. The Russian sergeant saved us, no doubt about that. Not only by the speed of his immediate reaction which we followed, but also in his identification of other, heavy gunfire as Russian. It was in that direction he led and we followed.

How far we followed a dried-out stream I cannot recall, then through woodland and there they were, a battery of four guns, equivalent perhaps of the German 88mms, maintaining continuous fire on the Wehrmacht counterattack.

We feared we had lost Bing, Sergeant Roberts and four of the escort, but Bing turned up safely, having been captured but then escaping by shooting his guard with a second pistol hidden on his person that his captors had failed to detect. The ever-resourceful Sergeant Roberts reappeared next morning. Separated from us, he had spent several hours submerged in a pool, breathing through reeds as a group of German soldiers rested nearby, on a bank above his head. Sadly, we had lost four of our escort, all killed in the initial attack.

It was a strange scene we then came upon, the artillery men stripped to the waist, serving their guns, behind them a longish wooden building with, outside, a dapper young NKVD officer, chatting to two attractive women NKVD members. They took no notice of us at all, but the thought struck me that if it was going to be the Lubianka, then I wouldn't mind if it was they who took me there!

However, our sergeant had other ideas. This strong, calm man, his face and neck burnt ochre, took his duties seriously. He was not going to leave us until we were in safe hands. In this he succeeded, no mean feat with long stretched lines of communication and a battle in progress.

A senior gunnery officer then took over to escort us across the river to Divisional HQ at Turnu Severin. It was then, and only then, that the sergeant left us, taking my hands and kissing me on both cheeks as I thanked him. 'Only my duty, Tovarich,' he said, saluting smartly and starting his way back to Klokosevac.

The bridge had been demolished, so crossing the Danube from Kladova to Turnu Severin by ferry, we saw the masts of several sunken vessels, victims of the Royal Air Force's mining campaign on the river. Later that evening we were interviewed by a senior staff officer. He clearly knew little of the Danube and whether or not he had received Colonel Sucharnikov's signal, it was difficult to say. He was courteous and correct, however, saying that accommodation was being arranged for us in town until a decision about us had been reached.

We were all very tired, relieved to be alive and, so far, free. As Dickie commented while we were being taken to a small but comfortable little house in the middle of town: 'If a bunch of ruffians claiming to be Russians without papers landed on a British HQ, I bet no one could understand them and they would be shot at once. Sleep well!'

This was to be the start of several weeks with the Russians, in which we witnessed the structure of Tolbukhin's 3rd Ukrainian Army, from front-line assault troops through divisional, corps and army HQs, with access at the highest level and minimum security restraint. After this initial period of what I would describe as hesitant caution at Turnu Severin, our party was to be allowed to travel together without security or escorts. This was to be an experience shared by few, or any other similar mission. Even today, I look back and still find that freedom of movement inexplicable, but something which I would not have missed for anything.

Those first days at Turnu Severin were, however, a little anxious, although full advantage was taken of them by Bing and Turpin. We were not housebound and they both got in touch with old Danube colleagues, from whom they derived much information. No doubt at all, the mining, which from early April had seen well over 1,200 mines 'sewn' in the river, had effectively closed the Danube, not only by direct results of the mining but also by the mass defection of barge crews. It was all very cheering, but we were still not certain where we stood, not least when Dickie, in his quiet way, whispered: 'I have just heard our guards dividing up our possessions.'

In fact, all was well, for the next day a senior naval officer on the staff of the Russians' Danube commander Admiral Sergei Georgiyevich Gorshkov[1] at Giurgiu, arrived to inform us that they had just been notified of our mission. He made no secret that the Admiral was anxious for all the technical help we could provide in clearing the river. They could not do it themselves. Could we help by pinpointing the particularly dangerous sectors?

The answer, responsibly, had to be no and without qualification! For a start, errors in where mines were dropped could be compounded by shifting currents, rendering pinpointing mere guesswork. The charts which Bari had provided Dickie before he was parachuted in had been lost when the Germans attacked our convoy. But there was a more compelling reason. Bari had forgotten to mark on the charts the sectors which had actually been mined. The charts were valueless; indeed it was just as well they had been lost!

What I could say, however, was that Commander Wolfson's minesweeping unit was waiting for a call to help. On hearing this, I was invited by the Russian Naval Officer to return to Giurgiu with him and join Admiral Gorshkov's staff as British Naval Liaison Officer (BNLO), Danube. I would have jumped at it, but the Russians' Division HQ decided that first the whole party of six of us had to proceed to Vidin for talks with Corps Commander, General N.A. Gagen.

This decision by the Red Army Command that we proceed to Sofia and not to Giurgiu, as invited by Admiral Gorshkov, has an intriguing 'might have been' consequence. With, unknown to us, Romania now formally an ally, elements of the British Control Commission were already in Bucharest. Among their number was a young officer, Malcolm Mackintosh, a fluent linguist, especially in the Cyrillic languages, with a distinguished career ahead of him in the Foreign Office and eastern European history. His first weeks were spent in a Russian transit camp, experiencing the same warm relations with fighting soldiers as we had, and this extended itself to a meeting with a small, tubby naval officer, powerful as a personality but jolly. This turned out to be Admiral Gorshkov himself, taking up his appointment as Admiral, Danube, with a well-manned Soviet Naval HQ at Giurgiu.

It was only many years later that Malcolm Mackintosh and I actually met and discovered how closely our paths had almost crossed. On the major issue, future control of the Danube, we both agree that little would have altered, that Soviet political control would have been complete. But had we been with the Admiral, as he wished, it is just possible that the Wolfson minesweeping unit might have been allowed to play a part, limited perhaps, but nonetheless helpful, in speeding the opening of some sectors of the Danube.

Meanwhile, back in Turnu Severin it was all becoming high drama in the Red Army hierarchy which we, as comparatively junior officers, could never have dreamt of entering. Comedy there would be, too, but a little later.

The journey to Vidin was by convoy, including American trucks and jeeps, as Dickie, with a much more discerning eye than mine, will describe later in Chapter 15. There was one nasty moment early on when the convoy suddenly halted in a nicely wooded hollow and we were ordered out. I thought Dickie's fear about the guards having divided up our possessions might have been right, but it was all quite innocent. The stop was 'for our comfort' they explained, for 'there might be fighting further on'.

There certainly was! We could see the effects of heavy shell fire and destroyed bridges being repaired by sappers, up to their shoulders in water. Then a stop for a meal at a large concentration of Russian troops. After the meal, I was invited to address a special Guard of Honour of some 100 Red Army soldiers. My pathetic effort in doing so I will leave to Dickie Franks to spell out also in Chapter 15. At least he seemed to enjoy it, even if everyone else was bewildered.

By nightfall, the convoy was reduced to a few trucks. Noise of shelling and mortar fire ahead broke the silence. Both grew in intensity and, with a good deal coming down around us, the truck suddenly lurched sideways, a rear wheel having come off. Out with all of us and the driver, one of those bottle-shouldered Russians, raised the truck high enough from the ground for the wheel to be shoved back on. He beckoned us in quickly, as too many shells were raining down, but I was perturbed. 'What about the wheel nuts?' I shouted. 'Nuts?' he replied, 'you bloody fool' (or some even stronger Russian oath), 'we lost them back in the Ukraine.'

We reached Vidin and were received by General Gagen the next morning. Once again, the extent of the mining was known, but detailed information was urgently needed and the idea of technical assistance appreciated. One comment of his was pertinent, to be repeated not infrequently later: 'I never thought much of you lot in warfare, are you American or British? It doesn't matter, but your mines are good, no doubt about that. You sunk three of my ships last night, more the night before. I am changing my mind about you.' And we ended the conversation by drinking vodka.

General Gagen confirmed our orders to proceed to Sofia, now unescorted, with rail warrants and no security. The train was due to leave Vidin at 10am. It was a charming little station, rich with roses along the single platform. At about 4pm there was still no train but a Red Army general with two ADCs arrived with a hamper full of hams, wines and vodka. He invited us to share. The train came in at about 7pm and we continued to share! All I recall is a rosy sunset when there was no more vodka or, for that matter, anything else. The General gave an order to his ADCs which I thought I understood. A few minutes later, the ADCs returned with a small can of petrol. The General poured it into our enamel mugs and, lighting his cigarette rather shakily over my mug, swigged it down as, very unwillingly, did the ADCs, who promptly keeled over.

'My apologies my friends,' said the General. 'Don't judge the Red Army by them. They can't hold their drink. They are wartime soldiers only.'

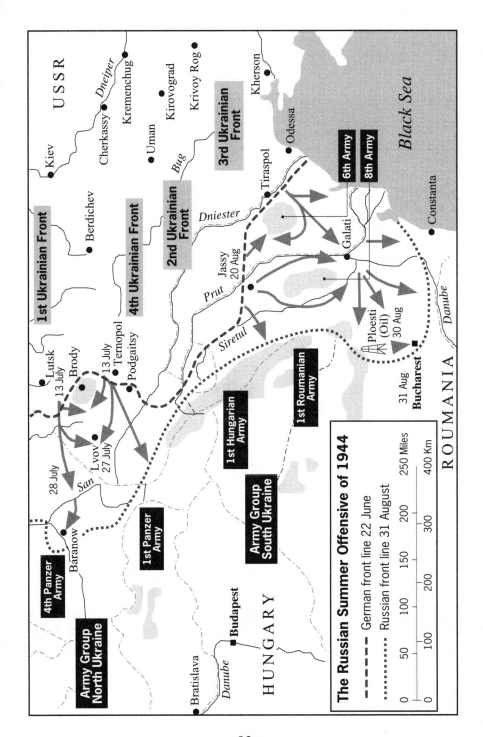

The Russian Summer Offensive of 1944

- - - - German front line 22 June
.... Russian front line 31 August

| 0 | 50 | 100 | 150 | 200 | 250 Miles |

| 0 | 100 | 200 | 300 | 400 Km |

USSR

Kiev
Dnieper
Cherkassy
Kremenchug
Kirovograd
Krivoy Rog
Uman
Bug
Berdichev
Kherson
Odessa

1st Ukrainian Front
2nd Ukrainian Front
3rd Ukrainian Front
4th Ukrainian Front

Black Sea

6th Army
8th Army

Constanta

Tiraspol
Galati
Dniester
Jassy
20 Aug
Prut
Siretul
Ploesti
(Oil)
30 Aug
Bucharest
31 Aug
Danube

Lutsk
13 July
Brody
Ternopol
13 July
Podgaitsy
Lvov
27 July
San
28 July
Baranow

4th Panzer Army
1st Panzer Army
Army Group North Ukraine

1st Hungarian Army
1st Roumanian Army
Army Group South Ukraine

ROUMANIA

HUNGARY
Budapest
Bratislava
Danube

93

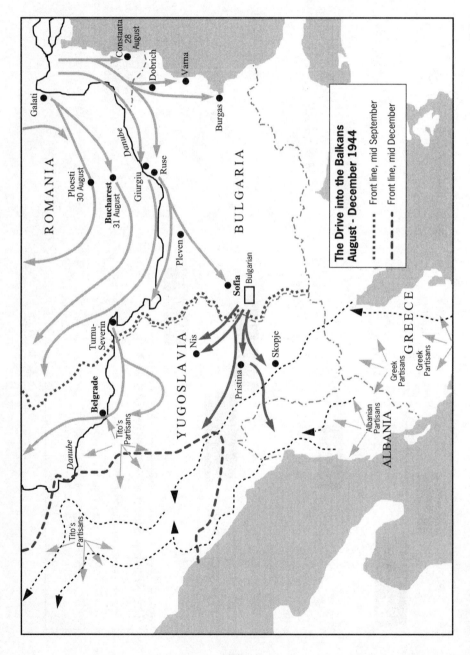

The Drive into the Balkans
August - December 1944

∙∙∙∙∙∙∙∙ Front line, mid September

– – – – – Front line, mid December

ROMANIA

Galati

Ploesti
30 August

Bucharest
31 August

Constanta
28 August

Dobrich

Varna

Burgas

Danube

Giurgiu

Ruse

Pleven

BULGARIA

Sofia   Bulgarian

Turnu-
Severin

Belgrade

Danube

Tito's
Partisans

YUGOSLAVIA

Nis

Pristina

Skopje

Tito's
Partisans

ALBANIA

Albanian
Partisans

GREECE

Greek
Partisans

Greek
Partisans

14

The Red Army

We arrived in Sofia the next morning. No sign of the General. No sign of his ADCs. Were they sleeping it off? Was it all just a dream? From what followed, it might well have been.

A taxi took us to the Balkan Hotel, full of Red Army officers, male and female, some of the women extremely attractive. We booked in as if it were peacetime, no identity required, although I did have an important-looking document from General Gagen.

We had baths and were deloused – which was more necessary than we had thought – then lunched well in the restaurant and I went off to Marshal Tolbukhin's HQ, as instructed, to present my credentials. A slight delay, very slight, then I was told to return at 1900 hours. When I returned I was ushered up a great staircase. On each step stood a Red Army soldier, arms at the present. Then along a corridor past one open door which revealed a table groaning under the weight of the banquet on it, and into a jet-black room.

A chair was found for me, there was a whirring noise and we watched a film of the march of German prisoners through Moscow. The lights went on and Marshal Tolbukhin, as broad as he was tall, greeted us, looking rather puzzled. It suddenly dawned on him that I was not who he thought I was. He was expecting to greet and fête a Bulgarian Partisan! No matter. He insisted I stay on whoever or whatever I was. I did and was treated to a tremendous evening of eating and drinking, during which time I met General Zeitzov, Marshal Tolbukhin's Chief of Staff, and Georgi Dimitrov, or I thought I did, and, in due course, I was returned to my hotel with all ceremony.

The next morning was hazy but I still remembered that I had to report to a senior member of the Marshal's staff at 1000 hours. Which one? I remembered well General Zeitzov who was, I thought, Chief of Staff, and had been very welcoming. In fact, I was mistaken, for the Chief of Staff was General Ulanov, a giant of a man with a great future ahead. General Zeitzov was, among other duties, Head of Security and it was to him that I reported – and possibly just as well, at that!

There was no discussion about British help in clearing the river; nor was there any talk about the efficiency of our mines. He simply wanted information on what areas were extensively mined and, rather as General Gagen, he made it clear he had no high opinion of Americans or British or whoever we might be. But, almost as an afterthought, he said I had to report to him every morning at the same time.

So I did. For the next two or three days our exchanges were, to say the least, brief and brusque. Then, on the fourth morning came a change. I received a relatively cheerful reception which was almost a replay of the Vidin situation. 'I might change my mind about you people,' said the General. 'Your mines are very good, sinking quite a few of my ships.' Alas, there was no vodka on this occasion, and no relaxation about British participation. This more cheerful but still non-productive response continued for a few more days and then ended as suddenly as it had begun.

This was the morning when the General looked pretty frightening. He glared and said: 'You people have made a mess of it. Your air force killed a Russian General in Macedonia yesterday. You must learn a lesson. You can't kill Russian Generals.' I thought that, at the very least, Siberia loomed. 'You must be taught a lesson.' I winced! 'You are going to march behind the coffin, eighteen miles or so, to where the Marshal himself will make an address.' I got out of that room pretty quick.

I did march behind the coffin. And I heard the Marshal's eulogy to the General, a victim of Fascist aggression. I kept quiet about his being actually a victim of British 20mm shells. And I lost my naval cap as a battery of heavy anti-tank guns fired a salute of live ammunition, there being no blanks available, more or less in the direction of the city.

Those few weeks I spent with them provided a profile of the 3rd Ukrainian Army from the most senior to the most junior rank. Compared with subsequent studies such as Anthony Beevor's masterpiece, *Stalingrad*,[1] mine can only be of modest significance. But it was of the moment.

The 3rd Ukrainian was a fast-moving army, already more than halfway towards its Berlin target; a force which had suffered early defeat and huge casualties but which now sighted victory. Officers and men of the Red Army were tasting a standard or quality of life totally new to them, although still relatively primitive to us.

We did not share in any major offensive, but the skirmishes were enough to convince us, if that was necessary, that these were hardened and seasoned troops whom one would not choose to fight against. One also learned the massive difference in quality between first-line and holding troops. Indeed, Colonel Sucharnikov had told me of the relative shortage of assault units and described how his unit could be, and was, moved from front to front to make the initial breakthrough before leaving the ground won to be held by other, inferior, soldiers.

In talking of Stalingrad itself, he recalled that the Officer Corps of his regiment was replaced three times over, perhaps more, and his memory of the days and nights of that incredible siege tally precisely in their endless horror with Anthony Beevor's brilliant account.

Not to be forgotten was the evening with the NKVD colonel who invited us to have a talk over supper, shortly after we had first made contact with the Red Army. Although probably only in his early forties, he was already grey and wizened, made old before his time by the action and privations he had lived through. 'I had my reservations about you,' he began, 'you will understand this army has moved many miles and every attempt is made to penetrate. However, Moscow has cleared you and it would be interesting to talk about our two countries.' He gave the impression that he believed all our factories were owned by lords wearing top hats, but wasn't clear as to whether we were British or American. I mentioned the support given by us to the supply routes to northern Russia, but this brought no response.

Dickie Franks turned the discussion back to the great distances over which the army moved and the impact of the different standard of life which the troops of all ranks were experiencing. Were there any dangers? His response was chilling: 'Certainly there are dangers,' he said, 'and we are prepared for them. There are several categories. Most of the men will simply pass through, loot, rape, enjoy and forget. Then there are those who may be influenced; they will go to re-educational units, two, three or five

97

years should suffice. Then the third category, those who draw conclusions. They will not see the Soviet Union again!'

Our minds turned to those assault troops, Sucharnikov's colleagues, some of them Stalingrad veterans, warm in their welcome, frank in their opinions of the new world they hoped for, for their children, and ours too. What would the future hold for them, or indeed for the Russian people who through history had suffered so much yet shown a capacity to overcome and win simply by holding on?

Our arrival in Sofia was the climax of our mission, as that of Dolphin's. We were, in fact, only a few days ahead of the British element of the Allied Control Commission, fortunately so, for in place of the relaxed Soviet security which we had enjoyed, the Soviet Command in Sofia under General Beresov had very different ideas as to what was permissible.

It was due to General Zeitzov, and not Beresov, that I was allowed to be present at Sofia airfield to meet General Oxley[2] and his colleagues, Mr W.E. Houston-Boswall,[3] the Diplomatic Representative, and, most important for me, the naval member, Captain Guy Maund, DSO, a Russian expert who had served so well as senior British naval officer (SBNO) at Archangel.

With this changing atmosphere, it was just as well, that same afternoon, that Dickie Franks, Turpin and Bing, with Sergeants Turner and Roberts, were able to leave by the returning Hudson. I was very sorry to see them go.

The Soviet authorities agreed that in my appointment as BNLO Danube I should be under Captain Maund as a 'Quasi member' of the British Mission, an ideal solution as it gave the opportunity of assessing information of the RAF's mining of the Danube, supplemented by what intelligence we might be able to obtain from the Danube ports, such as Rustchuk or, if possible, Giurgiu.

While this was to be meagre indeed, because of the Soviet restriction on travel, what had already been learned by our missions left no doubt that the combination of mining of the Danube and the bombing of Ploesti had inflicted lethal damage on the German war effort, both in regard to operations in the West and the Wehrmacht's withdrawal from the East. So the crunch question we had to face was: had we carried out the orders of the Commander-in-Chief Mediterranean; had we made a constructive contribution, or otherwise?

In tactical intelligence, I doubt what we provided would have altered the detail of daily operation. On a strategic, or longer-term assessment, specific intelligence on German failure to provide adequate minesweeping, flak defence and, in particular, the scale of desertion of Danube crews because of the mines, certainly was of value. This may have been enhanced by the fact, only known much later, that Bletchley Park received considerable intercepts from the Danube area but, because of the priority of major Allied operations in other theatres, were unable to process them.

We did make contact with the Red Army. But in September and not two months earlier. We had lost our W/T sets in the Wehrmacht counterattack and no provision had been made for that contingency. Access to the Soviet High Command had proved remarkably speedy, particularly significant being the visit to us in Turnu Severin of Admiral Gorshkov's Senior Staff Officer. In this, I believe the Soviet Command was in error in refusing his request that we accompany him to the Admiral's Naval HQ at Giurgiu and insisting, instead, that we proceed to Army HQ at Sofia.

In both cases we were able to warn of the scale of the mining but not the individual sectors in which mines had been laid, and also offer the early assistance of Commander Wolfson's minesweeping force in Istanbul. This force would unquestionably have speeded up the reopening of the river, with a corresponding reduction in Soviet losses. That Moscow, politically, was determined that the Danube would be under her sole control was evident enough, but it is open to question whether the combined efforts at Naval HQ at Giurgiu, in direct communication with both Moscow and Caserta, might have achieved a short-term compromise.

Could our missions have achieved more? By being earlier, yes, if we could have parachuted direct to the Red Army in July. And, in September, by establishing ourselves at Giurgiu instead of Sofia, as I have already said.

The overwhelming facts were the massive and successful scale of the mine laying of the Danube and the almost total destruction of Ploesti. In comparison with that, our missions were pygmies. But we were privileged to be among the very few at that time (indeed perhaps the only ones) to return safely from the other side of the Iron Curtain that was falling across Europe.

We had moved from one Red Army HQ to another, met and

planned with senior generals, travelled their fields of operation with minimum security, been with élite assault troops and low-quality holding troops. We had seen the structure from inside and from outside their operations and in several senses their morale – for criticism of the Communist regime and of Stalin himself was not absent.

It was for our seniors, and now for historians, to assess what our two missions achieved or failed to achieve in the context of the Danube. For us, it was very simple: an experience which in its richness of events one could never hope to share.

15

The Dolphin Mission

By the time Glen was parachuted into Yugoslavia, to join
what was known as the SOE's Twilfit Mission, the aerial
mining of the Danube – and the bombing of the Ploesti oil
fields – had been underway for about ten weeks. By the time
the Dolphin Mission, led by Captain Dickie Franks, joined
Twilfit three months later, their elaborate sabotage plans had
already been overtaken by events. But it was from Dolphin
that the Allies obtained confirmation of the enormous success
of the aerial mining of the Danube.

It was not really surprising that when SOE Bari and Cairo wanted
to capitalise on the Germans' disarray in the Balkans as 1944
unfolded, they should recall at least one of the few successful
operations of 1940 – the suborning of the Danube pilots, *writes
Leighton Bowen.*

It was a reason why they readily acceded to Glen's request that
two major figures in the 1940 Pilots Enticement Scheme – former
Danube pilot Ralf Navratil and Jaroslav Oldrich Vrana, a former
ship's engineer on the river – should be found and infiltrated into
his mission via Dolphin. Glen wanted their linguistic skills as
well as their local knowledge of people, areas and, crucially, the
Danube itself.

The two Czechs were carrying on their war against the Germans
in new guises, Navratil as Sub-Lieutenant Ralph Turpin of the
RNVR and Vrana as Flying Officer Peter Bing of the Royal Air
Force Volunteer Reserve, after both were evacuated to Britain following their success as ringleaders of the 1940 pilots' scheme.

A 'Danube Sabotage Progress Report' dated 28 March 1944[1]
and circulated on behalf of the SOE, recorded that Navratil 'has

been found and is willing to parachute' and Vrana 'has also been contacted by London. He is already parachute trained'. Navratil was to go 'as expert adviser to Iron Gates party' and Vrana 'with a view to organising subversive cells within barge or tug crews'.

But while the pragmatic Glen kept one eye on practical use of the river after the Germans had been driven from the area (eg to open it up to supply and transport Russian and other Allied forces) SOE Bari seemed almost wholly concerned with bringing the river to a standstill.

A suggested minute, dated 11 April 1944[2] for discussion among senior commanders and SOE's Director/Navy and their officer responsible for personnel and supplies, an Australian, Major F. Hilton B. Nixon (an old Section D hand referred to in the minute by his SOE operational code, DH/X) read:

> As the Russian advance continues, the importance of the Danube to the Germans as a military supply route is greatly increased. Any interference with the free operation of this line is of importance, such as bombing and mining, entice-ment of pilots away from their posts, alternatively their liquidation, sabotage of tugs, barges, shore and port instal-lations, pipelines etc. Also, since Joint Planning Staff cannot foresee any probable circumstances in which we shall need to make use of the Danube for military purposes, destruction of retaining, walls, dams etc., where possible should be laid on without regard to the possibility of such acts interfering with the navigation of the Danube in the immediate post-war period. Counter-scorching preparations to be laid on wherever possible, although it is recognised that little beyond intel-ligence of enemy preparations can be achieved by SOE field forces.

The reference to wholesale destruction without regard to the possible need for the Danube to be navigable was in direct con-trast with the paper prepared by Glen, in conjunction with Commander Dillon of the Naval Intelligence Division, for Admiral Sir John Cunningham. They stressed the need for a navigable river to be available to speed the Russian advance through the Balkans and in the hope of establishing international control of the Danube.

It is interesting to note, however, that when the Special Operations Mediterranean Danube Sub-Committee issued its first progress report[3] on 4 June 1944, just two days before the D-Day invasion of Normandy, it included under the subtitle 'Naval Operations', the following paragraph:

(a) It is understood that the C in C MED has instructed Flag Officer Levant and Eastern Mediterranean (FOLEM) to begin planning for the re-opening of the Danube to Allied navigation after enemy withdrawal, and for the establishment, in conjunction with the Soviet and appropriate other Allied authorities, of proper control over the river.

This is exactly what was contained in the Admiralty paper prepared by Glen and Commander Dillon and it comes as no surprise that alongside the typewritten paragraph referring to the reopening of the Danube there is a handwritten note: *The Navy had previously said they were NOT interested.*

When Glen linked up with the Partisans, the flow of traffic on the Danube was already being greatly reduced by the aerial mining. Apart from the destruction of tugs and oil-carrying barges, the mines were having a serious effect on the morale of river crews and those vital personnel, the pilots. Reports were reaching Glen and his party of wholesale defections, especially by crew members from countries other than Germany or Romania.

By the time the SOE infiltrated the Dolphin Mission under the command of Captain A.T. 'Dickie' Franks near the village of Sikole on the night of 14/15 September, so great had been the effects of mining and the bombing missions over the Ploesti oil fields themselves, that two of Dolphin's three main objectives (a) to carry out sabotage against enemy shipping on the Danube or to counter enemy scorch on port installations and canal routes; and (b) to secure key river personnel, had already been rendered obsolete. The third objective, (c) to supply all possible information on the river situation, was to prove invaluable and with Sub-Lieutenant Turpin, Flying Officer Bing and the wireless operator Sergeant Roberts among them having mastery of several local languages, a wealth of information was obtained in a short space of time.

As Glen has already written, a set of Danube charts were brought in by Captain Franks purporting to show the mined sections of the river. In fact, Bari had omitted to mark the sectors and the charts were, actually, blank! That they were lost during a German attack on Glen's Partisan convoy was therefore of no great concern. But the question must be asked whether the charts would have been helpful in the various meetings with the Soviet High Command?

Glen comments: 'It is not easy to be certain about this. With hindsight, we know, no matter what the wish of the Red Army Command locally to accept help in sweeping the river, Moscow would not have agreed. Accurate mine charts might have bolstered our case with the Red Army commanders and would have helped materially their own minesweeping operations.' In consequence, Glen considered himself remiss in not requesting a further set of correctly annotated charts from Bari, but as neither mission was at that time in radio contact with Bari, ·the question remains theoretical. This question of communications proved a fundamental weakness which should have been foreseen.

In his report on the Dolphin Mission[4] when he finally returned to Bari on 14 October 1944, Captain Franks referred to the differing attitudes of Partisan commanders towards their Western allies:

Strength of German forces in the area as a whole severely restricted Pzn [Partisan] movement, though Comdr. 23rd Div. was particularly uncooperative. The large numbers of German troops moving between Negotin and Kladova rendered the east side of the Danube loop impracticable as an approach to the river and we therefore decided to try and make for the Kazan area.

The initial plan was therefore to make our way with Pzn assistance to the Kazan Gorge and to investigate any signs of Hun scorch. From there, we intended to work round to the Iron Gates sector.

Up to this stage little river intelligence had been accessible to the Twilfit Mission and we stressed to the Div Comdr the urgent necessity for pressing on to the river.[5]

On 17th Sept. we were informed by Comdr. 23 Div. that he proposed transferring Lt Comdr Glen and the Dolphin party to the 25th Div. which had a Brigade working in the Sip area. We therefore separated from the Twilfit mission and moved to Klokocevac where HQ 25th Div. was located. Here, a completely different attitude was immediately noticeable and the Div. Comdr readily promised all possible support to get us to the river. He stated that the 16th Bde [Brigade] were then near Cerkesko and were under orders to move as quickly as possible to the area of the Iron Gates canal. He promised that we would be sent to this Bde the next day.

Next morning, 18th Sept. we found some 72 river men being marshalled into the village square as prisoners of the Pzns. Turpin immediately recognised among them men with whom he had worked on the river before the war and we requested permission to carry out interrogation. Request was granted on condition that no political questions were discussed and the interrogation confined to technical information.

A two-and-a-half hour interrogation of Kare Lanyi, a helmsman of Hungarian nationality provided first pictures of tremendous success of Danube mining policy and the disastrous results it produced upon this German supply route. There was no reason to doubt authenticity of this information and it was, in fact, subsequently cross-checked by other interrogations.

In the afternoon, we left for 16th Bde at Cerkesko accompanied by the river personnel and a small number of Volksdeutsch military prisoners.

A further interrogation was carried out during the day 19th Sept. Austrian ship's Captain Berndl corroborated the details given by Lanyi and gave clear indication of the eagerness with which all river workers awaited the return of the British representation on the river and of the numbers of such people who would be immediately available so soon as British influence re-appeared.

But the Dolphin Mission's plans to move closer to the river came to a sudden stop as German forces moved in strength in their area, attempting to evacuate themselves across the river. This meant the Partisans were committed to harassing the Germans as their major priority and the Dolphin party had to return to Partisan Divisional Headquarters in Rudna Glava.

105

While there, they decided to continue their interrogations[6] and learned of the desperate measures the Germans were taking to keep the river traffic moving:

> Interrogated Tug Captain Mihail Martinovic following day, obtaining further information regarding river personnel. Mining had produced such universal terror that wholesale escapes were organised by underground movement in Belgrade. Sole purpose behind these escapes was to get away from the river where Germans were enforcing compulsory river service on the crews in face of reprisals against their families. Groups of up to 300 in number had succeeded in getting away and planned to remain in other areas close to the river and there to await the re-appearance of the Allies.
>
> This confirmed opinion that there would never be any question of a shortage of river personnel if the British in fact 'set up shop' again on the Danube. His information also showed how the river workers fell into distinct categories according to their political tendencies or the degree of their fear of the mines. It might be necessary to discriminate carefully between those who had escaped and called themselves 'pro-Allied' but who had in reality served the Germans loyally until their terror became the stronger influence, and those who were undoubtedly pro-British and had escaped at the first opportunity.
>
> The majority of the Hungarians, Austrians and Germans with pro-Nazi sympathies departed with the Germans upstream.

Not included in this report but contained in another[7] prepared by Captain S.J. Sales, of the General Staff for distribution to London and the Commander of Force 133, the SOE Mission in Istanbul, is what happened when the Germans took over Captain Martinovic's Serbian tug, the *Jug Bogdan*. This is how Captain Sales related what Captain Martinovic told the Dolphin party:

> On June 9th of this year, Captain Martinovic's tug was taken over by the German Naval Authorities to be fitted out as a Minesweeper at Linz. The officer in charge of the minesweeping was Fregattenkapitan Heleparth whose Headquarters was at Kuchelau. The equipment fitted to the tug included a mag-

netic sweep made up of seven metal paravanes, arranged in diamond pattern, which were interconnected in a 3 cm insulated cable leading from a transformer situated on the after deck. In addition to this an Accoustic sweep was carried for'ard which consisted of a small Torpedo-like container in which a Rattler was rotated in the water.

During the first sweep 7 German Naval Ratings were on board, all of whom were terrified of mines. Captain Heleparth took no part in the operations afloat but he showed the greatest enthusiasm and energy directing operations from the bank! No mines were exploded. In addition to this type of surface sweeping, the Germans employed mine-sweeping aircraft, mostly JU 52s fitted with magnetic rings. Two of this type of aircraft were destroyed by exploding mines near Komoron about June 12. [Mines with AA settings were laid in certain sectors to deter this type of sweeping.]

Captain Heleparth's men were lucky that time. Using magnetic devices to sweep the mines laid by the RAF's 205 Group led to the loss of several Russian craft after they refused British minesweeping help.

Meanwhile, back with the Dolphin party, on 25 September, while delayed in Rudna Glavna because of various technical problems, including a fault in Glen's transmitter, the Mission received first news of the Red Army presence in the area and the following day, Glen and Franks had their historic meeting with the advance section of the Soviet Army at Klokosevac. It was the first meeting of West and East Allied combatants in the Balkans.

The Dolphin Mission were briefed by a Red Army political commissar, speaking in German, and were told that three Soviet divisions had crossed the Danube between Turnu Severin and Brza Palanka on 21/22 September and now held a line with advanced forces. But even as they were being briefed, strong German elements were gathering in the centre of the Danube loop and Soviet plans were to attack across the Timok river to complete a large-scale encirclement of the Wehrmacht troops. Captain Franks' report continued:[8]

Orders had been received from [Soviet] Div. HQ that we

107

should be given every attention and sent as soon as possible to Brza Palanka.

By now it had become obvious that para (a)[9] of our original intentions could not be carried out and the hand-over of the mining information had been presented to the Russians as the purpose of our present mission.

It had always been realised that the value of Turpin and Bing would not necessarily disappear because sabotage or pilot enticement ceased to be practicable objectives of the Dolphin party and the intention still remained to bring them on to the river so that their expert knowledge might be employed in the task of river clearance and re-opening, if in fact the Soviet authorities requested any assistance.

On morning 27 Sept. left for Div. HQ in three waggons with Russian drivers and Russian officer escort. We reached the river for the first time at the Jutz canal and found the shore navigation marks and marker buoys in position and the canal dykes undamaged. There was no traffic whatsoever on the river.

Shortly before reaching Miroc we encountered 32 German and Austrian prisoners who had given themselves up from Golubinje. Many of these had recently been in the Iron Gates area and stated that the canal had been handed over to the Russians undamaged.

Remained night at Miroc and resumed journey to Div. HQ early morning. Some five kilometres from Brza Palanka machine guns opened fire on us killing horses and two of the drivers, also, it is believed, our Russian officer escort. The whole party escaped down a river valley with the exception of the two W/T operators who were overrun by the Germans and were forced to lie low for two days, subsequently rejoining the party in Turnu Severin. F/O Bing was captured by three Cetniks in German uniform and obliged to surrender his pistol, watch and pullover. He managed to escape and shoot one of the Cetniks with a second pistol he had retained in a shoulder holster.

This German attack succeeded in re-occupying Brza Palanka.

This was the first point at which we had observed any MT [motor transport] in use by the Red Army. American two-and-a-half ton Dodges were being employed for Russian

108

Artillery and troops and about a dozen jeeps were concentrated in the neighbourhood of Div. GQ then in Grabovica. Several Rumanian and German 2–3 tonners were employed for troop carrying and also the standard Russian 20 Cwt [hundredweight] truck of very old pattern which was in most general use over the whole of this front.

Still treated with courtesy but with some suspicion by the Red Army officer with whom they came in contact, the Dolphin Mission moved across the Danube in barges to join the Soviet Corps HQ at Turnu Severin. They stayed there for the period 29 September/1 October, during which time they gathered considerably more corroborative and fresh information about the effects of mining the river and, through Turpin and Bing, who found many old contacts in the town, the steps taken by the Russians towards river organisation.

With the arrival of a naval colonel on the staff of Admiral Gorshkov, Captain Franks considered the mission had now assumed an entirely naval aspect and there was no need for himself and Sergeant Roberts to remain. His report continued:[10]

F/O Bing at this time had become concerned over his pseudo-British status and cover name, *vis à vis* the Russians, and had requested that he might return to Italy. I therefore suggested that I returned to Jugoslavia with Bing and Sgt Roberts to contact Bari through a Partisan mission, obtain the mine pinpoints which had been lost during the attack on our waggons and request orders for myself. The remainder of the party, under Lt Comdr Glen was to proceed to Giurgiu.

Chief of Staff at Corps refused permission for the party to split, on the grounds that he had received clear orders from High Command that the whole British mission was to proceed to Army HQ. Any decisions regarding co-operation with the Soviet Navy would be made at that HQ.

On 2 Oct. the entire party again crossed the river to Brza Palanka, the new location of Corps HQ. Our W/T equipment had re-appeared in Turnu Severin the previous day, hopelessly smashed but complete down to the batteries.

It is worth noting that a razor sharpening machine which F/O Bing kept inside his haversack had been placed with this equipment. To a non-technical person this might have seemed like a wireless store, but only careful sorting of all our kit could have produced it from the three cartloads of material which were abandoned during the attack.

In Brza Palanka we were first told we would be spending the night there and then ordered to be ready to move to Vidin in quarter of an hour. The Soviet officers were most concerned to ensure that we had every piece of our totally useless W/T equipment on the truck before we left.

Upon arrival at Brza Palanka and during the subsequent journey south we observed many groups of barges either sunk or gutted along the banks as far as Prahova. Just above Brza Palanka a considerable number of apparently sound units were moored to the bank.

At Prahova, the Danube was blocked completely by four warships and four or five barges which had sunk in a line across the river, but the port workings had somehow been preserved and were all in working order. After several mishaps on their journey, including the loss of a wheel on the 20cwt, the party were eventually ferried across the Danube – all bridges in the area had been destroyed and Russian sappers were building replacements from nearby trees – and walked into Bregova, normally a small village but at that time swollen by the 20,000 Soviet troops concentrated in it.

It was here that Glen experienced one of his most peculiar moments of the war. For after lunch, he was invited to address a special guard of about 100 Soviet troops which had been paraded in honour of the British mission.

Glen recalls:

I had an interpreter, of course. What could you say to these people but something like what a great lot they were and that sort of thing? At the time, this Red Army battalion's name sounded something like a Christian battalion and I congratulated them on all being Christians. But that threw the interpreter entirely. 'You've said the wrong thing there,' he said. 'They're all totally puzzled by all this.' Well, I replied, I'm not all that clear on this myself. That was quite an experience among a people whose reactions are rarely quite what

110

you expect. We saw quite a bit of the Red Army, a good cross-section of them certainly among the assault troops. They were generally magnificent troops and we had a great welcome from them, a great warmth.

These front-line units were vastly different from the holding battalions coming up. They poked Tommy-guns into peoples' tummies and stole their watches. Well I've never worn a watch, they don't seem to go on me, so when this chap came along with his Tommy-gun, I pulled up my sleeve and showed I didn't have a watch. He was astonished and said, 'You've got no watches, you are Tovarich, you must have one of mine.' With that he took off one of the 10 or 12 watches he was wearing and insisted I had it. Most extraordinary!

The Dolphin Mission was certainly a success because of the first-hand information they were able to glean from the river personnel with whom they came into contact, and supplied to their HQ in Bari. In his general conclusions on the Dolphin Mission, Captain Franks said:[11]

Before the infiltration of the Dolphin Mission it seemed clear that in view of the speed of the Russian advance there was no great likelihood of any sabotage targets presenting themselves. But in view of the complete lack of information on the Danube situation, the obvious value of Turpin and Bing as qualified observers and Lt. Cmdr Glen's request for them from the field, it was decided to infiltrate the mission. Moreover the brief of this party was so comprehensive that accepting absence of target and even scorch, and given fair measure Partisan and Soviet co-operation there was every chance of its producing valuable results.

Some disappointment was naturally felt when it became apparent that we were too late to employ the special equipment waiting in Bari, but as mining successes unfolded themselves after each interrogation it was appreciated that an odd ship sunk through our efforts could never have produced a hundredth part of the effect resulting from the Danube mining.

There is no doubt that Bing and Turpin were quite invaluable throughout, not only in their acquaintance with many of

111

the river men responsible for providing most of the information, but also in their language qualifications whereby they were able to understand everything, whether spoken in Serbo-Croat, Russian, Roumanian or Bulgarian. They were thus able not only to acquire concrete information regarding events on the Danube but also to assess local reactions to such events. Furthermore, due to their previous knowledge of the Danube organisation and personalities they were able to supply us with their conclusions upon these different events and reactions.

After speculating on future possible representation on the Danube, now that the greater part of the river lay in Russian theatres of operation, Captain Franks added:

During discussion with the Soviet Corps HQ and General HQ the impression was very strong that whilst technical assistance would be welcomed by the Red Navy, Soviet preparedness to accept British Naval parties would be limited by suspicion of their political intentions.

It is therefore submitted that the Dolphin party has achieved a twofold result. Firstly it has collected sufficient accurate information to enable departments to assess with fair reliability the effects of the economic disaster sustained by Germany on the Danube over the period of the last six months. Secondly it has been able to appraise the present position on the river and supply certain details as to the organisation being set in motion there by the Soviet forces, as well as to present some indication of their intentions.

In conclusion I would add that F/O Bing acted throughout with the highest sense of duty and responsibility. He was shrewd and careful in his dealings with the Roumanian and Bulgarian contacts and always acted strictly in accordance with orders given him. I recommend that he be found employment on the Danube whether in the capacity of a British officer or civilian of his own nationality. He has made a request for nationalisation [sic] as a British subject.

Sub Lieut Turpin was more than excellent during the whole time of our approach to the river.

So Captain Franks returned to Bari, satisfied with a job well done and went on in the post-war years to reach the very top in the Intelligence service, at one time serving as the Head of MI6.

16

Allied Air and Naval Build-up

The Allied landings in Italy and availability of major bases around Foggia and Bari had brought the hitherto remote enemy installations and communications in the Balkans for the first time within range of Allied attack. To maximise this new potential, the 15th United States Army Air Force (USAAF) was consolidated with 205 Group of the Royal Air Force into the new Mediterranean Allied Strategic Air Force (MASAF) at Allied HQ in Caserta, under the command of General Ira C. Eaker of the USAAF with Air Marshal Sir John C. Slessor as his Deputy and Air Vice Marshal George E.B. Baker as Slessor's Senior Air Staff Officer.

Their objective was the immediate denial to Germany of her supplies of oil from Romania and the cutting of supplies of all kinds to German forces on the south-eastern front. Ploesti and the Danube were the main targets, together with other producing, refining and distribution centres, this to be achieved by daylight bombing by the Americans and night bombing by the British, who also had sole responsibility for the mining of the Danube.

Mining of the Danube had been under the planning microscope since the early days of the war, but the distances involved from other bases and the restriction of range of aircraft had rendered the project almost impossible, save for occasional one-off operations. By the end of 1943 however, with Italian bases available, these restrictions no longer applied and the twin-purpose operation was aimed to start not later than April 1944, two months prior to the projected date for D-Day, the invasion of Normandy.

In the case of the mine laying it is strange, however, that the Naval Staff history states: 'A detailed search of all records, including the papers of Chiefs of Staff, has failed to reveal when and by whom a decision was taken to undertake the actual operation'.

From the scale and speed of action taken by both 205 Group and the naval authorities in Italy and in the UK, there was no evidence of lethargy or ambiguity. The Danube was a combined operation in every sense: the adaptation and training of aircraft and aircrew, the design and effectiveness of the mines to be used, together with absolute confidence that stocks would always more than meet immediate needs.

Design and production was the responsibility of HMS *Vernon*,[1] the Torpedo and Mines Establishment of the Admiralty. Their history[2] written years after the war, reveals how thoroughly this task was undertaken, not least in the essential liaison with 205 Group in Italy, to ensure total compatibility. That this was achieved owed much to the availability of a remarkable naval officer, then on the Staff as Torpedo Officer of the Commander-in-Chief Mediterranean, Commander Roger Lewis, DSO, RN,[3] who had made his mark very early in the war.

In the first months of the war, Hitler unleashed his first secret weapon, a magnetic mine, against the British east coast convoys. No counter was known to this new weapon, which caused havoc and brought increasing shipping losses. On the evening of 22 November 1939, the Luftwaffe dropped 14 of these mines off Southend, one of which was seen to land on a mudflat near Shoeburyness. Action was swift. Churchill, then First Lord of the Admiralty, was informed and by midnight he and the First Sea Lord, Admiral Dudley Pound, had given their brief to do their best to two young officers who had been driven post haste from HMS *Vernon*, Lieutenant-Commander Roger Lewis and Lieutenant John Ouvry, RNVR.

Lewis and Ouvry were on the mudflat before dawn. The mine was still above water and although they had never seen its like before, they managed to defuse it, an act of cold skill and courage that was recognised with the first DSO awards of the war. The mine, still intact, was taken back to *Vernon* for examination and the knowledge thus gained led to a degaussing system being developed to make shipping less vulnerable to magnetic mines. The number of craft and lives saved by this action can only be a matter of speculation, but it must have been considerable.

In January 1944, Roger Lewis, by then a Commander and shortly to be promoted Captain RN, was appointed by Admiral Sir John Cunningham to be in charge of all preparations for the

Danube operations and naval liaison with MASAF. To carry out these duties, he joined the Staff of FOTALI (Flag Officer Taranto, Adriatic and Liaison Italy), giving him supervision over the stock of mines being established at Taranto from HMS *Vernon* and immediate liaison with 205 Group.

Both AMk1 IV and AMk V mines were provided. Each normally required a depth of 30 feet but were modified to accept a depth of only 10, if dropped from low level. As the *Vernon* history relates, the 205 Group Wellingtons could carry the larger magnetic acoustic AMk1 IV and V mines but the US Liberators only the smaller versions. This, in practice, proved no great disadvantage as the Germans, untypically, were inept at dealing with both.

Cooperation between the Royal Navy and 205 Group was, as usual, excellent but there could have been problems with MASAF, as it was one of the first occasions when the Royal Air Force came under the operational control of another country, in this case the United States. In fact, it proved an harmonious association, one in which Roger Lewis played his part but also in which another exceptional officer, Group Captain J.A. 'Speedy' Powell, DSO, DFC, OBE, made a very special contribution as liaison officer between the RAF and the 15th AF.

A jaunty, bold and courageous officer, Powell was a born leader. When he took command of the newly-formed 330 Wing (142 and 150 Squadrons) of 205 Group in North Africa, he brought his own brand of leadership. In briefing before an operation, he carried his trademark fly swatter like a swagger stick. Then, standing very erect, very calm and with arms folded, his send-off line never varied: 'Well, off you go and don't do anything I wouldn't do.' Crews knew exactly what he meant. There was very little Speedy Powell wouldn't do!

Months before he joined MASAF, Powell had won a reputation among the Americans with an extraordinary feat. Just as he had let General Jimmy Doolittle fly on 150 Squadron night mission raids, Doolittle allowed Powell to go on a B-24 (Liberator) daylight raid. The pilot and navigator were killed when the plane was attacked and badly beaten up and incredibly, Powell, who had never flown a four-engined B-24 before, brought the stricken aircraft in for a crash landing on a beach. The surviving American aircrew recommended him for an American DFC. Ironically, the

DFC arrived in Doolittle's office two days after Powell, who as a Staff Officer had no need ever to fly again, was killed flying over Yugoslavia with 19 Fighter Squadron in August 1944.

There may not have been too many Americans taking up an offer to dip into Powell's gold-plated snuff box – an offer he made to men regardless of rank before a raid – but they would never forget a fearless and flamboyant officer who did so much to cement HQ relations between the two air forces.

In January 1944, when 205 Group joined the 15th USAAF in Bari, the immediate task of the Strategic Air Forces, both in the UK and in the Mediterranean, was Operation Point Blank. This called for the destruction of German air power, to reduce resistance to the increasing Allied bomber offensive on the Continent, especially enemy opposition in the air when the planned invasion of Europe got under way.

By March, MASAF turned its attention to other targets. The Bulgarian railway system was one and, later, they carried out heavy attacks on key marshalling yards throughout the Balkans, aimed at disrupting communications in south-east Europe to assist the Russian advance from the East.

April was the month designated for MASAF to start its attacks on the heavily-defended oil refineries at Ploesti – and for the mining of the Danube. The mining operation was given the green light on 30 March with a directive that defined the period of operations and the general area to be visited, but left the selection of exact positions and the scale of the diversionary bombing effort to be decided by MASAF, in conjunction with 205 Group, who would lay the mines.

205 Group (motto: *'Through darkness to light'*) then comprised four wings of two squadrons, five of the squadrons experienced in mine laying, as follows:

231 WING **No. 37 Squadron** (Wellingtons); motto: *'Wise without eyes'*; based Cerignola from 14 December 1943, moved to Tortorella 29 December 1943 until October 1945.

No. 70 Squadron (Wellingtons); motto: *'Usquam'* ('Anywhere'); based at Cerignola from 7 December 1943 until October 1945.

117

236 WING **No. 40 Squadron** (Wellingtons); motto: '*Hostem Coelo Expellere*' ('To drive the enemy from the sky'); based at Cerignola 16 December 1943, moved to Foggia Main 30 December 1943 until 25 October 1945.

No. 104 Squadron (Wellingtons); motto: '*Strike hard*'; based Cerignola from 14 December 1943 (ground crews), 20 December 1943 (air crews); moved to Foggia Main 30 December 1943 until October 1945.

240 WING **No. 178 Squadron** (Liberators); motto: '*Irae Emissarii*' ('Emissaries of wrath'); 178 Squadron was formed at Shandur on 15 January 1943 from a detachment of 160 Squadron and began bombing operations the same day; in March 1944 they moved to Celone and in July 1944 they moved again to Amendola, where they stayed until August 1945.

No. 614 Squadron (Halifaxes); motto: '*Codaf i Geislo*' ('I rise and search'); arrived Celone 3 March 1944, moved to Stornara 10 May 1944, moved to Amendola 15 July 1944 until 27 July 1945. **614** were the Group's pathfinders.

330 WING **No. 142 Squadron** (Wellingtons); motto: '*Determination*'; ground crew arrived Cerignola 16 December 1943, air crew 20 December, moved to Amendola 14 February 1944, based at Regina from 3 July 1944 until 5 October 1944.

No. 150 Squadron (Wellingtons); motto: '*Always Ahead*'; arrived Cerignola 12 December 1943, moved to Amendola 14 February 1944, based Regina from 3 July to 5 October 1944.

They were later supplemented by elements of 31 and 34 Squadrons of the South African Air Force, a formidable force, as events were to prove.

17

The Attack On and Defence of Ploesti, 1944

As we met the Red Army in September, it looked as if our earlier fears that we were late were to be realised. However, the situation was more complex than we then knew. True, the mining of the Danube had been carried out over six months from April and, if our responsibilities to the Red Army in acquainting them of the danger areas were to be fulfilled, we should have been in direct contact with them much earlier.

In fact, although the Red Army reached the Iron Gates sector of the Middle Danube in September, the HQ and major force only reached the Lower Danube, including Giurgiu, at the same time. Admiral Gorshkov had just set up his Naval HQ Danube and Marshal Tolbukhin, in command of his 3rd Ukrainian Army, his own HQ in Sofia. Had we been allowed, as I described earlier, to join Admiral Gorshkov, as he wished, it is not impossible that he would have accepted the Wolfson minesweeping force at least for an initial period, perhaps under joint command.

However, the overall strategic situation in the area was seriously deteriorating, from the Germans' viewpoint, and improved greatly from that of the Allies. From the Spring of 1944, the mining operations against the Danube were having a sustained and cumulative impact, as did the massive bombing of the source of the oil itself, the Ploesti complex.

The size, complexity, history and the defences of Ploesti must be understood. These were as clear to the Germans as to the British, as critical and as fragile. Ploesti was no mere centre, no concentrated production area; it was a vast complex of wells, refineries, huge storage tanks, petrochemical plants, marshalling yards and endless networks of pipelines, rail tracks and roadways. With settlements and office buildings, above all defences of every type, shelters and, to add to the complexity, camouflage and mock structures built to deceive, Ploesti must have stretched 40 miles or more in one direction and perhaps half as much in another.

I remember my one and only visit to Ploesti in early 1940. It was a cold and miserable day, the road from Bucharest snowbound and our driver a lunatic determined only to knock as many peasant troikas as possible off the road. When we finally stopped in a chaos of installations, I asked where was Ploesti? The answer given by our host, an oil-man, was: 'Everywhere as far as you can see and further still.'

A settlement in the sixteenth century, by the 1850s Ploesti had grown into a small town and it was then the first evidence of the riches below its soil was found. Growth was not slow, British interests joining those of others. By 1913, Ploesti had become the single largest producer of oil in Continental Europe, its output of 1.9 million tons exceeding that even of the prolific Dutch East Indies. By the start of the Second World War, 26 years later, it had also become Germany's principal source of petroleum products, initially amounting to some 120,000 tons per month, soon to increase to more than 200,000 tons.

The history of Ploesti held quite a few lessons for both Germany and Britain. In the First World War, for instance, Romania had tried to remain neutral, but in 1916 slid into hostilities against Austro-Hungary and later also against Germany, up to then a major buyer of her oil and grain. As General Ludendorff stated: 'We should not have been able to exist, let alone carry on the war, without Romania's corn and oil.' Very quickly indeed, in 1916, German forces broke through Romanian defences to secure Ploesti.

On that occasion, the oil companies (British, French and Romanian) moved still faster. A scorched earth policy was their riposte, destroying with primitive means their life's work. Wells were blocked or fired, machinery sabotaged and the smaller refineries wrecked. This Germany never forgot. In the years ahead they were to make Ploesti the most heavily-defended area in the whole of Europe – and Romania secure! Unfortunately, the British did not forget, either. They continued to believe Romania to be a trusted and reliable ally, committed to repeat, if necessary, the destruction of the oil fields.

Times and circumstances had changed, however. Within the first

12 months of the war, the perception and thoroughness of Canaris had ensured German control of Romania, with the effect that any attempts within Ploesti itself were frustrated. All that might still be possible were limited attempts against the Danube and its traffic, but these, in comparison, were pinpricks.

In short, Germany could feel its resources in Romania were secure, bolstered by confidence in the estimates of their scientists, in the development of enormous supplies of synthetic oil. In practice, this confidence was not justified.

Ploesti's geographic location made it immune from Allied attacks for the greater part of the war. There was a weak and ineffective raid by the Russians in June 1941 but with the speed of the Wehrmacht advance eastwards, the German High Command had little to fear from that direction. Twelve months later, however, the first warning of future threat came from the Halverson raid involving 13 B-24 Liberators flown from El Fayid in Egypt, on 12 June 1942. Complete surprise was achieved and they dropped their 4,000lb bombs through cloud from 10,000ft. Seven aircraft returned safely, six ending up in Syria and Turkey, where they were interned. Heroic as was the venture, its results were limited, if not minimal. Indeed, the raid may have been negative in alerting the Germans to the fact that Ploesti was no longer immune from attack by air.

Defences in and around Ploesti were speedily strengthened. As well as additional fighter squadrons, this involved rings of search-lights and anti aircraft batteries, heavy and light gunnery, state of the art control systems, smokescreen devices and further deception in the form of mock buildings and structures. Nor was damage control overlooked and a capacity for speedy repair and replacement was set up which was to prove outstandingly successful.

Much of this new defence system was operational when, on 1 August 1943, the next Allied attack was launched by the USAAF, codenamed Operation Tidal Wave. The 44th, 93rd and 389th Bombardment Groups of the 8th Air Force were combined in Libya with the 98th and 376th Groups of the 9th Air Force. Some 177 of these aircraft were assembled at Benghazi for the round flight of some 2,700 miles to Ploesti, each aircraft carrying, typically, 3,100 US gallons of fuel and 5,000lbs of bombs and incendiaries. The force was under the command of General Lewis Bretherton, one-time air chief to General MacArthur in the

Philippines, who had no illusions as to the dangers ahead and who warned his crews of potential 50 per cent casualties.

He was not mistaken. Problems developed after take-off, the aircraft carrying the lead navigator crashing and that of his backup having to abort. Weather over Greece after their low-level flight deteriorated, a wrong turn was made towards Bucharest instead of Ploesti and any element of surprise was forfeited. Nevertheless, the remaining aircraft swept in, some as low as 50 or 100ft. The barrage of fire encountered was so thick that one pilot said afterwards you could have walked on it. As the second wave came in, they came under attack from Luftwaffe ME 109s and Romanian JAR 80As, both skilfully directed.

The outcome was 43 US aircraft destroyed, 15 forced to land nearby and another 8 in Turkey, with 14 aborted. All but 35 of the surviving aircraft suffered combat damage and the last one home reached base after 14 hours, holed in more than 300 places.

The aircrew involved in Tidal Wave numbered 1,726; of these 532, or 32 per cent, were lost, fewer perhaps than General Bretherton had warned, but still heavy indeed. The courage with which the attack was maintained after surprise was lost was outstanding and its recognition as the most highly decorated operation by the US Air Forces during the entire war was thoroughly merited. The mission received a total of seven Medals of Honor.

The damage inflicted on Ploesti, sadly, was less than the effort exerted or the loss of life incurred. Of the seven refineries targeted, two received effective damage, two were reported out of action for six months, two suffered light damage and one none at all. At the time it was claimed that some 42 per cent of Ploesti had been destroyed. But the complex at the time of the raid was operating at only around 60 per cent capacity. Within six weeks, Ploesti was not only producing at its normal capacity but at a higher rate than before.

No longer, however, could the German High Command believe that only one-off or occasional raids could be mounted against Ploesti. The defences they already had in place had shown their capacity against Tidal Wave. With the Allied landings in Italy, Ploesti inevitably would come under sustained and regular attack and even further strengthening of its defences became an absolute priority.

General Alfred Gerstenberg was a sound choice when Hitler

appointed him to be in command of the air defences of Ploesti and formidable indeed were they to prove. But time by then had deserted the Germans, as shown by Hitler's own comment to the General much later, in August 1944: 'If we lose the oil fields, we lose the war'. By the time the Führer made that observation, most of the oil fields had been lost, distribution disrupted on a grand scale and supply to Germany, as well as to the Wehrmacht and Luftwaffe, in full retreat from the south-east, in crisis.

The MASAF had planned its tactics well. Day bombing of Ploesti and related targets by the 15th US Air Force was coordinated with night attacks by the RAF's 205 Group, which was also responsible for the mine laying operations. Both groups undertook other operations, equally related, on distribution targets such as the huge storage depots at Turnu Severin, the major Danube port of Giurgiu, smaller refineries such as Prahova and key bridges, railways and marshalling yards in Yugoslavia and Bulgaria as well as Romania.

Oil might escape destruction in Ploesti but on its long route to Germany it was under constant threat in pipeline or storage tank, on rail or in a Danube tanker. It was in Ploesti, however, that the German defences were strongest and a heavy price was to be exacted of the attackers, particularly in daylight.

After an attack by 220 Flying Fortresses and 93 Liberators, supported by 1,120 fighters, on the main railway station in north-west Bucharest on 4 April 1944, which cost ten aircraft against an estimated enemy loss of 50 fighters, the following day the 15th US Air Force launched the first of their 20 attacks against Ploesti itself. Again with strong fighter support, 256 aircraft bombed the extensive rail system, also damaging nearby installations with the loss of 13 aircraft. This was only the beginning. A second attack was then made on Turnu Severin.

In early May, 205 Group made a particularly successful night attack on the Steau Romana refinery and adjacent marshalling yards with the loss of three Wellingtons, and two days later a brilliant low-level destruction of a strategic bridge involved the loss of the aircraft but not of its crew, who were rescued and taken to safety by a Yugoslav Cetnik band.

That same day the 15th Air Force again hit Ploesti with 486 bombers dropping 1,225 tons of high explosive. Their fighter escort shot down 23 enemy aircraft but 18 bombers were lost.

Extensive damage was caused, later reconnaissance showing that the Astra Romana, Phoenix and Orion installations, among others, had suffered heavily.

In addition, daylight onslaughts by the Allies were extended deep into Romania. Brasov was heavily bombed, along with Turnu Severin, Craiova and, on 7 May, Bucharest, where 269 B-24 Liberators and B-17 Flying Fortresses dropped some 1,100 tons of bombs, protected by 230 P-38 Lightning and P-51 Mustang fighters.

Attacks on Ploesti had, by the end of May, become more selective. On 31 May, 382 aircraft dropped more than 1,100 tons of bombs with the loss of 15 aircraft, 13 of them by flak. Defence was still uncowed and German initiative in damage control and repair quite outstanding. Ploesti was showing itself as a formidable fortress with a capacity to become even more so.

With the Normandy landings on 6 June came orders to both the US 8th Air Force in Britain and the 15th in Italy from General Carl Spaatz,[1] the new Commander-in-Chief United States Strategic Air Forces Europe (USSAFE) that the cutting of oil supplies to German Forces was the priority. Already, with the RAF's Bomber Command and the 8th US Air Force battering synthetic plants from their bases in the UK and the 15th Air Force and 205 Group hammering production complexes, marshalling yards and supply routes along the Danube, there was evidence that synthetic output was reduced by more than 50 per cent and refined output by some 45 per cent.

The Balkan opportunities were widened most unexpectedly by the Russians granting the 15th Air Force bases in the Soviet Union. In what was appropriately named Operation Frantic, the Americans were now able to attack new targets in Transylvania, including the important rail centre at Simeria, and the air base at Galati.

However, June was to be a month of mixed fortunes for the Americans. Their strength had been increased to 60 squadrons of Liberators and 24 squadrons of Fortresses. The escort wing had also been strengthened to seven groups with nine squadrons each of Lightnings and Mustangs and four squadrons of P-47 Thunderbolts. Formidable as this force was and despite the fact that it inflicted heavy and widespread damage during daylight raids, it was also to suffer heavy losses.

D-Day was celebrated by a 359-ton bombing of Galati, 700 tons on Ploesti, 320 tons on Brasov, an attack on the Iron Gates by 28 Fortresses and on the railway yards at Piesti by 31 Liberators. Four days later came a change of tactics when a force of P-38 Lightning fighters were converted to dive bombers in a bid to overcome the increasing use of smoke in German defences, which had so hampered the heavy bombers. But it was a costly experiment, with the loss of 24 out of the 46 P-38s involved. A total of 26 enemy aircraft were downed with one young US pilot, Lieutenant Hatch, making no fewer than five credited kills.

After that, the P-38s were restored to their proper role as fighters, proving their worth over the Giurgiu depot and port the very next day, 11 June, when 264 Liberators were attacked by some 70 German and Romanian fighters. The P-38s drove them off without loss and this success was to be repeated over Constanta when US fighters shot down 14 enemy planes with the loss of three bombers and five fighters.

Ploesti was attacked again on 23 and 24 June, for the first time using Pathfinders against the Zenia and Concordia refineries. Night raids by 205 Group Wellingtons were also becoming increasingly effective against Ploesti and the important Prahova refinery near Bucharest, despite the increasingly effective use of smoke by the German and Romanian defences.

July was to record no fewer than five US daylight attacks on Ploesti, with a total of 4,641 tons of bombs dropped at a cost of 73 aircraft, bringing the total lost to date to 185 over the four months of action. These losses included incidents in which Medals of Honor were awarded posthumously to two brave airmen. On 23 June, Second Lieutenant David Kingsley, on his twentieth mission as a Bombardier, selflessly took off his own parachute and put it on a badly-wounded tail-gunner after the order had been given to abandon their stricken plane. The last paragraph of his citation read: 'Moments later, on the order to jump, Lieutenant Kingsley helped both wounded men to bale out through the open bomb bay. He was last seen by surviving crew members standing by the bomb bay catwalk. The plane went into a spin and crashed and his body was later recovered from the wreckage'.

On 9 July, the second and final Medal of Honor of the Ploesti Campaign was awarded to First Lieutenant Donald D. Pucket, of the 98th Bombardment Group. His aircraft was severely damaged and he ordered his crew to abandon ship. Three of them lost their nerve and refused. Pucket refused to leave and instead fought to regain control of his aircraft which, despite his effort, hit a mountainside.

Attacks on Ploesti were now becoming more and more selective in the choice of individual targets and on 9 July the Xenia and Concordia refineries were bombed by 222 Liberators and Fortresses. Although no enemy fighters were engaged, ground fire accounted for six aircraft. On 15 July, a huge force of 604 bombers shed 1,521 tons of high explosives on the major Romana Americana refinery and this was again the target for three more attacks that month. Again, little trouble was had from enemy fighters but losses were suffered through continued heavy and accurate flak.

What was also remarkable was the continued ability of the Germans to maintain damage control. Time and again an installation would be confirmed as destroyed, only to be found a few days later to be back in production. Cannibalisation from minor to major installations by the Germans (and no doubt Romanians) was brilliantly organised and effected, the scale of reconstruction between day and night raids exceeding any rational expectation. This enabled production at Ploesti, despite the weight of attacks, to *increase* in July from that of June. However, the MASAF policy of continued attack elsewhere, on distribution and stocking centres and transport, meant little of this extra output reached it destinations.

By the early days of August, the cumulative impact of day and night attacks had, at last, outweighed German damage limitation capacity. There was, after all, little left from which to cannibalise and the Romana Americana was one of the few major refineries still left in effective production. That this became the major objective for Allied attack both by night from the Wellingtons and Halifaxes of 205 Group, and by day from the Liberators and Fortresses of the 15th Air Force, was clear enough. What was not so clear at the time was the German ability to still be able to concentrate ground defences so powerfully. Smoke was particularly effective in screening targets while night-fighter intervention over Yugoslavia much increased, with the result that on the night of 9/10 August 205 Group had 11 of their 81 aircraft shot down.

Meanwhile, the 15th Air Force were completing their 20 missions involving direct attacks on Ploesti itself with the last four between 10 and 19 August. These included attacks on the Steaua Romana refinery at Cimpina, and the Romana Americana, Astra Romana, Unirea, Dacia and Xenia refineries (or what was left of them). A total of almost 2,500 tons of bombs were dropped, but despite an absence of enemy fighters, the Allies lost 45 aircraft, a tribute to the undiminished morale and skill of German ground defences.

But the end had come. Ten days after the final attack on Ploesti, elements of the Red Army were in the complex, finding a desolation of mangled steel and fires burning everywhere. MASAF had accomplished its task but it had taken five months with the loss by the 15th US Air Force of 239 aircraft and in the night operations by 205 Group of 46 aircraft. Hundreds of aircrew were killed or captured, those caught by the Romanians often treated abominably, others rescued by Yugoslavs, mostly Cetniks.

A breakdown of bombing operations may be found in Appendix 3.

18

Allied Mining of the Danube

Mining missions, due to begin on the night of 6/7 April 1944, got off to a depressing start when bad weather caused the cancellation of the first two raids planned for successive nights. All 205 Group activities were night-time operations and, in fact, most of the April moon period was deemed unsuitable.

Aerial mine laying called for precision and the considerable cloud and haze hanging over the river made accurate mine-laying within the required parameters almost impossible.

To ensure maximum accuracy, and comply with shallow water restrictions, aircraft were obliged to come down to 200ft before release, one reason why beds for the night-time operations were chosen where the surrounding countryside was flat. Much of the Danube is shielded by high-banking landscape, making mine-laying runs hazardous.

Despite the atrocious weather conditions, 205 Group still managed 54 sorties over three nights during April, laying a total of 179 A Mk I-IV and A Mk V mines in beds ranging between Turnu Magurele and a position ten miles north of Baja.

Losses for those initial three raids were disappointing: one Wellington of 70 Squadron was shot down into the river east of Belgrade and two Liberators of 178 Squadron unfortunately crashed on take-off. These two crashes occurred on the night of 14/15 April when Liberator 'R' (Skipper, Lieutenant Shaw) crashed immediately after take-off and three of the crew were killed; Liberator 'D' (Skipper, Lieutenant Rogan) crashed after take-off one kilometre east of San Marco, all the crew being killed. The cold facts set out in the Group's ORB (Operations Record Book) fail utterly to convey the sense of futility at the loss of ten aircrew and two aircraft that was not due to enemy action.

Wellington B of 70 Squadron (Skipper, Pilot Officer Gibson) ditched in the Danube after being hit by flak just before releasing its mines; the captain and bomb aimer survived to return to squadron but the remainder of the crew perished.

In addition to mine laying, some Wellingtons and Liberators also beat up river craft during their sorties and it was with some glee that a cipher to the War Office in London reported that observers had seen three oil-carrying barges set alight, the first eye-witness account of damage to Germany-bound craft. In fact, damage to river craft and to the morale of their crews from those first three missions had an immediate impact, bringing some sections of the river to a temporary standstill.

This extract from the MEW Intelligence Weekly Report No. 119, for week-ending 11 May 1944 tells an encouraging story:

A report states that on 20th April all commercial traffic on the Danube between Hungary and Bulgaria had been stopped. A ban on passenger traffic had been imposed on or about 17th April, as a result of intensive mine-laying in the lower and middle reaches of the Danube and commercial traffic was evidently banned at the same time. Amongst the commodities known to have been held up are coal, chemicals and machinery bound downstream and agricultural produce bound upstream. This appears to have led to considerable congestion at both Upper and Lower Danube ports, particularly in those in Bulgaria where warehouse accommodation is already overtaxed.

How long the ban will last it is impossible to say. Up to the present there is no information to suggest that it has been raised. Though local traffic in the affected area may be rapidly resumed, through traffic between the Upper and Lower Danube is unlikely to be resumed on anything approaching a normal scale until such time as Germany has been able to provide means for mine clearance, a task for which she has apparently made no preparations in the Middle and Upper reaches of the river.

So results were not slow in coming, and the German High Command had been caught unprepared. This surprised the Admiralty, considering the great thought and care that had been put into protecting the Danube in previous years. Perhaps the reverses in the Russian Front and the imminent threat of invasion in western Europe had caused them to take their eye off this particular ball. Whatever the reasons, 205 Group were ready to press home their advantage.

During May, four highly successful Danube mining missions were undertaken involving 104 sorties dropping a total of 361 mines, mostly of the 1,000lb A Mk V type. The month had started disappointingly, as in April, with the first mission planned for the night of 4/5 May called off because of bad weather. Liberators of 240 Wing were due to have been in operation but they were stood down as late as 1800 hours. The delay lasted only 24 hours. On the night of 5/6 May, the first of four heavy nights of mine laying began and by the end of the month, 205 Group intelligence officers reported: 'Mining of the Danube was again carried out successfully on four nights and reports since received indicate that there has been much interference with traffic on the river, particularly the vital oil traffic'. This corroborated eye-witness reports of damage done to Danube traffic, received by the FOTALI from various observers and aerial reconnaissance.

For some, the mining sorties came as a relief from missions flown over much more heavily-defended targets such as Ploesti and the huge Giurgiu storage depot and marshalling yards. We are indebted to Paul Long, the six-foot son of the 5ft 4in bomb-aimer John 'Shorty' Long of 150 Squadron for permission to reprint this extract from his father's book *It's a Long Story*, published in 1990. Extra information on the six-hour round-trip from Amendola (by Wellington Mk X HE606, Squadron Code JN-Y for Yorker) on the moonlit night of 5/6 May is provided by Paul and appears in the brackets:

Mine-laying in the Danube was fun! We flew to yet another capital of the Balkans, Belgrade in Yugoslavia, and identified the stretch of the river, south of the city, that had been allocated to us (It was east of the city toward Novi Sad). We were loaded with two 1,000lb mines which were equipped with parachutes which opened quickly to lower the mines gently into the water to avoid detonation on impact. To successfully plant the mines we had to get down between 50 and 150ft above the water. This precision flying and spot on delivery was just what appealed to our illustrious skipper

130

(Flt. Lt. Norman W. Thomas, DFC, of Swansea, South Wales). Down we went, me in my usual prone position ready to press the bomb release when Tommy gave the word. Lower and lower we went with no illumination other than the reflections from the river, which I could see flashing below, through the bombing panel. Jerry could have thrown stones at us, much less AAA, small arms fire and the kitchen sink, if necessary.

We hit the 50ft mark, flying very carefully straight and level because one false move and we're in the drink. 'Let 'em go Shorty,' yelled Tommy ... and a few seconds later Geoff (Woods, the rear gunner) called excitedly over the intercom, 'There they go. Chutes are open. Hey what a splash!' Without a word fired in anger by the Jerries we were climbing away from the river, with me humming *The Blue Danube* waltz to the rest of the crew.

Apart from the flak experienced by Danube mining missions, 'Shorty' Long, originally from Bristol but who emigrated to Canada after the war and died there in the summer of 2001, reminds us of another hazard to the low-flying aircraft of high-tension wires strung across the river at many strategic points and almost impossible to see during the night operations. No wonder Paul Long says: 'The flying skill was equal to that of the Dambusters of 617 Squadron but very little was ever said about these exploits'.

But the irrepressible 'Shorty' Long even has an anecdote about the potentially lethal high-tension wire:

One particularly 'bolshie' Australian crew was carrying an extra front gunner who was British (a Pom as they called him). He was a very conscientious gunner who did his job well whilst the Aussie crew, while good, had little respect for regulations and doing it by the book. They also a wicked Australian sense of humour. The pilot called the gunner and told him to watch for wires stretched across the river. The gunner asked what signal he should use to inform the pilot of the impending danger. 'Oh don't worry about that,' said the Aussie pilot, 'when yer head comes through the front bulkhead, I'll know we've 'it one'.

131

As Paul Long says: 'We will not see their like again'.

But the down side of the four mining missions in May, was that one Liberator of 240 Wing crashed on landing back at base, killing all the crew and there was one fatality on another sortie when the rear gunner, Pilot Officer Allingham, was killed following three direct hits on his Liberator. The aircraft, however, was piloted home safely.

For the first time, operations were extended into the Upper Danube, releasing 72 A Mk V mines either side of Komoron in a raid mounted on the night of 29/30 May by 12 Liberators of 240 Wing. May also saw 614 Squadron (County of Glamorgan) move to Stornara and pass from the command of 240 Wing to the 'administrative and operational control' of HQ 205 Group, amid worries about morale on squadron. It was feared some aircrew, who flew Halifaxes and lit the targets as pathfinders for the following heavy bombers, were dispirited because their target-marking technique was being used sparingly on operations. The Group's ORB reported: 'Also, every failure to date has been hailed as proof that they cannot do their job. Until these are overcome and some failures accepted as inevitable, 614 Squadron's training is likely to be dispirited and disinterested'.

However, whatever problems 614 Squadron had, real or imagined, they pulled themselves together and as the campaign wore on they engaged in some outstanding precision marking.

But while 240 Wing 'lost control' of 614 Squadron, they welcomed, towards the end of the month, 31 Squadron (South African Air Force), thus adding a second Liberator squadron to join the Wing's 178 Squadron. They joined 205 Group at a time of buoyancy over mining operations, despite some disappointment that there would be no mining during June because all resources were to be directed at oil production targets. There was time to reflect on progress so far, and perhaps to bask in a little glory.

The first Progress Report of the SOE's SOM (Special Operations Mediterranean) Danube Sub-Committee covering the period 1 April to 2 June 1944 and dated 4 June, included the following item:

Mining Operations

There is reason to believe that the mining operations carried out during the April and May moons have caused the enemy considerable embarrassment and, in particular, have brought about the total suspension of traffic on different stretches of the river during periods of at least five days. When it is considered that a single day's traffic may amount to over 20,000 tons, the overall result can be appreciated. The recent intensification of mining, together with bombing attacks, should considerably increase the enemy's difficulties.

Such progress reports, along with various eye-witness accounts were later treated with some scepticism because they were so close to the events. The Admiralty admitted it was almost impossible to make a strictly accurate analysis of the results because of so many imponderables; so many necessary facts and figures then being unobtainable. But subsequent records of the Inspector of Minesweeping, Danube, the Admiral Danube and those of the German Danube Shipping Authority, allied to reasonably accurate figures for shipping losses, provide a wealth of material to piece together a general picture.

The April mining operations certainly took the enemy completely by surprise, and this unpreparedness caused a chaos that was exacerbated by the four heavy mining missions carried out during the May moon period. Eyewitness and documentary evidence show an instant reduction in traffic and the monthly tonnage of oil and other imports into Germany via the Danube. These had averaged 177,724 tons in 1943, dropped to an estimated total of 124,827 tons in April and, as the mines began increasingly to have effect, slumped to an astonishing 48,319 tons during May.

Exports via the Danube, mainly made up of stores for the German armies and their allies in the south-east, were similarly affected. That these reductions were brought about by the mining campaign is borne out by the fact that the two-way traffic for March, the month preceding the start of mining, had exceeded the average for 1943. It was certainly not due to adverse weather or ice because 1944 was an exceptionally mild year.

The Germans, initially caught unprepared, were stung into action. Before April was out they had appointed an Inspector of Minesweeping to coordinate countermeasures. An experienced captain, he immediately began the task of organising defences. He split the river into three operational sectors: the Upper Danube from the German border to Bratislava; the Middle Danube from Bratislava to Moldova; and the Lower Danube from Moldova to Braila, establishing Sector Headquarters at Vienna, Belgrade and Rustchuk. Vessels for sweeping were selected from among the numerous river tugs, while the Luftwaffe provided fixed flak batteries near and around the Iron Gates Canal, a prime target for blockage because of its narrow passage.

This concentration of defences may also have been influenced by the attack on the Iron Gates on the night of 31 May/1 June when 11 Halifaxes, 25 Wellington and two Liberators of 205 Group dropped 83 tons of bombs. Subsequent photographic reconnaissance showed the bridge joining the Iron Gates installations with the main road destroyed, and an ammunition dump among military property hit, causing considerable damage to surrounding buildings. But neither the track nor the locomotive sheds were seriously damaged, which meant the Allies were bound to continue attacking the Iron Gates, and particularly its barge-towing facilities, as a priority target.

The Germans also set up mobile floating batteries which could be switched to positions anywhere between Novi Sad and Bazias; degaussing stations were established at Vienna and Rustchuk and an extensive organisation of minespotters was put into operation.

This mine-watching operation (apparently something on the lines of Britain's Royal Observer Corps) worked efficiently from early on and greatly assisted in assessing the mining threat at any given point. Yet this advantage was minimised for several months by a lack of sweepers to reopen the waterways after attack, due in turn to the delay in getting magnetic minesweeping equipment into the area.

This is where chaos was compounded after the four heavy mining attacks in May. Although the Germans quickly set up a sound countermeasure organisation, they just didn't have the equipment ready to take advantage of it. For instance, at the beginning of May only five minesweepers were in operation between Mohacs and Braila; a month later, only 12 sets of magnetic sweep gear were available for use in all three sectors. The establishment of flak defences also took more time that it should have, with the result that it was not until July that they began to have effect.

For those first two months, the brunt of sweeping fell on just 15 aircraft operating from Budapest, Belgrade and Craiova, which accounted for 55 of the 85 mines swept. And although they achieved some success, there were simply too few of them to cope adequately with the plethora of mines laid. As a result, shipping casualties, which totalled 15 in April shot up to 81 in May. (The majority of shipping casualties occurred among barges and tanker barges, but all total figures given include other craft such as tugs, motor vessels and miscellaneous other craft.) These losses in themselves were serious, especially when allied to the frequent and lengthy closures of many sections of the river.

But there soon surfaced other side-effects that were to cause just as much trouble for the enemy. Almost immediately after the casualties had started to mount, the crews of all but German-owned vessels began openly demonstrating their reluctance to move on the river. Desertions, particularly among Yugoslavs, escalated at an alarming rate. This unwillingness on the part of civilians to accept the risk was understandable. The explosion of a 1,000lb mine in a shallow river is not something to be taken lightly as an everyday event. As many of the barges being towed included fuel tankers, the conflagration brought about by hitting a mine was both spectacular and daunting!

The Danubian shipping companies were the first to reflect this caution, tending to halt their vessels for longer periods than the Germans. One Hungarian shipping firm, presumably bolder than the rest in the face of German control, went into liquidation as a result of its losses.

This dislocation and disorganisation of what was normally an efficient river transport system led to goods and supplies piling up at various points. Some freight rates doubled; certain storage companies refused to accept any responsibility for goods stored in the event of attack; and coal traffic from the Pernik mines was virtually suspended because of overcrowding in Bulgarian ports.

Where the Germans normally operated with order and precision, there was suddenly chaos. At the end of May the Hungarian representative of the German Danube Shipping Authority wrote a lengthy memorandum to his board which supports the early reports of the success of the mine laying. He began by saying the purpose of his report was to draw attention to:

the almost hopeless state in which the Danube Shipping finds itself since the enemy started mining the waterway... All the interested parties, especially those in shipping, have pointed out the immense danger that the Danube might suddenly become no longer navigable, and this danger grows daily as more ships are sunk in the narrow and shallow parts of the fairway.

After dealing at some considerable length with the inadequacies of Germany's minesweeping organisation, this report went on to say:

In the meantime the same hopeless struggle against the mines continues, with the Hungarian section of the Danube now open, now closed, depending on the urgency of supplies to the front. The latest mined area was re-opened on 22nd May and the result was that, within 24 hours, from 23rd to 24th, no less than 13 ships ran on mines; whereupon this danger-ous stretch has again been closed, with a net profit of three tank barges with petrol passed through the area against the 13 vessels sunk or damaged.
   The Hungarians, Roumanians, Bulgarians, Slovaks etc. are not sailing at all, because they justifiably consider the situation too dangerous. And so, in the past few days it has been only the German companies that have risked – and lost – their ships and crews. The reason why the Hungarians and Slovaks do not sail in these conditions is that there is no war compen-sation law whereby their ships would be replaced or repaired. Nor is any provision made by these countries for the depen-dents of crew members who lose their lives on war service.

If the Germans did not realise themselves the implications of the British mining operation, the Hungarian spelled it out for them:

If some energetic action is not taken now, and if mine-sweeping aircraft and mine-sweeping gear do not arrive quickly in adequate quantities, then the Danube will soon be so jammed with sunken vessels, at certain points, that navi-gation will become entirely impossible; for even the salvage gear, although receiving attention, is not nearly ready for operational use. There is no need for me to go into details of what the loss of the Danube, as a supply line, would mean.

There certainly was not! The German Supreme Command was well aware of the gravity of the situation as it affected both imports and supplies to the army. And so, it seemed, was Adolf Hitler!

The advance of the Russian armies towards Ploesti and the bombing of oil targets throughout Europe, which started in May and quickly reduced output by an overall 50 per cent, served only to underline the importance of the Romanian source. At the end of May, the German Naval Staff drew the attention of the Inspector of Minesweeping to 'the decisive importance of maintaining a clear passage through the Danube'. At the same time, Hitler became involved personally. Told that around 10,000 tons of ammunition, enough to satisfy all the deficiencies on the southern front, was held up on the river, the Führer repeated an urgent call to the Kriegsmarine (German Navy) and the Luftwaffe to do everything possible to keep the Danube waterway open. No doubt as a result of his personal intervention, by the third week in June the minesweeping capability on the Danube had increased considerably. On 20 June, there were 22 minesweepers operational, with 13 more due to complete in a few days and 11 refitting, and all types of sweep were available. The number of minesweeping aircraft had been boosted to 24.

From then on, there were sufficient resources. But there was little easing of the traffic problem, increasingly because of desertions by the crews of river craft. It was reported that there were 78 casualties from mining during June, the majority of them vessels carrying army stores eastwards for German troops being driven back by the Red Army. Traffic flowing towards Germany had lessened, for by then the output from Ploesti had been considerably reduced by the bombing. What oil cargoes there were went often only as far as Novi Sad before being transferred to the railway system.

Even so, the Germans swept a total of 139 mines during the month, with no new ones being laid. But Allied plans were for further major missions during July. And to help them, No. 2 Wing South African Air Force were on their way from North Africa to join the MASAF and elements of No. 31 Squadron were also arriving in Italy to take part in mining operations.

In the meantime, on 24 June, Hitler tried to achieve some coordination of effort by appointing a plenipotentiary for the Danube. The Führer decreed:

The maintenance of an unrestricted passage for shipping on the Danube is of decisive importance for the supply of the troops on the south-eastern front, as well as for the transportation of important war materials to and from the south-east, in particular, oil, chrome and other mining products. Enemy activity has placed this most important waterway in the gravest danger. I therefore order:

1. All implicated military and civil offices and organisations are placed under the unified command of a military plenipotentiary.
2. I appoint General-Admiral Marschall to this post, and he is directly subordinated to me. His headquarters are in Vienna.

General-Admiral Marschall assumed his duties at a time when river defences were near their strongest, in terms of equipment. There were 11 minesweepers in the Upper Danube, 18 in the Central Danube and 20 in the Lower Danube. In addition to the fixed flak batteries at the Iron Gates and floating batteries spread between Novi Sad and Bazias, a balloon barrage had been established near the Iron Gates and three squadrons of night fighters were stationed near Bucharest. Night fighters, however, were largely ineffective against mine laying, mainly because of the poor spotting service in Yugoslavia and the slow communications, which usually failed to provide sufficient time for interception – especially when operations were concentrated over the Central Danube. The mobile flak batteries met with greater – and instant – success when mining operations resumed in July.

On the night of 27/28 June, Sergeant Turner and I were dropped into the Nis area of Yugoslavia to link up with the 23rd Partisan Brigade and seek intelligence on the effects of the mining. Initial reports were more than encouraging, albeit limited, as they were not of first-hand origin. It was against this background of early success that mining operations resumed with a vengeance on the first two nights of July, 251 mines being laid in beds covering 810 miles of the river from Komoron to Giurgiu, again bringing traffic to almost a complete halt. Only a fraction of these mines had been swept by mid-month when Admiral Marschall, in desperation, ordered the resumption of military and civil shipping movement over the whole waterway.

The Admiral was prepared to accept heavy casualties. His fears were not confirmed. After that early stoppage, there was considerable river movement up to the end of the month but on the night of 31 July, a further 178 mines were laid between Giurgiu and Belgrade, once again restricting traffic in the lower reaches of the river.

It was not all gloom for the Germans. Their mobile flak batteries were an instant success when mining was resumed on the night of 1 July, shooting down four Wellingtons. This brought an immediate rethink by MASAF which led to a change in mine laying tactics. After 1 July, aircraft preferred to lay their mines while heading across the river, causing more mines to miss their targets and fall on land. Until this change in tactics, the only mines recovered by the enemy, according to their own reports, had been 3 in April, 2 in May and 1 in June. But in July they recovered and dismantled 11 and in August, 17. German minesweepers also claimed some successes, accounting for 109 mines during the month.

Nevertheless, the overall number of mines remaining unaccounted for by sweeping casualties, or other causes such as self-detonation, rose to 369 by the end of July, compared with a total of 106 in June. This accumulation increased gradually thereafter until the end of mining operations.

Shipping casualties for the month of July were down to only 18. But this was almost certainly due to the lack of movement on the river in the first half of the month. Surely little cause for any self-congratulation by Admiral Marschall and his men.

In truth, conditions on the river were giving the Admiral cause for even greater concern, particularly the most urgent problems of shortage of crews and lack of traffic discipline. Even the German minesweepers were being 70 per cent manned by foreigners, described in one German report as 'not to be trusted to execute their tasks in accordance with their orders'.

At the beginning of the month, Admiral Marschall sent an urgent message to the Naval Staff demanding experienced, reliable NCOs to man the minesweepers, describing the situation as 'militarily intolerable as well as damaging to the navy's image'.

He pointed out, as typical of the situation, one minesweeper whose commanding officer was Yugoslav and whose crew was composed of 'unreliable foreigners who were doing all in their power to get their ship out of service'.

But for all the backing of Hitler behind him, the Admiral's pleas fell on deaf ears. There simply were no naval ratings available! A later demand for the staffing of a convoy organisation also went unsatisfied.

With the resumption of the mining campaign came the news that Brigadier J.T. Durrant, DFC, of No. 3 South African Air Force Wing, would arrive at HQ on 25 July to take over command of the Group from Air Commodore J.H.T. Simpson, DSC, from 3 August. Also, 205 Group was strengthened by the addition of a new Liberator squadron, 34 Squadron South Africa Air Force began to arrive at the Celone base in early June and, together with 31 Squadron, formed the new 2 Wing SAAF. Thus, by the end of July, 205 Group was operating five wings.

Most of the mine laying action took place on the first two nights of the July moon period. The crew of Wellington aircraft 'N' of 40 Squadron, skippered by Sergeant Booth, had a remarkable escape on the night of 1 July. Hit by flak near Belgrade, the port engine was put out of action, the hydraulic system damaged and the wireless operator slightly wounded. As the aircraft could not gain any height, the crew baled out, landed safely and made contact with a group of Cetniks. Only two months earlier, in May 1944, British missions in Cetnik-held territory had been withdrawn, along with British support for the men led by Mihailovic. Yet Sergeant Booth's crew were greeted warmly and spent 40 days in the care of the Cetniks before being evacuated by air.

The raid on the night of 1 July had been particularly ambitious, covering a 350-plus mile stretch of the Danube from Bazias on the Romanian border 50 miles upstream from the Hungarian capital, Budapest. Even with the loss of four aircraft, it was a successful mission, as was the one the following night when ten Liberators dropped 60 × 1,000lb mines in eight beds between Viskovar and Giurgiu.

On the night of 30/31 July, target sectors ranged from Mohacs in southern Hungary and Kovin east of Belgrade to two at Giurgiu and Orsova in Romania. Although there was some light flak at some points and unidentified planes spotted, all aircraft returned safely and some even took time out to beat up barges and other river traffic. Some flak positions were also machine-gunned.

Some mines were laid in the channel leading to the Iron Gates Canal, where the terrain on either side towers steeply hundreds of feet above the water, requiring skilful handling of the heavy bombers flying sometimes as low as 500ft. It was here that one of the 1940 sabotage schemes, to mine the cliffs on the Yugoslav side and cause them to slide into the channel, thus blocking the Danube, had failed. This new aerial sabotage by mine laying was more efficient.

August proved a truly grim month for Admiral Marschall, with mining casualties mounting to 32 and little improvement in the general situation on the river. It was also a grim month for Germany in general. The rapid Russian advance which reached Galatz on 24 August, brought about further crumbling of the Axis, when both Romania and Bulgaria switched allegiance from Germany and joined the Allies.

Mining went on steadily, with five missions during the month and a total of 220 mines being laid. Operations were also continued upstream of Bazias, as soon as Bulgaria and Romania were out of the war. Minesweeping accounted for 130 mines and during the month a *CAM-Sperrbrecher*[1] became operational for use in the shallower stretches of the river. But she was also needed to help out in the defence of river positions against the Russians and succeeded in sweeping only eight mines in total. It was a most happy situation for Brigadier Durrant, who took over as Commanding Officer of 205 Group on 3 August.

Many years later, an entertaining account of what happened to him on one of these Danube mining missions was written by Flight Sergeant Alan Bates, an Air Bomber of 31 Squadron South African Air Force:[2]

These operations always coincided with the full moon and even today I think of the full moon as the Danube Moon. The hazards of flying alone in bright moonlight rather than in the protection of a bomber stream were easily outweighed by the absence of a heavily-defended target. Three or four aircraft shared each 'bed' and each of us would plant six 'vegetables' (mines).

We were rather concerned to find that we would be

141

carrying a passenger from our sister squadron, 34 SAAF, which had shared the airfield with us for some time now but had only just become 'operational'.

The briefing confirmed our guess that the target was the Danube and our 'beds' lay between two small islets near to Turnu Magurele. Our passenger turned out to be an extremely aggressive youth and, on the assumption that attack is the best form of defence, he told us with some degree of conviction that he would be flying in the rear turret. We all turned towards Bill Cross, the Rear Gunner, to observe his reaction. The deep-set eyes of the Lancastrian gunner glowed and the heavy jowl moved. 'Tha'll be on t'beam guns,' he said. Our guest appeared to appreciate that although Bill may not have the gift of rhetoric his few words had the ring of finality. He looked for a moment at Taff Lewis, the little Welsh Mid-Upper Gunner and saw that a similar demand was unlikely to succeed. I moved discreetly away lest the cuckoo in our nest should decide that he would like to drop the mines. Beam guns it would have to be. We consoled our friend with the thought that he would at least get into the war before Errol Flynn and John Wayne wrapped the whole thing up.

We took off at dusk and once out to sea, the guns were tested. A couple of short bursts from Bill in the rear turret and his flat Lancashire voice came through the intercom 'Rear guns OK, skipper'. Then two quick squirts from the Mid-Upper and the sing-song Welsh voice gave the same affirmative.

At this point quite a minor air battle developed as 34 Squadron's representative decided to test the port beam gun. He was in danger of running out of ammunition before a few well-chosen words from the captain brought the battle to an end.

We crossed the Yugoslav coast on course and I passed the time taking drift readings and toying with the new-fangled GEE box,[3] both of which I hoped would be of some assistance to Noel Sleed, our Navigator, who busied himself at a small table between me and the nose wheel door.

It was not long before a staccato warning came from the Rear Gunner – 'Fighter seven o'clock down, Skipper –

142

Round the clock 1: An RAF Wellington waits for the USAAF B-17 Flying Fortress returning from a daylight mission to land before setting off itself for a night-time bombing raid over Ploesti.

Photo: Imperial War Museum CNA2830

Round the clock 2: An American Air Force crew just back from a daylight bombing raid over Ploesti pause to wish 'all the best' to their RAF colleagues about to embark on a daylight sortie. Yanks and Limeys sharing the same bases in Italy enjoyed good relations.

Photo: Imperial War Museum CNA2785

Bombs Away! Waves of USAAF B-24 Liberators leave the Concordia Vega Refinery in ruins in a daylight mission on May 31st, 1944, despite the heavy flak to be seen exploding around the aircraft.

Photo: Imperial War Museum

Menace in the skies: An American B-24 Liberator drops its bombs despite the thick smoke and heavy flak in this low-level daylight attack over the Ploesti oilfields in Romania.

Photo: Imperial War Museum *ZZZ*11980F

weave, he's closing'. Taff confirmed the sighting and the pilot started evasive action. We all waited anxiously for things to start humming. The aircraft corkscrewed around the sky and the tension was increased by a burst of fire from one of the beam guns. Our enthusiastic friend from 34 Squadron was silenced by a few uncomplimentary words from Taffy in the Mid-Upper Turret. The silence continued for several seconds and the Skipper's voice came over the intercom inquiring impatiently what was happening in the rear. Eventually Taffy broke the silence with an apologetic chuckle – 'Sorry Skipper, it was only the moon coming up over the horizon'. The rest of the journey out passed quietly and soon the broad band of the Danube came into sight. My little strip with its two small islets was easily distinguishable. This was my moment of glory. The Bomb-Aimer is somewhat akin to the triangle player in an orchestra who, at some particular moment in the piece, stops smiling at the girls in the stalls, puts on his white gloves and with triangle held high goes 'ting'. Before going 'ting' it was my job to talk the pilot down to 100 feet in a correct line for the mine drop.

Everything was going well until we reached around 100 feet and we were still losing height. It appeared that the pilot was using his altimeter, which had been set at airfield height and the target was a few hundred feet higher. I called over the intercom 'Level out now – we are a bit low'. This did not produce results and we drifted lower still. I saw two large oil drums, one stacked on the other, on the shore of the first islet. I hardly noticed that our passenger was raking the left bank with his .5 Browning as the oil drums came hurtling towards us. All attempts at a calm and assured intercom manner were abandoned as I screamed for height. Fortunately, the Skipper must have raised his eyes from the altimeter and he lifted the aircraft over the island, missing the oil drums by a whisker.

I collected my thoughts. We were on target and were far too low. I had rehearsed the procedure for the drop many times. I would drop Number 1 mine and then count 1, 2, drop until all six had gone. I started quite well, keeping to the waltz time until Number 4 mine when I realised I was running out of river and the last two mines were dispatched in quick-step. As we pulled away from the Danube a light gun opened up at us and some form of rocket fizzed past under the port wing. We climbed steadily away and set course for home. We were then delighted to hear the plaintive voice of our guest on the intercom complaining that he was wet through. It appears that we were so low that each time a mine hit the river it flew up a column of water which lifted into the bomb bays and found its way to our favourite beam gunner. He was invited on to the flight deck for the remainder of the journey. We landed after a round trip of 4 hours and said 'goodbye' to 34 Squadron after debriefing and so to bed. Just another little one for the Log Book.

The Red Army entered Ploesti on 30 August, taking over an area of incredible mass destruction. They arrived at Turnu Severin on 2 September. Although the Russians were held in that general area for some time, allowing the Germans breathing space to evacuate stores and equipment upstream, by then the Axis situation was lost.

Not all Soviet commanders had shown themselves averse to accepting British assistance in clearing the river, nor did they underestimate the impact of the mines themselves. Admiral Gorshkov, in particular, was clear they could not do it themselves. Moscow, however, was equally clear that control over the Danube was theirs, to be shared with no other power, a decision that was not altogether a surprise to Allied commanders in the earlier plans for a cooperative approach.

How much the consequences of 'going it alone in clearing the river' cost the Red Army is impossible to calculate. Their speed of advance across Romania into Yugoslavia and northwards suggests not much; but in human terms, it could be different!

What might also have been different was the Allied decision to reduce the scale of mine laying in late September, a total of 137 mines having been laid in the Middle Danube during the first ten days of the month. Enemy shipping losses were believed to be about 39 during that period, with the number of mines swept estimated at around 60, although records were by then rather dubious as retreat and disarray among the Wehrmacht escalated.

The enemy were concentrating their efforts on salvaging shipping and equipment for use up-river. Their withdrawal was by no means

144

haphazard. In his survey of the situation for mid-September to mid-November, the German Inspector of Mining expressed surprise that the reduction of the length of the river under German control, as a result of the Red Army's advance, had not been exploited more effectively by the Allied air forces. The Inspector reported:

> If the enemy had taken the chance presented to him, he could have carried out large-scale mining of the shortened waterway and inflicted very heavy damage on the vast withdrawal of shipping and cargoes towards German territory. But the expected mining did not take place. The last enemy lay was on 4th October 1944 ... they laid about 51 mines but all available (minesweeping) forces were used and, during the prevailing low water period, it was possible to clear the waterway without even having to close the channel because of wrecks.

A reason may have been the problem of 'co-ordinated Allied with Soviet and Partisan land operations', but the outcome was only four mining operations were carried out during this last period of targeting the Danube.

September also saw the last operation carried out by 142 and 150 Squadrons on the night of 26/27. During early October both squadrons and their 330 Wing Headquarters were disbanded, in accordance with the Group Rearmament Programme, the aircraft, equipment and the majority of personnel being absorbed by other units of the Group.

No. 330 Wing had first came under the operational control of No. 205 Group in early July 1943, and two months later was transferred to the complete control of that Group. During 15 months with Group, the Wing took part in every important operation and attacked every type of target assigned to them, flying 4,723 operational sorties and dropping a total of 8,050 (American) tons of bombs and mines.

The very last mining operation took place on the night of 4/5 October when 22 aircraft dropped 58 mines. Surprisingly, the Germans still managed to put up a stiff ack-ack defence and one Wellington of 40 Squadron was shot down in flames into the river near Kisbodak, the eleventh and final casualty of the mining campaign.

19

Aftermath

The end of August saw the cessation of Ploesti production, the virtual destruction of the complex itself and its occupation by the Red Army. The MASAF had performed its task in the obliteration of the refineries, distribution lines and storage centres while on the Danube, 205 Group's low-level night operations had been mightily successful with the loss of only 11 aircraft. As the official history of HMS *Vernon* described it: 'Statistically the most effective mining operation of the war in terms of aircraft lost'.

The supply of petroleum products from Romania to Germany had ceased!

But there is another side. The tenacity, courage and resourcefulness of the German and Romanian defenders of Ploesti. To have held firm for five months of massive onslaught day and night, to have continued to man the warning systems, fight the missiles, the guns, heavy and light, within surroundings all immediately inflammable and explosive, must rank among the great defensive epics.

Yet they did more than that! Their damage control and repair was unbelievable, cannibalisation effected until there was nothing more from which to cannibalise; an existence which can only have been, day and night, an inferno, comparable with Stalingrad and, like Stalingrad, which in the end could only promise early death or a more lingering one as a prisoner of the Red Army.

No matter the repugnant nature of the Nazi regime, the men and women of Ploesti were brave indeed.

On the Danube, German defences, on the contrary, seemed unprepared and wavering. Whether they did not believe that we could or would mount such an intensive aerial mining operation is difficult to comprehend. Defence of a fixed target such as Ploesti is one thing; defence of near to nine hundred miles of river is quite another matter. The Iron Gates Canal, for instance, was well defended because of its particular vulnerability, but elsewhere there was little available until too late of minesweepers or other equipment to give any extensive cover to this massive target.

Kriegsmarine officers and men, trained and responsible, were just not available for drafting to Danube duties, the result of the havoc wreaked on the U-boats and their bases by Allied sea and air attacks in northern Europe. What is strange is the German surprise that Yugoslav, Hungarian and Romanian crew members deserted in huge numbers, rather than face the hazards of 1,000lb mines exploding underneath their craft.

By Autumn 1944, it was no longer the shadow of Moscow control that was spreading over the Balkan lands and the Danube. It was the reality. Churchill and Stalin had signed a scrap of paper, a 75:25 agreement, simple in itself but hiding a multitude of interpretations. For the Romanians, their pre-war nightmare scenario of Russian occupation was realised and Stalinist at that – and it occurred after a sequence of events strange in the extreme.

At the end of 1943, the SOE sent a Mission to Romania under Colonel Gardyne de Chastelain.[1] They were captured almost immediately, but instead of the fate they expected, their treatment was more than correct, including contact with the Prime Minister, Ion Antonescu, which resulted in the latter sending a personal envoy to Cairo in mid-March 1944. This envoy was Prince Barbu Stirby, father-in-law of Colonel Edward Boxshall, head of the SOE Romanian Desk in London.[2]

It might then have seemed possible that an armistice could have been negotiated, although German forces were still in control of much of the country. Juliu Maniu[3] still had influence, as Hugh Seton Watson had predicted when, years earlier, it seemed like cloud-cuckoo land. But the Russians held back, suspicious and confused. De Chastelain found himself back in prison.

Romania was still hoping that, as there was now no German protector, as in 1940, Britain or the United States might be benevolent, perhaps even return parts of Transylvania to them. In August 1944, King Michael had Antonescu arrested, a new government was set up and De Chastelain was accepted as British representative in Bucharest, together with an Allied Control Commission.

It was all pretence, of course. Moscow was in control and the

147

pretence ended in December 1947 with the abdication of King Michael. Earlier, the Soviets had already shown their colours at the Danube Conference where the ghastly Anna Pauker left no one in doubt as to the brutal absolutism of Soviet purpose, which was to apply throughout Romania and persist for half a century.

In Bulgaria, the outcome was similar, but was speeded up by the Russian refusal to accept an armistice from them in August 1944 and instead declaring war. The Red Army occupied Sofia in the early days of September 1944 and on 10 September, Marshal Tolbukhin established his 3rd Ukrainian Army HQ in the Bulgarian capital.

The shape of east and south-east Europe seemed clear enough: a Moscow-controlled collection of subservient states, individual only in name. Events in Yugoslavia reinforced this, if indeed reinforcement was needed. Despite earlier signs of friction between the Red Army and the Partisans, Marshal Tito's armies and those of the Soviet Union joined together effectively to liberate Belgrade, with enough of the credit going to Tito as the only liberator in Europe of their own land.

There had been evidence earlier in 1944 of a hard attitude against any direct Allied military intervention in Yugoslavia, but not on a scale to anticipate the near collision of forces which was to ensue in Carinthia and over Trieste. With mass movements of displaced persons and little foodstuffs or shelter, the situation was critical, in itself. The new Yugoslav Army, as the Partisans were now designating themselves, were on the rampage to seize Trieste and much of Istria. They would have occupied both and inflicted further reprisals on Italians as they did on Cossacks and their own fellow countrymen, had it not been for the resolve of the British Command and not least the initiative of young British Officers such as the then Major (later Major General) Abraham, MC, of the 12th Lancers.

Churchill was already changing his mind about Tito; the Levanting from Vis to Moscow after their meeting had been a sore disenchantment. Were they the trusted friends whom the Western Allies had supported when no Russian help was forthcoming against the Axis occupiers of their country? Where was the good will Fitzroy Maclean had claimed? Was this the Resistance force we had hoped to help create in 1941?

As to the last, it was the opposite. The Communists had taken

148

no action in the earlier part of the war against Germany, which they dismissed merely as an imperialist struggle. They only reacted when Germany turned against their beloved Soviet Union. In contrast, the Serbs carried out their *coup* on 27 March 1941 and virtually invited German attack, which took place within the next ten days and, after the collapse of the Yugoslav armies, it was Serb units which regrouped in the mountains under Draza Mihailovic and became the Cetnik units of initial resistance.

For the Communists, however, once Russia was invaded there arrived not only a cause for which to fight but also an objective of their own: a Communist Yugoslavia. That, to the Royalist Cetniks, was to make them as dangerous an enemy as the Germans and more so than the Italians.

There was another factor, however, that we British in particular were slow and reluctant to understand. This was the impact on Mihailovic, and many Serbs, of the memory of the appalling losses they sustained in the First World War and their determination that Serbian lives would not be squandered until the moment was ripe, which they, and not we, would determine. They, too, failed to comprehend how this would jeopardise their relations with London and Washington.

The war between the Partisans and the Cetniks, as between both of them with the Croat Ustachi, seems to me sadly to have been inevitable. The reprisals levied by the winner on the loser fall into the same category and, had the situation been reversed, I doubt if it would have been different. But the Partisans' open hostility towards the western Allies as the war ended seems contrary to Tito's normal caution, and despite all the excuses and explanations of his colleagues, I remain perplexed.

A bleak picture it certainly then seemed. A Cold War with the whole of south-central Europe under Soviet remit and Yugoslavia bristling among the most hostile. A pretty reward for the West after all the support which had been provided. Then, in 1948, came the thunderblast, the breach of relations between Moscow and Belgrade. Surely Tito would yield, surely he could not survive and surely, militarily and/or politically, Russia would reestablish control?

Now, almost 55 years later, it is tempting to assume that danger for Tito was limited to the months immediately following the receipt of Stalin's letter of bitter denunciation. This was not so.

The ferocity of criticism from the Comminform and its members was predictable, their fury at this treachery as they saw it. But the internal reaction within the Yugoslav Communist Party was critical too, and it was the care with which this was handled by the leadership and especially by Tito himself that secured internal stability, a stability Tito never ceased to underestimate in his later relations with local party cadres. Nor externally in the Western world was there immediate sympathy or support. Bevin and the Labour Government in London were inclined to let him stew in his own juice, Washington was perhaps less disinterested, France hostile. Anxious years for the West were to ensue, with the Korean War a distraction for them from the problems of a Tito who too often had shown his ability to accept every benefit from the West and give nothing in return.

Moscow seriously considered invasion, but Stalin was cautious, and it was only well into 1949 that the Defence Chiefs in Washington began seriously to consider whether support of Yugoslavia against Soviet attack might be in the interests of Western security. There would be prices to pay, not excluding cessation by Belgrade of support for the Greek communists, and both Washington and London were no longer trusting as to Tito's promises. Nonetheless the strategic situation was recognised as having altered, and aid from the West, financial, economic as well as military began to flow. Within the country its effects were visible quickly enough, relaxing party harshness, a gradual improvement in the quality of life, but no suggestion of any retreat from a one-Party structure, because of Tito's sense of obligation to the Party for its support.

Was Communist control of the country inevitable? From the arrival of the Red Army in Autumn 1944 I believe, yes, and probably in any event when even greater suffering and loss could have ensued. With Communist control and the regime's hostility to the West, a rupture between Moscow and Belgrade could not seem on the cards, certainly not in any foreseeable future.

There were not a few who deemed Maclean's war-time advice mistaken and irresponsible, yet he never ceased to believe that a break would occur. He was right and both Deakin and he were to play very positive parts in the years ahead.

As the 1950s passed on, Yugoslavia, although still a Communist state, appeared a relatively relaxed society. It was possible for people to travel abroad, even to have an overseas bank account. A good life with a boat and a small holiday home on the Adriatic was not impossible. Tourism was encouraged and an increasing number enjoyed the glories of Dubrovnik and Split, the monasteries of Ochrid, or skiing at Pale.

True, there were islands where the tourists couldn't go, such as Goli Otok where, for those incarcerated, the regime was harsh indeed. But it seemed a happy enough society, certainly in comparison with life over the borders in Hungary or Bulgaria. The young, in particular, seemed proud of this new Yugoslavia, even if some of this talented people were seeking success and fortune in the United States or various parts of Europe. Their elders might not have shared this enthusiasm or confidence, but there was little reluctance in expressing doubts or criticisms openly.

I certainly do not suggest that Yugoslavia was a democracy. Far from it! It remained a dictatorship, benevolent in some respects but with restraints which could be harsh. Political rectitude was one and, as corruption grew among the ruling élite (not least their wives), those who were brave enough to write and speak out, such as Milovan Djilas, found tolerance was minimal.

In the universities, too, there were pressures on academics, threats of dismissal and loss of pensions. In one case, at Belgrade University, Antony Kenny, the Master of Balliol, who despite Secret Police intervention had been holding his small seminars in Prague, intervened and, with a minor input on my part with certain old Partisan friends, succeeded in securing the careers of seven senior professors. But such success was as rare as the courage and vision of Djilas.

To look back now, however, those years of the 1970s seem like a dream in comparison with the nightmare that the later 1980s and 1990s were to bring: the country broken up and divided; the Federal army employed to bombard open towns such as Vukovar; war between Serbs, Croats, Bosnian Muslims and Albanians; war of a brutality that killer squads bring; neighbour against neighbour with old scores rediscovered and a new greed for this or that irresistible. That a city of old cultures such as Sarajevo could be under siege for months was unthinkable. But it was! Massacres such as that at Srbenica and elsewhere were equally unthinkable in a country which a generation or two before had suffered German occupation. But they took place! Few can be innocent,

151

many guilty, but remembering the evil of Slobodan Milosevic in Belgrade and that of Tudjman in Zagreb, there are many who should stand in the dock. Could it have been averted; could it have been just different?

I should explain that in the 1960s and 1970s, my Yugoslav-born wife and I spent a good amount of time there. Zorica's first cousin was Olga Humo, one of Tito's two secretaries who was with him throughout the war and was married to Avdo Humo, a young Partisan leader in Bosnia. Avdo was later a member of the Praesidium and close to Tito, until he fell from favour by drawing attention to problems developing in Bosnia.

I remember so clearly our first meeting with Avdo. It was in the bad years before the break. I had been asked by the Foreign Office, who knew of our relationship, to pass a personal plea for moderating intemperate exchanges on some issue at the time, I think involving Greek children. We were due to dine privately with Olga and Avdo but Zorica had arranged a drinks party beforehand with her 'cousins'. I had expected 4 or 5 – in fact there must have been 30 or 40. I had to drink a raki with most, if not all, present.

By the time we reached Avdo's, I was indeed drunk but holding onto one thing: delivery of the message. Their flat was tiny. Moving into the kitchen I managed to get Avdo jammed in a corner, my arm across his chest, and delivered my message in no diplomatic terms.

Zorica was staying in Belgrade but I had to leave by the midnight train. I woke up near the border with a hell of a head and a worse conscience. What balls-up had I created? As soon as I could get to a telephone I called Zorica. She seemed quite unconcerned and told me: 'Avdo simply said that up to now he had thought the British rather shy and reserved'.

Avdo Humo was one who saw very clearly the dangers ahead in Bosnia. His political courage was the equal of the physical courage he had shown during the war. But at that time, President Tito did not want to know. Avdo's fall from grace lost Tito a talented and selfless younger minister.

We were fortunate to enjoy the close friendship of so many. Orecanin and his wife Sonja, a member of that great Montenegran Dapcevic family, paid many visits to our Cotswold home. Orecanin had commanded in Croatia, was especially close to Tito during the anxious days of the break, and later was a highly successful Ambassador to London.

Vladko Velebit we got to know through Fitzroy and Veronica Maclean and watched his remarkable career from the earliest days in Zagreb to success both as Minister of Foreign Affairs and in the highest posts in the United Nations.

There are too many to mention but we owe much to all. Not least to Fitzroy as to Veronica and to Bill Deakin, for all that I have learned from each; for their friendship over long years in Strachur and in France. Their achievement, each in their own way, is remarkable in gaining the trust of a hard man, Tito, a Moscow Communist, and influencing him to a vastly wider and positive world role.

Earlier, as Chairman of the Export Council for Europe, I took part in a number of trade missions to Belgrade and Zagreb. These visits involved lasting contacts with bankers and industrialists, as well as ministers, and discussions on the problems facing the country were frank indeed. Later, in the 1970s, when I was Chairman of the British Tourist Authority, a more specialist relationship developed as the Yugoslavs sought our guidance as to the development of their resources.

On one of these visits we were in Sveti Stefan and received an invitation to call on General Tempo Vukmanovic, who had commanded the Partisans in Macedonia and South Serbia. I was surprised because in wartime, Tempo had the reputation of being totally averse to anything British, apart from British weapons. In his small house above a rocky cove, we found a wise and kindly man, willing to talk not only over old days, but of future ones too. He was not complacent and had just returned from spending a few days with Tito, who he had found deeply depressed. When Tempo asked him about the state of the Communist Party and of the country, Tito had replied: 'There is no party and soon there will be no country'.

Some years later, we were in Zagreb for a tourism conference, when early one morning the telephone rang. It was Vladamir Bakaric, then Prime Minister of Croatia, calling from his home and inviting Zorica and myself to lunch with him, just the three of us, simply and quietly. Bakaric had been one of Tito's closest colleagues from the early days, a quiet, thoughtful man, modest in demeanour and always courteous.

He was very serious. These were 'dangerous times' he said, with Ustachi influence strengthening along with other activists and the students. There was corruption and mismanagement in high places, both in Belgrade and Zagreb. Then he turned to tourism and looking directly at me asked: 'These great hotels we are building for our own people, aren't they like prisons, with the daily routine all prescribed?'

His worry was that there was no settled succession and he said very sadly, 'The old man [Tito] knows it and he knows he is losing his grip'.

In truth, of course, Nationalism had never withered in Croatia or Serbia. The reverse was the case, while new ambitions were smouldering in Bosnia and Kosova.

Tito was only too aware of the dangers: of Serb revenge for Ustachi horrors; of Croat and Slovene resentment of Belgrade centralism. He shaped and reshaped the constitution to offset these trends; in Bosnia to balance Muslim rights against Bosnian Serb pretensions; in Kosova some protection, as a federal republic to the growing Albanian majority and the dwindling Serb minority in this most sacred of Serbian lands.

'Where Serbian foot has trod, where Serbian blood has shed, is Serbian land'. A heavy legacy, one not lightly to be yielded by a determined people who in their history, recent as well as aged, had shown their conviction that defeat and death are preferable to dishonour. Less recognisable but perhaps as strong, is the Croat memory of their place in an old and proud empire, the successor of Charlemagne and the ultimate defender of the Roman faith.

More immediate and more everyday problems were those of administration, not least in terms of money. The industrial and financial structure of the country was most advanced in Croatia and Slovenia. Governmental and financial decision-taking was over-concentrated in Belgrade. Funds for development earmarked for further profitable investment tended to be siphoned off or diverted elsewhere, and, inevitably, when graft and corruption had their share, Croatia and Slovenia were the losers.

Nonetheless, helped by massive loans from overseas, Yugoslavia managed to hold together until, in 1980 Tito died.

'Soon there will be no country.' Tito's own forecast to General Tempo Vukmanovic was only too correct. No succession, instead a system of rotating presidents from each of the republics, Communism discredited, corruption increasing and Nationalism seeking its own discordant opportunity.

This is not an attempt to write history, it is merely perception and the strongest came after Milosevic, as Prime Minister of Serbia, having disentangled himself from his former Titoist identity, announced that a memorial in honour of the old Cetnik commander Draza Mihailovic was to be established. Julian Amery and I were both invited, with others, to its inauguration. Julian called to suggest we go together. I declined. When he asked me why, I replied that this was the formal rebirth of a Greater Serbian creed. It would mean the end of Yugoslavia as we had known and admired it. It is one occasion when my perception was more accurate than Julian's.

Can one think forwards and not backwards? Are old feuds, old hopes and alliances fulfilled or repudiated the only determinants? I think of the speed of changing events, Yugoslavia itself, only 20 years in its existence between 1921 and 1941 when the Germans invaded, followed by 5 years of dismemberment by the Axis. Yet Tito kept this disparate country together again for 35 years.

We may fail to realise the German Nazi empire lasted for only 12 years, yet its world impact was tumultuous; the Soviet Empire lasted some 70 years when its inherent weakness and the Cold War brought about its collapse. Lest we forget, that ramshackle structure of Mussolini's had a short enough life also, even if the trains did run on time and the castor oil was less obnoxious than the measures used by others.

A European Community? If it can prevent Europe from again tearing itself to pieces, the concept, and its partial existence today, must compel support. But can it? The nation state is already a much eroded entity in a global world with much of industry, finance and defence already in global or wider structures. Yet it is in this very Europe, in the south-east and east, that raw nationalism has caused misery and suffering on a scale comparable with the Second World War.

The Church of Rome and the Orthodox Church seem able still to invoke the worst of old feuds and hatreds, however unintended in their leadership this may be, and they certainly provide enough followers in Croatia and Serbia with fervour to do their worst. Enter the Albanians in Kosova, where Western intervention simply moved control from one dominant rule to another, and in Bosnia, where the brutality and clumsiness of Karadic led to the strange and no doubt temporary marriage between Catholic Croats and Muslims, the last of Turkish and Slav descent.

The West can find no reason except to be humble. Peacemakers given neither armed support nor immediate sanction; rules of engagement that stymied the best and bravest of soldiers in doing their job, human as well as military. These in a land renowned for implacable resistance, for the cheapness of life and merciless killing, as well as the skill in doing it. A reliance on air power and not on the ground, making it easy for a determined enemy to make a Mickey of NATO and UN forces.

I asked if one can look ahead, not only backwards over that short period which in our lifetime has seen empires rise and fall. The old danger zones are there: the historic fracture zone between Western culture and a Western Church and an Eastern culture and an Eastern Church, not only in the South Slav lands, but in eastern Hungary and Romania as well. Montenegro is showing its own schisms, both in its Church and its politic; that poor land of great warriors and beautiful women, which deserves so much better.

So many economies ruined, infrastructures damaged if not destroyed and yet thought and discussion still concentrates on old hatreds, old feuds. Can this turn into thoughts on reconstruction, on economic cooperation as opposed to mutual slaughter? Umpteen Customs posts, as many currencies, all the barriers to trade small or large, is there not a place for at least a move towards economic association, however unpalatable it may be to many?

Marshall Aid surely taught its lesson in a Europe more damaged and divided 50 years ago. If rebuilding Germany then caused some to choke, we might reflect that there is little to choose between Serb and Croat practice on each other, except that Serbia has shown herself to be a staunch but foolhardy ally when the going was hard for her friends.

With the overthrow of the Milosevic regime and Milosevic himself on trial in The Hague, and with international capital becoming available for industrial reconstruction there is a new hope for Serbian recovery. It would be idle to deny, however, the threat internally of those interests in the country who profited from the old regime, including the mafias. In fear of their own skins, they could be as vicious as rattlesnakes and more adept in adjusting their colour to new environments. Equally what must not be overlooked are the aspirations of those previously discriminated against who have found power and are determined not to yield it.

NATO so far has had to take responsibility for measured intervention in the most difficult of circumstances. No matter what Brussels would like to pretend, no other force combines the quality, experience or the overall potential than NATO. One must hope that the European Community can live up to its pretensions. Will it so do?

This final Chapter is concerned almost exclusively with events in the former Yugoslavia and excludes the developments in Romania, with which the early part of the book was equally concerned. The reason is simple in that so much of my business and personal life these last 50 years was related to Belgrade and Zagreb and none, sadly, to Bucharest. As this book is so largely anecdotal, the gap is there. However, a brief summary would seem necessary, not least because its development, despite the appalling years of Soviet control and Ceasescu frenzy which brought such suffering, now would appear to have made effective recovery a realistic hope.

Poverty overall is still widespread but for Romania now to have prospect of acceptance both in Membership of an enlarged European Community and of NATO, would have seemed a pipe dream only a brief period before. Even more, the presence of Romanian forces, not large but there, with Western Allies in Afghanistan is a welcome fact, one that I am sure disproves the reputation in my days of their officers as 'cocktail party heroes' and vindicates the true toughness of the ordinary folk of that country, of whom others more knowledgeable than I have much to write.

And, as the subject of this book is the Danube, the relief that the great wet land of its massive delta, with its wealth of bird life and ecological treasure is again secure, rescued from the destruction threatened by the Ceasescu regime.

APPENDIX 1

Mining Operations

This is how the Danube was mined, as reported in Group 205 Operations Record Book:

APRIL

Night of 6/7

'Target – mining the River Danube: operation cancelled.'

Night of 7/8

'Target – mining the River Danube: operation cancelled.'

8/9 (target: mining in Danube between Bazias and Belgrade, 22 sorties)

'19 Wellingtons of No. 231 Wing and 3 Liberators of No. 240 Wing successfully laid mines in the areas specified. One Wellington "B" of No. 70 Squadron [skipper, Pilot Officer Gibson], ditched in the river as a result of being hit by flak just prior to dropping its mines. The Captain and Bomb Aimer have since returned to their Unit, but the remaining members of the crew are thought to have been killed. All the other aircraft returned to base safely. One Liberator raked the decks of shipping on the river with machine gun fire, observing many strikes.'

9/10 (target: completion of mining in Danube)

'Operation cancelled 20.20hrs.'

10/11 (target: mining in Danube)

'Operation cancelled.'

14/15 (mining in Danube, 11 sorties)

'Eleven Liberators of No. 240 Wing operated, four successfully dropped their mines in the river between Prahovo and Turnu Magurele; one dropped mines 15 miles due south of Craiova in the River Jiul and four aircraft were unable to locate the target owing to considerable haze and poor visibility and brought mines back. One Liberator "R" [skipper, Lieut. Shaw] crashed immediately after take-off and three of the crew were killed; another Liberator "D" [skipper, Lieut. Rogan] crashed after take-off one kilometre east of San Marco, all the crew being killed. 30 mines were laid in the Rivers Danube and Jiul.'

15/16th (mining in the Danube)

'Operation cancelled.'

MAY

5/6 (target: mining in Danube, 31 sorties)

'20 Wellingtons of 330 Wing and 11 Liberators of 240 Wing operated successfully, all the mines being dropped, except one which hung-up and was brought back. A total of 105 mines was dropped, most aircraft being able to see the parachutes open; all the aircraft saw splashes in the water. On leaving the target area at 10,000ft, one aircraft saw a large explosion in the vicinity of the river. Many aircraft fired at barges on the river, a large concentration being observed at Smederevo, and tracer fire was returned. One fire is believed to have been started in a tug, under way towing barges. One aircraft of No. 178 Squadron received three direct hits in the rear of the aircraft, which riddled the rear turret, fins and rudders, and killed the rear gunner, Pilot Officer Allingham. This aircraft returned safely and no aircraft are missing.'

9/10 (mining in Danube, 8 sorties)

'Eight Liberators of No. 240 Wing dropped 48 × 1,000lb mines in the area stipulated, one returning early with electrical trouble. Parachutes were seen to open and most crews counted the required number of splashes. The river was in flood at several points. There appeared to be no shipping active on the Danube but some barges were reported, apparently anchored. No attacks were made on these barges.'

29/30 (mining in Danube, 12 sorties)

'12 Liberators of No. 240 Wing carried out a most successful operation [they laid 72 A Mk V mines in the Upper Danube, either side of Komorom]. The weather was excellent, all crews saw parachutes open and splashes were observed in the water in every case. A total of 72 × 1,000lb Mk V mines was dropped. Several barges were shot up by one aircraft but no results were observed.'

31 May/1 June (mining in Danube, 52 sorties)

'42 Wellingtons of Nos. 231 and 236 Wings and 10 Liberators of No. 240 Wing operated. 4 Wellingtons returned early for various reasons and one Liberator "L" [skipper, Lieut. Hall] crashed on landing and burnt out, all the crew being killed. No aircraft are missing. All mines [a total of 136 A Mk V 1,000lb] were successfully dropped in the specified areas [in a variety of beds between Bazias and a position ten miles north of Baja], apart from two which were slightly outside their area, owing to an error in pinpointing. Several aircraft machine-gunned barges and gun positions in the mining areas, observing strikes but no other results.'

JUNE

No mining operations were carried out this month as top priority was given to the bombing of the Ploesti oil terminals and its internal rail systems along with other primary targets such as marshalling yards and oil storage terminals.

JULY

1/2 (mining in Danube, 76 sorties)

'57 Wellingtons of Nos 231, 236 and 330 Wings and 16 Liberators of No. 240 Wing operated with 3 Halifaxes of 614 squadron marking the route. Two Wellingtons returned early and two aircraft jettisoned, one after a hang-up and the other after being hit by flak. 192 mines were dropped in beds between Nyergsujafalu (30 miles east of Komarom) and Bazia (40 miles east of Belgrade).

'Mining was generally accurate, crews seeing parachutes opening and splashes in the correct positions, but five aircraft mined outside their allotted areas, four due to incorrect identification and one due to flak hits. Tugs and barges were strafed, strikes and one explosion being observed. Much accurate light flak was encountered, several aircraft being hit and sustaining casualties and there were some reports of aircraft being seen to crash, hit by flak. Fighter opposition was slight.

'Four Wellingtons were reported missing, "A" of 40 Squadron [Sgt. Waddell], "H" of 104 Squadron, "L" of 104 Squadron [Sgt. Hunt] and "N" of 40 Squadron [Sgt. Booth].'

2/3rd (mining in Danube, 10 sorties)

'This was a most successful operation. 10 Liberators of 240 Wing dropped 60 × 1,000lb mines in eight beds between Vikovar and Giurgiu. All aircraft identified the correct positions and in all cases splashes were observed. There was no opposition.'

30/31st (mining in Danube, 52 sorties)

'34 Wellingtons of Nos 231, 236 and 330 Wings and 18 Liberators of No. 240 Wing and 2, SAAF Wings, operated and dropped 175 mines in 13 beds on the following stretches: Giurgiu/Vrata – Ogradina/Orsova – Gradiste/Mohacs – Kovin/Bazias.

'With the exception of one mine jettisoned and two mines dropped outside the allotted bed, all mines were laid correctly, many crews seeing parachutes open and splashes. Barges and light flak positions were strafed. Light flak was encountered at many places along the river and accurate heavy flak at Paracin. Some unidentified aircraft were seen but no encounters took place.'

AUGUST

7/8 (mining in Danube, 2 sorties)

'2 Liberators of No. 240 Wing successfully dropped 12 × 1,000lb mines in 2 beds situated between Mohacs and 10 miles north of Baja. The only opposition was slight machine gun fire from barges in the target area.'

10/11 (mining in Danube, 13 sorties)

'13 Liberators of No. 240 Wing and 2 SAAF Wing dropped '78 × 1,000lb mines in widely separated beds between Batina and Nokopol. 12 aircraft dropped their loads in the correct beds but one had to make several runs owing to thick haze and finally two of its mines fell on land. Light flak and machine gun fire was encountered at many places along the bank, the largest concentration being at Batina. One Ju 88 was sighted but did not attack.'

27/28 (mining in Danube, 7 sorties)

'7 Liberators of No. 240 Wing were despatched and six successfully dropped 36 mines in two beds in the Dalj and Dubovac/Bazias areas.

'The other aircraft "E" of 178 Squadron [F/Sgt Ansell] is missing. Light flak and machine-gun fire was encountered at many points along the river banks but was mainly inaccurate.'

28/29 (mining in Danube, 10 sorties)

'10 Liberators of No. 2 SAAAF Wing operated and 9 dropped 54 mines in three beds in the Orsova, Mohacs, Baja and Kaloca/Belcke areas. One mine possibly fell on land and one crew did not observe results but all other mines fell into the correct areas. One aircraft "F" of No. 34 SAAAF squadron [Captain Munro] was seen to fall in flames and explode on the ground near Mohacs. Much light flak was encountered along the river, and four fighters sighted, one of which made two attacks, but these were evaded.'

29/30 (mining in Danube, 7 sorties)

'Seven Liberators of No. 240 Wing successfully laid 42 mines in the Orsova and Barina stretches without loss. Only slight flak was encountered and an aircraft machine gunned 30 barges without observing results.'

SEPTEMBER

5/6th (target: mining in Danube, 12 sorties)

'12 Wellingtons of No. 236 Wing operated and 11 of them successfully dropped 22 mines in three beds Cortovici/Gardinovici – Fajs/7 miles south – Jabouka/5 miles north. One aircraft overshot and dropped two mines in the river near Peks. Balloons and flak positions were strafed with only slight return fire.'

6/7 (target: mining in Danube, 18 sorties)

18 Wellingtons of 330 Wing were despatched. One returned early but the remaining 17 carried out a very successful operation. 34 mines were lain in two beds Dunasfeldvar/Dunapentele and Jabouka/5 miles north. All mines were seen to enter the water in the correct positions. Light flak was reported at many places in the mining areas, being accurate at Dunsfeldvar and Kisepostag but no aircraft was hit.'

10/11 (target: mining in Danube, 29 sorties)

'17 Wellingtons of No. 231 Wing, 11 Liberators of Nos. 240 and 2 SAAF Wings and 1 Halifax of 614 Squadron operated. The Halifax marked the route and illuminated the Komarom area. This was the first occasion on which illumination had been used in the mining operation and crews reported that it was most useful. 25 aircraft mined successfully, laying 82 mines in four beds between Esztergom and Szap. 1 Liberator returned early, 1 could not identify the target area and 1, 'Q' of No. 34 SAAF Squadron [Captain Capstick] is missing. Accurate flak was encountered along the river but no aircraft was hit.'

OCTOBER

4/5 (target: mining in Danube, 22 sorties)

'18 Wellingtons of No. 236 Wing and four Liberators of Nos. 240 and 2 SAAF Wings operated and all reached the mining areas. 17 aircraft dropped 50 mines in 5 beds between Bratislava and Esztergom and four aircraft dropped eight mines at short distances outside the correct beds, owing to over-shooting. 13 balloons were reported in the Nyergesujfalu

163

area and much light flak in the mining areas. This was generally inaccurate but Wellington "A" of No. 40 Squadron [Captain, Warrant Officer Mayers] was seen shot down in flames into the river near Kisbodak.'

APPENDIX 2

USAAF and RAF Squadrons: How the Allied and Axis Aircraft Lined Up

The Mediterranean Allied Air Force (MAAF) and the Mediterranean Allied Strategic Air Force (MASAF) were made up of the American 15th Air Force and 205 Group of the Royal Air Force augmented by two squadrons of the South African Air Force which formed its own Wing within 205 Group. Members of 205 Group also included strong representations of Australians, Canadians and New Zealanders. Midway through the Bombing of Ploesti and the mining of the Danube campaigns, the Balkan Air Force was formed, mainly to coordinate and support missions in the Mediterranean theatre and the Balkans.

The Air Commander-in-Chief of the Mediterranean Allied Air Force was Lieutenant-General Ira C. Eaker and the Deputy Air Commander-in-Chief of MAAF, and also Commander-in-Chief of the Royal Air Force (Mediterranean) was Air Marshal Sir John Slessor, DSO. Major-General Nathan F. Twining, of the United States Army Air Force, was Commanding General of the American 15th Air Force, and he said of the Battle of Ploesti:

> The Battle of Ploesti was won by airmen who flew through the best defences of modern fighter aircraft and flak which a determined enemy could concentrate over his most valuable resource.
>
> The formations never turned back until their bombs had been dropped on the target. Some of our bomber crews and escort pilots did not return. Of all airmen who flew against Ploesti, these gave the most...

Air Commodore J.H.T. Simpson, DSO, was Air Officer Commanding 205 Group when the bombing and mining campaigns began and continued until 3 August 1944, when he was succeeded by Brigadier J.T. Durrant, CB, DFC, of the South African Air Force. The Group's Senior Air Staff Officers were Group Captain D.I.P. McNair and (from 19 June 1944) Group Captain L.E. Jarman, DFC.

The structure of 205 Group, made up for four Wings, was as follows (all personnel RAF unless stated):

165

231 WING: OC, Group Captain P.R. Beare, DSO, DFC; **37 Squadron** Wing Commander R.P. Widdowson, DFC (22 April 1944 until 28 August), Squadron leader P.E.B. Forsyth, DFC (temporary appointment until 12 September), Wing Commander Henry Langton, DSO, DFC; **70 Squadron** Wing Commander C.P. Barber, DFC (until 27 June 1944), Wing Commander R.R. Banker, DSO, DFC.

236 WING: Group Captain P.J. Harris, DFC; **40 Squadron** Wing Commander J.D. Kirwan, DFC, was appointed OC from March 1944 but with Kirwan ill, Squadron Leader C.F. Mervyn-Jones, DFC, was Acting OC from mid-April until 24 August); **104 Squadron** Wing Commander H.G. Turner, DSO, DFC, from 2 December 1943, Wing Commander C.F. Mervyn-Jones, DFC, from 31 October 1944.

240 WING: Group Captain J.J. McKay, DSO, DFC, Royal New Zealand Air Force; **31 Squadron, South African Air Force** Lieutenant-Colonel D.U. Nel, DFC, SAAF; **178 Squadron** Wing Commander D. Smythe, DSO, GM; **614 (Target Marking) Squadron** Wing Commander J.S. Laird.

330 WING: Group Captain J.C. Morris; **142 Squadron** Wing Commander A.R. Gibbs, Royal Australian Air Force, Wing Commander A.G.C. Maclean, from 29 March 1944; **150 Squadron** Wing Commander E.R.A. Walker.

The 15th Air Force comprised the XVth Fighter Group (Prov) and XV Air Force Service Command; 5th Photo Group recon and the 885th Bombardier Squadron (H) (Special). The breakdown:

5th BOMB WING (B-17 Flying Fortresses). **Bomber Groups (BGs):** 2nd, 97th, 99th, 301st, 463rd, 483rd.
47th BOMB WING (B-24 Liberators). **BGs:** 98th, 376th, 449th, 450th.
49th BOMB WING (B-24 Liberators). **BGs:** 451st, 461st, 484th.
55th BOMB WING (B-24 Liberators). **BGs:** 460th, 464th, 465th, 485th.
304th BOMB WING (B-24 Liberators). **BGs:** 454th, 455th, 456th, 459th.
305th FIGHTER WING (Prov) (P-38 Lightnings). **Fighter Groups (FGs):** 1st, 14th, 82nd.
306th FIGHTER WING (P-51 Mustangs). **FGs:** 31st, 52nd, 325th, 332nd.
5th PHOTO GROUP RECONNAISSANCE. 15th Photo Recon Squadron, 4th Photo Tech Squadron, 32nd Photo Recon Squadron.
XVth AF SERVICE COMMAND. 18th and 41st A.D.G.; **Service Groups:** 37th, 38th, 43rd, 60th, 62nd, 96th, 323rd, 324th.

ALLIES vs AXIS: THE AIRCRAFT

Here is a run-down of the Allied aircraft involved in the bombing and mining campaigns – and the Axis fighters lined up to stop them...

205 GROUP

VICKERS WELLINGTON: When that most imaginative of designer/inventors Barnes Wallis first saw his prototype Wellington bomber (K4049) fly in June 1936, he could hardly have expected that eight years later, his twin-engined 'baby' would still be in the forefront of the struggle.

Wellingtons were involved in the first bombing missions over Germany on 4 September 1939, became the backbone of Bomber Command until superseded in 1943 by the real heavies, the Avro Manchester/Lancaster, the Handley Page Halifax and the Short Stirling, and then carved a whole new vital role for themselves in the Middle East and the Mediterranean theatres of operation.

The Vickers Wellington – mostly known to its crewmen affectionately as the 'Wimpy' after the character J. Wellington Wimpy in the American Popeye animated cartoon – could be ranked with the Lancaster, the de Havilland Mosquito and the Junkers Ju 88, as the most versatile of aircraft for overall mission capability.

Coastal Command anti-submarine hunter, mine-exploder, night torpedo bomber, parachute trainer, crew trainer and, of course, strategic bomber, the Wimpy could count its performance as a low-level mine layer on the Danube night missions as among its finest moments, often flying at 100ft or below. Not least of its many and various qualities was its ability to carry the 4,000lb 'cookie' – a devastating parcel to drop on the enemy! For an aircraft deemed to be approaching obsolescence by 1943, it had a remarkably long and deadly life.

A fully-loaded and crewed B-17 Fortress or B-24 Liberator could carry only about 4,500lbs of its lethal cargo on a daylight operation. The Wellington, much smaller and cheaper to produce than the American giants, regularly flew with this same load. A typical bomb load for short to medium distances was 9 × 500lb MC bombs or 810 × 4lb incendiaries. But some records show that in the summer of 1944 loads approaching 6,500lb were carried over short distances in the tactical role. A specially-modified bomb bay allowed the Wellington to carry the 4,000lb HC 'cookie' or 'blockbuster' and most squadrons had at least two 'cookie kites' modified to carry the 4,000-pounder partly inside and partly outside the aircraft. It could also carry two 1,000lb magnetic or acoustic naval mines, as it did during operations to mine the Danube; it was also able to carry two naval torpedoes as an anti-shipping night torpedo bomber or four Torpex depth charges and a Leigh Light for anti-submarine patrol.

For its mine laying mission on the Danube, the Wellington bomb bays had to be redesigned and adapted to enable them to carry the smaller and lighter bombs, and mines which were developed by Commander Roger Lewis and his experts at HMS *Vernon*.

The Wellington was well beloved of its crews. The fabric covering the incredibly strong but flexible 'geodetic' construction allowed flak and cannon shells to pass through without doing serious structural damage – unless they hit something vital. Unlike an aircraft with a monocoque construction, the covering of the Wellington served only to streamline it and to keep out the draughts.

Since each section of the geodetic construction distributed weight and stress in many directions, great chunks could be shot away and the aircraft could still be flown home. There are stories of aircraft returning with no fabric at all on parts of the tail or wings.

The Wimpy always seemed a mystery to American crews. They called it 'the rag bomber', 'the paper covered kite' and even 'canvas covered coffins'. They often failed to appreciate the genius of Barnes Wallis invention – a flexible and incredibly strong aircraft for the minimum required weight.

Apart from its vital and well-documented role as the backbone of Bomber Command over Europe, the Wellington served in the Middle East with 202 and 205 Groups from 1940 and was involved in the bombing of ports at Tripoli, Benghazi and Bizerte to smash Rommel's supply lines, as well as supporting the British Eighth Army in their efforts to defeat Rommel's Afrika Korps.

It would not have been possible without the skill and dedication of the ground crew, the fitters, riggers and armourers who serviced the Wellingtons. They mostly had to work in conditions of extreme heat, dust and very poor living conditions and quality of food, but they kept the Wellington fleet at an incredible level of serviceability, especially considering that every spare part, every tyre, every nut and bolt and every bomb and round of ammunition had to reach them from the United Kingdom or North America.

A total of 11,461 Wellingtons of varying Marks rolled off the Vickers assembly line, compared with 7,000-plus Lancasters, making it the most numerous bomber in the Royal Air Force. The Wellington was in on the first bombing mission over Germany in 1939 and she dropped her last bomb (yes, a 4,000-pounder) over Trieste on 13 March 1945.

So Barnes Wallis' inspiration served from the first day of the war to near the end as a front-line aircraft – an enormous tribute to her designer and to the people at Vickers who put her together.

HANDLEY PAGE HALIFAX: The Halifax, the second British four-engine bomber to enter combat behind the Stirling, flew its first mission with No. 35 Squadron in March 1941. In spite of a number of teething problems, it went through several Marks to become very successful at its job although, unfortunately, overshadowed by its stablemate, the Lancaster, much as the B-24 Liberator was overshadowed by the B-17 Fortress. The 'Halibag' was much loved by its crews and was used in a greater variety of jobs than most heavy bombers. In the Battle of Ploesti and the mining of the Danube, the Halifax doubled up as target-marking pathfinder and heavy bomber. The last Halifaxes were retired from service as late as the early 1950s.

THE 15TH AIR FORCE

CONSOLIDATED B-24 LIBERATOR: First flown in December 1939, the Consolidated B-24 Liberator ended the war as the most produced American aircraft in history at 18,000 examples, thanks in large measure to Henry Ford and the harnessing of American industry. Overshadowed in publicity by its stablemate, the B-17 (the Flying Fortress), the Liberator served in every theatre of war with almost every Allied nation, *including the Danube mining campaign with 205 Group.*

The Liberator's most famous mission was the low-level strike against Ploesti in Operation Tidal Wave on 1 August 1943.

BOEING B-17 FLYING FORTRESS: America's most famous aircraft, it seems, was almost stillborn. During the summer 1935 fly-off competition with its rival Douglas B-18, the control locks of the B-17 were not removed and the prototype Model 299 crashed, leaving victory to the converted Douglas airliner. Fortunately, the promise of this heavy bomber brought an initial purchase of 13 test aircraft as coastal defence weapons, an extension of coastal artillery. An offensive weapon (says *Jane's*) would never have got past an isolationist Congress. Though the RAF had very poor results with their early Fortresses, the USAAF built its strategic bombing doctrine around the B-17, particularly in Europe.

LOCKHEED P-38 LIGHTNING: The most advanced aircraft of its day when it first flew on 27 January 1939, Lockheed designer Kelly Johnson's P-38 Lightning became one of America's more famous aircraft in the Second World War as both a fighter and photo-reconnaissance platform. The P-38 is included here, among the bombers, because on 10 June 1944, the 15th Air Force configured 46 of them as dive bombers for an all-P-38 bombing mission over Ploesti in an effort to beat its effective smokescreen.

THE AXIS DEFENDERS

FOCKE-WULF FW 190: When the 190A version entered combat in the summer of 1941, according to *Jane's*, it outclassed the Spitfire, which was made to look sluggish by comparison. Designed by the chief company designer Kurt Tank, it was Germany's most potent piston-powered fighter aircraft of the war and, despite severe problems with the BMW 801 engine, the 190 kept even or ahead of Allied fighters through successive versions.

The Focke-Wulf was not only fast but its superior handling and fast roll rate gave it an edge even in the hands of less experienced pilots. Such sparkling performance combined with the 190's superior armament presented Allied pilots with a real challenge until German pilot training began to drop in quality. The 190 was also one of the first fighters to feature a clear rear canopy, allowing pilots to keep an excellent lookout for enemy fighters.

MESSERSCHMITT BF 109: Willy Messerschmitt designed the 109 in 1934 for the Bayerische Flugzeugwerke (Bf) and the small fighter captured the imagination from the start. It became Germany's premier fighter aircraft in 1939 and it established its superiority over most of Europe through to the summer of 1940 when it met the Hurricanes and Spitfires of the Royal Air Force during the Battle of Britain. Hampered by being at the end of their flight range, German pilots did not have time to use many of the fighter's sterling qualities and they were unable to prevent an RAF victory.

Even though the Fw 190 came along in 1941, the 109 kept up with Allied fighters through successive versions until the end of the war. A tricky aircraft on take-off and landing, the Messerschmitt required skill and experience to bring out its best. Most of Germany's leading aces, including Erich Hartmann, the all-time leader with 352 victims, got their kills in 109s and preferred to fly them even when newer fighters became available.

When the American daylight bombing campaign was at its height, the 109 was lightened and used as a top cover fighter while heavier Fw 190s attacked the bombers, a testimony to the Messerschmitt's handling. Final versions of the 109 included a high altitude fighter with a pressurised cockpit. After the war, the 109 was built in Czechoslovakia and then in Spain until 1956. A total of 35,000 examples were assembled – one of the largest production runs in history.

MESSERSCHMITT BF 110: After being well beaten during the Battle of Britain, the ME110 became an outstanding night fighter, opposing the four night raids by 205 Group on the Ploesti oil fields and in their sorties over other targets. Like many other twin-engined fighters developed by many nations in the late 1930s, the Bf 110 was underpowered and vulnerable to single-engine opponents. It had the range needed to protect bombers but not the manoeuvrability needed to beat the likes of the Hurricane and Spitfire and it got shot to pieces during the Battle of Britain. It might have faded away completely had night fighters not become desperately needed in 1942 to stem the tide of Bomber Command.

JUNKERS JU 88: This was another civil airliner converted into a bomber. It flew for the first time in December 1936 and was immediately regarded as the ideal *Schnellbomber* (high-speed bomber) around which to build the burgeoning Luftwaffe. It entered service just days after the start of the Second World War and the Ju 88 soon became an airframe modified for several different missions, used in more varying roles than any single German wartime aircraft – bomber, fighter, night fighter, destroyer, tank buster, reconnaissance, dive bomber and anything else Berlin could think of. Almost 15,000 Ju 88s were built and the night fighter, which could carry an impressive combination of radar and weapons, was the most successful of all types in downing RAF bombers.

APPENDIX 3

Statistical Summary of 15th US Bombing Raids on Ploesti

One of the most decisive single battles of the Second World War was waged five miles above the rolling plains of Romania for five bitterly-contested months: the attempt to eliminate the vast oil-producing area of Ploesti, the greatest single source of oil available to the Axis.

Over those five months, B-24 Liberators and B-17 Flying Fortresses of the United States' 15th Air Force based around the east coast of Italy launched 5,446 effective bomber sorties against the oil installations in 20 daylight raids, during which 13,286 tons of bombs were unleashed. Four further night attacks by 205 Group of the Royal Air Force were described by Major General Nathan F. Twining, Commanding General of the 15th American Air Force as 'attacks which contributed substantially to the overall success of the campaign'.

However, the bulk of the campaign was carried out so effectively by the 'Fighting 15th' that by the time the advancing Russian Red Army reached Ploesti at the end of August, they found most of the area smoking ruins. Here is the month-by-month account of how victory was achieved – and at what cost.[1]

Table 1 Statistics of the Ploesti campaign

	5 April	14 April	24 April	April Total	5 May	6 May	18 May	31 May	May Total	Cumulative April & May
Bombers Airborne	285	188	313	786	522	151	420	542	1635	2421
Less Early Returns*	29	8	11	48	23	11	22	36	92	140
Sorties	256	180	302	738	499	140	398	506	1543	2281
Less Non-Effective Sorties	26	43	12	81	14	5	192	25	236	317
Effective Sorties	230	137	290	657	485	135	206	481	1307	1964
Tonnage Dropped	587	316	793	1696	1230	329	493	1113	3165	4861
Bomber losses by enemy A/c	11	1	3	15	6	3	8	1	18	33
By Flak	2	2	5	9	12	3	5	13	33	42
Other Causes	—	—	—	—	—	—	1	2	3	3
Total	13	3	8	24	18	6	14	16	54	78
Enemy A/c destroyed in air	4	1	11	53	22	14	25	19	80	133

	8 June	10 June (all P-38s)	23 June	24 June	June Total	Cumulative April, May and June
Bombers Airborne	361	46	241	160	808	3229
Less Early Returns*	31	1	61	11	104	244
Sorties	330	45	180	149	704	2985
Less Non Effective Sorties	20	7	41	14	82	399
Effective Sorties	310	38	139	135	622	2586
Tonnage Dropped	698	19	283	329	1329	6171
Bomber losses by enemy Aircraft	10	2	3	8	23	56
By Flak	3	7	3	4	17	59
By Other Causes	1	—	—	2	3	6
Total Bombers lost	14	9	6	14	43	121
Enemy A/c destroyed in air	17	7	10	11	45	178

	9 July	15 July	22 July	28 July	31 July	July Total	Cumulative April, May, June, July
Bombers Airborne	247	705	618	403	168	2141	5325
Less Early Returns*	10	51	59	56	8	184	427
Sorties	237	654	559	347	160	1957	4897
Less Non Effective Sorties	15	50	100	23	6	194	586
Effective Sorties	222	604	459	324	154	1763	4311
Tonnage Dropped	605	1521	1238	842	435	4641	10812
Bomber losses by enemy Aircraft	1	—	2	—	—	3	57
By Flak	5	13	15	11	2	46	98
By Other Causes	—	7	9	8	—	24	30
Total Bombers lost	6	20	26	19	2	73	185
Enemy A/c destroyed in air	8	2	5	—	—	15	193

	10 August	17 August	18 August	19 August	August Total	Cumulative April, May June, July, August
Bombers Airborne	477	325	441	79	1322	6692
Less Early Returns*	32	31	37	6	106	534
Sorties	445	294	404	73	1216	6158
Less Non Effective Sorties	31	49	31	8	119	712
Effective Sorties	414	245	373	65	1097	5446
Tonnage Dropped	952	534	825	144	2455	13286
Bomber losses by enemy Aircraft	—	—	—	—	—	59
By Flak	11	19	5	1	36	141
Other Causes	6	—	2	1	9	39
Total Bombers lost	17	19	7	2	45	239+
Enemy A/c destroyed in air	1	2	—	—	3	197

*Early Returns: Aircraft airborne failing to reach enemy lines

+230 Heavy Bombers
9 P-38 Dive Bombers
───
239 Total

NOTE:

1. The Air Battle of Ploesti, PRO, Kew, AIR 23/7776; tables Ref: II.

LIST OF ABBREVIATIONS

ADNI	Assistant Director of Naval Intelligence
AOC	Air Officer Commanding
BNLO	British Naval Liaison Officer
CIGS	Chief of the Imperial General Staff
CO	Commanding Officer
DNI	Director of Naval Intelligence
FOTALI	Flag Officer Taranto and Liaison Italy
MASAF	Mediterranean Allied Strategic Air Force
MEW	Ministry of Economic Warfare
MI(R)	Military Intelligence (Research)
NCO	Non-Commissioned Officer
NID	Naval Intelligence Division
NKVD	Narodnyi Kommissariat Vnutrennykh Del, the Soviet Secret Police and counter-intelligence organisation
ORB	Operations Record Book
RAF	Royal Air Force
RCOS	Royal Corps of Signals
RN	Royal Navy
RNVR	Royal Navy Volunteer Reserve
SASO	Senior Air Staff Officer
SBNO	Senior British Naval Officer
SIS	Secret Intelligence Service (British)
SOE	Special Operations Executive
SOM	Special Operations (Mediterranean)
USAAF	United States Army Air Force
USSAFE	United States Strategic Air Force in Europe
W/T	Wireless Telegraph

SOURCES and NOTES

1 THE DANUBE: GERMANY'S ACHILLES HEEL

*1 General Ira C. Eaker: born in 1896, the formidable Ira C. Eaker died in 1987 at the age of 91. He was US Commander of Strategic Air Forces in Europe and a vociferous advocate of strategic bombing. It was Eaker who established the American Army Bomber Command in England, the nucleus of the 8th Air Force, and supervised the first action, against marshalling yards near Rouen, in August 1942. He was appointed Commander of the 8th Air Force in December that year and set about rebutting criticism, notably from the Commander-in-Chief (C-in-C) Bomber Command, Air Marshal Harris, and Winston Churchill, about the effectiveness of precision daylight bombing. He took his view to the Casablanca Conference and won support for what became known as the Eaker Plan, the Joint Bombing Offensive under which Eaker's daylight raids complemented the RAF's night bombing offensives. He was promoted to Lieutenant-General in June 1943 when he succeeded Air Chief Marshal Sir Arthur Tedder as C-in-C Mediterranean Allied Air Forces. In August that year, when the Battle of Ploesti was effectively won, he took command of Allied air forces for the invasion of southern France.

2 Air Marshal Sir John Slessor (1897–1979): as Group Captain John Slessor, he was Director of Plans at the Air Ministry at the outbreak of war in September 1939. Singled out as an outstanding officer from an early age, he took part in the 1941 Anglo-American staff discussions in Washington that first formulated the 'Europe first' strategy in the event of American entry into the conflict. He commanded No. 5 Bomber Group before taking over as Air Officer Commanding Coastal Command and, working closely with the Royal Navy and American naval forces, improved the effectiveness of campaigns against the German U-boat wolf-packs in the Battle of the Atlantic. He commanded RAF units in the Mediterranean, where he later became Deputy C-in-C Allied Air Forces. In 1950 he became Chief of the Air Staff. As with Admiral Sir John Cunningham, his understanding of the new atomic age proved to be outstanding.

3 Air Vice Marshal George Baker had an earlier association with Air Marshal Sir John Slessor at Coastal Command where he also first came

into contact with Glen. In 1942, Glen was Naval Liaison Officer with the first VLR (very long range) Catalina flights around the Arctic Circle by Coastal Command and struck up an excellent working acquaintanceship with Baker. Slessor later took over as AOC-in-C Coastal Command and in another coincidence also knew Glen from meetings between the two shortly before war was declared in 1939.

4 Admiral Sir John H.D. Cunningham, GCB, succeeded his namesake, Admiral of the Fleet Sir Andrew Cunningham, as the C-in-C Mediterranean Fleet on 15 October 1943, while already holding the post of C-in-C Allied Naval Expeditionary Force (Med.) and held the joint responsibility until 1946. Previously: Assistant Chief of the Naval Staff 1936–37; Chief of Naval Air Service 1938; Vice-Admiral 1st Cruiser Squadron 1938–41; Fourth Sea Lord and Chief of Supplies and Transport April 1941 to May 1943; C-in-C Levant 1943. He became Chief of the Naval Staff 1945–49 and was regarded as one of the outstanding brains of the navy with an exceptional grasp of future warfare as Britain entered the nuclear age.

5 HMS *Vernon*: this potted history of HMS *Vernon* is taken from *The Oxford Illustrated History of the Royal Navy* (Oxford University Press, 1995). Page 270: 'In the late 1860s Mr Robert Whitehead, manager of an engineering factory in Fiume, developed a self-propelling, depth-keeping torpedo, which the Admiralty bought a licence to manufacture after successful trials in Sheerness in 1870. In 1872, the frigate *Vernon*, which was then a hulk serving as a coaling jetty at Portland, Dorset, was brought round to Portsmouth and fitted out as a torpedo instructional ship. She was still a tender to *Excellent* in September 1872 for 'torpedo instruction'. *Vernon* broke away from *Excellent* and was commissioned as a separate command in 1876. Through the years, *Vernon* accumulated various other hulks around her for accommodation and instructional purposes which all moved to Porchester Creek in 1895. Finally, in 1923, *Vernon* moved ashore to the Gunwharf in Portsmouth Harbour, where the Mining School was already established. The Torpedo Branch became responsible for all aspects of torpedo and mine warfare, and also for ships' installation. Training and instruction, for both officers and ratings, including ships' divers, was carried out at *Vernon*.' So the experience of more than 80 years went into the preparation of the mines used to turn the Blue Danube red with blood and black with the oil spilling from the crippled barges bound for Germany.

6 Professor Sir Edward Victor Appleton won the Nobel prize for physics in 1947, was a pioneer in electronic engineering and was closely involved in the development of radar and the planning of the chain of radar stations around the east and south coasts leading up to the Second World War; he served on the War Cabinet RDF (Radio Direction-Finding) Policy Sub-Committee. He was one of the distinguished Senior Scientific Advisers to the government during the war and was highly regarded for his calm judgement. Bradford-born Professor Appleton, knighted in 1941, was decorated by France and Norway and held honorary doctorates in distinguished universities in America, Canada, Australia, Germany and, of course, the United Kingdom. He was later appointed Rector of Edinburgh University.

7 RADAR: an acronym for **RA**dio **D**irection **A**nd **R**anging, was not coined until 1943 when the Americans came up with it. Until then the top-secret weapon had been known as Radio Direction Finding and radar stations had been known either as RDF stations or Air Ministry Experimental Establishments (AMES).

8 Professor Robert Watson Watt (later Sir Robert Watson-Watt, hyphenating his name at the time of his knighthood) was generally regarded as the 'father' of radar development, although the first proven experiment was conducted by one of his assistants, Mr Arnold Wilkins. Professor Watt envisaged the ring of detection stations around the British coast which became known as the Home Chain and was encouraged in his experiments by Air Chief Marshal Sir Hugh (Stuffy) Dowding while Dowding was Development Officer at the Air Ministry. When Dowding became Air Officer C-in-C of Fighter Command, he was thus well placed to use RDF effectively and help him win the Battle of Britain.

9 Admiral John Godfrey was appointed Director of Naval Intelligence in 1939 at a time when the Naval Intelligence Division was at a low ebb following stagnation in the years between the two world wars. Under the unorthodox directorship of Sir Reggie 'Blinker' Hall during the First World War, the Division had gained an enormous reputation for efficiency and resourcefulness. Admiral Godfrey set about restoring that reputation in the manner of Sir Reggie, trawling through the professions of law, academia, science, finance and journalism for the right sort of recruits. One of his notable 'captures' was Ian Fleming, later to become the creator of James Bond. Fleming was appointed Lieutenant in the Royal Naval Volunteer Reserve in July 1939 and he became Admiral Godfrey's personal assistant. In 1943, Admiral Godfrey was appointed Flag Officer of the Royal Indian Navy.

10 Captain Max Despard, DSC, RN, was First Lieutenant on HMS *Broke* in 1917 when the captain, Commander E.R.G.R. Evans, later Admiral Lord Mountevans of Broke, embarked on one of the most spectacular, and brilliantly-successful naval battles of the First World War, in which the *Broke* and HMS *Swift* engaged and defeated six German destroyers.

2 YUGOSLAVIA AND ROMANIA

1 *World War Two: Nation By Nation* by J. Lee Ready (Arms and Armour, an imprint of the Cassell Group, 1995) hereafter to be referred to as J. Lee Ready.

2 The Ustachi (or Ustache): began life as a secret Fascist organisation formed in about 1929 by Ante Pavelic, a fanatical Croatian nationalist. The organisation operated violent terrorist actions against the Orthodox Serb establishment of Yugoslavia throughout the 1930s, often from bases in Hungary, Austria and Italy. Pavelic and the Ustachi were put in control of the nominally-independent kingdom of Croatia after the fall of Yugoslavia in 1941 and perpetrated appallingly brutal purges against non-Croat nation-

alities such as Orthodox Serbs, Muslims and Jews. At the end of the war, while revenge had its opportunity against Ustachi sympathisers, Pavelic escaped to Spain and subsequently to Argentina. The Ustachi survived as a separatist terrorist movement however and continued to be responsible for terrorist activities. (Source: *The Macmillan Dictionary of the Second World War*, updated edition, 1995.)

3 Source: *The Luftwaffe: A Photographic Record 1919–1945* by Karl Ries (Batsford, 1987). Translated from *Luftwaffe Photo-Report* by Dipl.Ing. Karl Ries, published by Motorbuch-Verlag, Stuttgart, 1983.

4 J. Lee Ready.

3 BRITISH AND GERMAN SECRET OPERATIONS IN THE BALKANS

1 Bletchley Park: the Buckinghamshire HQ of the government's Code and Cipher School, known to those who worked in it and supplied it during the war as Station X. The School was moved to Bletchley in 1938 and its contribution to the war effort is thought by many historians to have shortened the conflict by as much as two years, and saved many thousands of lives. Its most famous coup was the unpicking of Germany's Enigma Code, believed by Hitler and the German High Command to be unbreakable. This belief encouraged them to 'discuss' details of many planned operations, not knowing their message traffic was being read at Bletchley. But the complex technical nature of the work carried out led to many other achievements. In 1943 Colossus, the world's first electronic programmable computer was developed, breaking high-grade German codes, including those used by Hitler himself. The work at Bletchley remained secret for many years after the war and the real and factual story of Enigma did not really start unfolding until the mid-1970s. Bletchley Park, a former manor house, is now administered by the Bletchley Park Trust. Bletchley hit the newspaper headlines again in 2000 when an Enigma machine was stolen and a ransom demanded. It was eventually returned via a surprised Jeremy Paxman, the BBC TV presenter.

2 Lieutenant-Colonel (later Major-General) Lawrence Grand: former head of Section D which was later absorbed into the Special Operations Executive. Grand, who had been commissioned into the Royal Engineers, was an elegant, distinguished-looking man who usually wore civilian clothes, even after war broke out. A regular red carnation and a long cigarette holder added to his flamboyance but he was generally regarded while at Section D as far-sighted and imaginative, with fine organisational qualities. Like others before and after him, he was hampered by lack of official funds for much of his work. His response was to persuade the mining magnate Chester Beatty to second mining engineers to Section D while keeping them on his (Beatty's) payroll. Grand gave Section D its early flourish and impetus, although his methods were not always to the liking of his superiors. He was dismissed by SOE's boss, Dr Hugh Dalton, the Minister of Economic

Warfare, in September 1940 in an acrimonious dispute. Dalton nicknamed him 'King Bomba' and had to withstand pressure from Grand's 'high friends' in the Foreign Office to make the dismissal stick. Grand then reverted to normal army duties, rising to the rank of Major-General.

3 Colonel (later Major-General) J.C.F. Holland (1897–1957): head of MI(R) when war broke out, when his chief assistant was Major (later Lieutenant-Colonel) Colin Gubbins, later Head of the SOE. Like Lawrence Grand, Joe Holland was commissioned into the Royal Engineers. Interested in 'irregular warfare' in 1938 he was posted to a small branch of the War Office known as General Staff (R), the R standing for 'Research'. Later it was renamed MI(R) and the research Holland was most interested in was guerrilla warfare; he was soon acknowledged as the driving force behind the organisation. When MI(R) became part of SO2, under the Special Operations Executive, Holland was again involved in subversive warfare and, with Gubbins, was responsible for the publication of pamphlets on guerrilla warfare and sabotage, some of which were translated into many languages and dropped into occupied countries.

4 Admiral Wilhelm Franz Canaris (1887–1945): head of the Abwehr, the German Military Intelligence organisation from 1935 to 1944. He joined the Navy as a cadet in 1905 and saw service on the cruiser *Dresden* in the Battle of the Falklands in the First World War. He escaped internment after the scuttling of his ship and succeeded in making his way back to Germany despite having to pass through British control points. This daring and resourceful exercise brought him to the attention of German Military Intelligence. In 1935 he succeeded Conrad Patzigas as head of the Abwehr, then a small but important department. Canaris built it up significantly by the time the Second World War broke out. An enigmatic figure, Canaris, who came from a wealthy, military background, was brilliant at his job, although he detested National Socialism and feared for the consequences for Germany. There were many suspicions that Canaris actively worked against the Nazis, including, after the invasion of Poland, sending a covert warning to Denmark, Belgium, the Netherlands and Norway that they would soon be on Hitler's invasion list. A pre-war opponent of Hitler and Naziism, he came under suspicion by the SS and Gestapo in 1943 and their constant surveillance made Canaris' resistance work against the Hitler regime largely ineffective. Although Canaris was not directly involved in the 1944 July bomb plot on Hitler's life by Count Stauffenberg's group, he was, like hundreds of others, caught in the fallout. He was arrested, tried for treason and imprisoned. Transferred to a series of camps and prisons, he was executed by the SS at Flossenburg in the last few days of the war.

5 Colin McVean Gubbins, later Sir Colin (1896–1976): Acting Brigadier in 1940, Lieutenant Colonel in 1941; Colonel in 1942; Temporary Major General in 1943; Director of Operations and Training at the SOE 1940–42; Deputy Head at the SOE 1942–43; Head of the SOE 1943–45. A former stalwart of Section D, Gubbins was a short, wiry Highlander with a trademark toothbrush moustache. He had been commissioned into the Royal Artillery. He was born in Japan, where his father was a consular official,

was fluent in French and German and had an understanding of Russian. He was decorated for gallantry under fire in the First World War. Gubbins was a close colleague of his Head at Section D, Major Joe Holland.

6 Source: a paper on '*SOE and Romania*' by Dr Maurice Pearton of London University, which was delivered at a conference on The Special Operations Executive at the Imperial War Museum on Thursday, 29 October 1998; hereafter this source will be referred to simply as Pearton.

7 Colonel Alfred Gerstenberg: the German Air Attaché in Bucharest, had a direct line to Reichsmarshall Herman Goering, with whom Gerstenberg had seen First World War service in the air squadron led by Richtofen, the legendary Red Baron. Because of this, Gerstenberg was considered as important a figure in Bucharest as Dr Wilhelm Fabricius, the German minister or his successor, Von Killinger. Later, as General Gerstenberg, he was appointed by Hitler as the officer responsible for the air defence of the Ploesti oil fields.

8 Source: *Canaris*, a biography by Andre Brissaud, first published in France, 1970; English translation Weidenfeld & Nicolson, 1973; translated and introduction by Ian Colvin; hereafter this source will be referred to simply as *Canaris*.

9 Colonel (later Lieutenant-General) Erwin Lahousen: Chief of Austria Counter-Espionage at the time of the *Anschluss* and later became Deputy Chief of Abwehr Section I, Espionage.

10 Colonel (later General) Egbert von Bentivegni: Chief of Abwehr Section III, Security, masterminded the plans and disposition of the undercover Brandenburg Regiment which frustrated so many of the sabotage attempts on and around the Danube.

11 *Canaris*.

12 Ronald H. Cross, later Sir Ronald, 1st Bart (1896–1968): Minister for Economic Warfare 1939–40; Shipping 1940–41. Conservative MP for Rossendale 1931–45; Ormskirk 1950–51; Junior Minister 1938–39; High Commissioner to Australia, 1941–45.

13 Sir Frederick William Leith-Ross (1887–1968): Deputy Controller of Finance at the Treasury 1925–32; Chief Economic Adviser to British Government 1932–46; Member of Economic Committee of the League of Nations 1932–39.

14 Hugh Todd Naylor Gaitskell (1906–63): Labour MP for South Leeds 1945–63. Principal Private Secretary to Hugh Dalton as Minister for Economic Warfare 1940–42; Principal Assistant Secretary to Board of Trade 1942–45; Parliamentary Secretary, Minister of Fuel and Power 1946–47; Minister of Fuel and Power 1947–50; Minister of State for Economic Affairs 1950; Chancellor of the Exchequer 1950–51; Leader of the Labour Party 1955–63.

15 Sir George Binney, DSO: in his days at Oxford in 1920–24 organised and led the first of a series of expeditions to the Arctic which were to become such a feature of university life over the following 19 years. He then worked with the Hudson Bay Company in Canada until joining the steel industry. In 1939 he joined the Ministry of Economic Warfare and,

with the Admiralty and Section D, organised and commanded Operation Rubble. This cut out from Gothenburg, four fast Norwegian cargo liners loaded with precious ball bearings. He sailed them successfully through the German blockade control of the Skaggerak to the UK. Binney was knighted for this brilliant feat, worthy of Horatio Hornblower himself. He also received the Distinguished Service Order for further similar operations, some involving fast Motor Gunboats. He was made a Captain in the RNVR. After the war he was a director of many companies but a serious heart attack caused him to take early retirement, during which he devoted himself to work for English Heritage. He turned Horham Hall in Essex into a showpiece. His stepson, Marcus Binney, followed Sir George's tastes, becoming one of the most discerning of writers on historic houses and churches, indeed on the heritage issue as a whole.

4 CANARIS SHAPES ROMANIA TO HIS DESIGN

1 General Alfred Josef Jodl (1890–1946): Hitler's Chief of Operations for the OKW (Oberkommando der Wehrmacht), the German Armed Forces' High Command, from 1939. Another of Hitler's high-ranking officers who disapproved of National Socialism, Jodl was nevertheless a loyal and trusted aide of the Führer, so much so that when he asked for a field command in 1942, Hitler turned down his request to keep him on his staff. Jodl was injured while standing next to Hitler in the bomb plot of July 1944 and it was he who, in May 1945, signed the unconditional surrender document of the government then being run by Admiral Doenitz. Jodl was tried at Nuremberg as 'a planner of aggressive war', found guilty and hanged.
2 *Canaris*.
3 Ibid.
4 Admiral Sir Andrew B. Cunningham. (1883–1963): a highly-successful First World War destroyer captain, Admiral Cunningham became the star of Britain's operational wartime naval leaders after taking over command of the Mediterranean Fleet in 1939. Although outnumbered by the Italian navy after they entered the war in June 1940, Admiral Cunningham followed a series of operations with hugely successful attacks on Italian warships at Taranto and Cape Matapan that established a superiority over Italian surface forces that he never relinquished. He later helped keep supply lines open to beleaguered Malta and North Africa, became C-in-C of the larger Anglo-American Force covering the Torch landings in north-west Africa and was responsible for the planning and execution of the amphibious landings in Sicily and Italy. Following the death of Sir Dudley Pound in October 1943, he was appointed the First Sea Lord. He was succeeded as C-in-C Mediterranean by his namesake, but no relation, Admiral Sir John Cunningham.

5 SUMMER 1940: EUROPE AND LONDON

1 Clement Richard Attlee (1883–1967): later 1st Earl Attlee; Labour MP for Limehouse 1922–50; West Walthamstow 1950–55; Under-Secretary of State for War 1924; Chancellor of the Duchy of Lancaster 1930–31; Postmaster-General 1931; Lord Privy Seal 1940–42; Deputy Prime Minister 1942–45; Secretary of State for Dominion Affairs 1942–45; Prime Minister 1945–51; Minister of Defence 1945–46; Leader of the Labour Party 1935–55.

2 Lord Halifax: Foreign Secretary 1938 to 22 December 1940 when he became British Ambassador to the United States, a post he held until 1946, although he was still nominally a member of Churchill's War Cabinet. He was nicknamed The Holy Fox because he was a devout Anglican and a keen huntsman.

3 Ernest Bevin (1881–1951): Labour MP for Central Wandsworth 1940–50; East Woolwich 1950–51; Minister of Labour and National Service 1940–45; Secretary of State for Foreign Affairs 1945–51; Lord Privy Seal 1951; Member of the General Council of the Trades Union Congress (TUC) 1925–40; National Organiser of the Dockers' Union 1910–21; General Secretary of the Transport and General Workers' Union (TGWU) 1925–40.

4 Edward Hugh John Neale Dalton, later Baron (1887–1962): Labour MP for Peckham 1924–29; Bishop Auckland 1929–31 and 1935–59; Under-Secretary of State for Foreign Affairs 1929–31; Minister of Economic Warfare 1940–42; President of the Board of Trade 1942–45; Chancellor of the Exchequer 1945–47; Chancellor of the Duchy of Lancaster 1948–50; Minister of Town and Country Planning 1950–51; Minister of Local Government and Planning 1951.

5 Sir Alexander Cadogan: Permanent Under-Secretary to the Foreign Office 1938–46.

6 Field Marshal Sir Alan Brooke, later 1st Viscount Alanbrooke (1883–1963): generally regarded as one of Britain's most brilliant strategists and field generals providing decisive and cohesive leadership. As commander of the 2nd Corps, British Expeditionary Force in France in 1940, he played a large and significant part in directing defensive operations which enabled so many Allied soldiers to be evacuated from Dunkirk. He served briefly as C-in-C Home Forces before replacing Sir John Dill as Chief of the Imperial General Staff in 1941. From June 1942 he was Chairman of the Chiefs of Staff Committee. An Ulsterman by birth, Alanbrooke grew up in France and spoke French before he learned to speak English. The other side of this immensely professional soldier was a warm and affectionate person, dedicated sportsman and a lover of nature, particularly ornithology. No greater tribute to Alanbrooke's qualities as a soldier and leader could be made than that of General Hastings 'Pug' Ismay (later Lord Ismay), Churchill's representative on the Chiefs of Staff Committee and later first Secretary-General of NATO, in his memoirs published in 1960: 'His self-lessness, integrity and mastery of his profession earned him the complete confidence, not only of his political chiefs and his colleagues in Whitehall,

but also of all the commanders in the field. On that account alone, he was worth his weight in gold. In the course of my eighteen years' service in Whitehall, I saw the work of eight different Chiefs of the Imperial General Staff at close quarters and I would unhesitatingly say that Brooke was the best of them all.'

7 Independent Companies: Britain, the first nation to form commando units, raised ten Independent Companies for the Norway campaign in 1940 but only five were used. Independent Companies joined commando units on early raids but were later absorbed into the battalion-sized commando units raised to carry out hit-and-run raids in Europe.

8 Sir Frank Nelson: then Executive Director of SO2, the SOE's sabotage section, codenamed CD. Sir Frank (1883–1966) was Conservative MP for Stroud 1924–31; Vice-Consul in Basle 1939; served as Executive Director of SO2 from its formation in 1940 until 1942 when he moved to Washington as Wing Commander, Air Intelligence; between 1945–46 he was Air Commodore in command of Air Intelligence at the Allied Control Commission, Germany.

9 Colonel Harry N. Sporborg (1905–85): a banker, solicitor (a partner with the City firm of Slaughter and May) and businessman. He joined the Ministry of Economic Warfare in 1939 and when the SOE was formed in 1940, he took charge of the Norwegian Bureau and later, from 1940 until 1943, headed the Executive's Western Directorate, being responsible for liaison with General Charles de Gaulle's Secret Service. From 1943 until 1946 (the year the SOE was disbanded) Sporborg was the SOE's Vice-Chief. After the war he returned to banking and became Managing Director of Hambro's Bank. In his book *Between Silk and Cyanide*, about the SOE's wartime coding operations, Leo Marks refers to Sporborg wearing an eye patch and comments: 'Sporborg could see more from his single orb than most with two.'

10 Charles J. Hambro, later Sir Charles, (1897–1963): merchant banker and Director of the Bank of England. Deputy Head of SO2 1940–42; Executive Director of SOE May 1942 to September 1943, when he fell out with Dalton's successor, Lord Selborne. Like Nelson, Hambro was also given a job in America where he became concerned with liaison between the two great Allies on the exchange of nuclear information. While serving with the Coldstream Guards in the First World War, Hambro won the Military Cross in France before he was 21; afterwards he was a director of the Bank of England before he was 30 and was General Manager, later Chairman, of the Great Western Railway. One of his early claims to fame was as Captain of Eton when he once took six Winchester wickets for just six runs.

11 Captain Peter Wilkinson: described by Glen as 'one of the great professionals of the Great Game'. He was a regular soldier who, after the war joined the Diplomatic Service and carved out a distinguished career. His father, Captain Osborn Cecil Wilkinson, was killed in action in 1915, the year after Peter was born. Educated at Rugby and Corpus Christi College, Cambridge, Peter Allix Wilkinson was commissioned into the Second Battalion of the Royal Fusiliers in 1935 and saw action in Poland (where

he was mentioned in dispatches), the Mediterranean, Italy, the Balkans and Central Europe. He commanded No. 6 Special Force of the SOE 1943–45 during which time, in 1944, he won the DSO and was awarded the OBE. In 1947 he joined the Foreign Office and was appointed First Secretary at the British Legation in Vienna. Subsequently he was appointed First Secretary at British Embassy, Washington, 1952; Secretary-General of Heads of Government Meeting in Geneva, 1955; Counsellor at HM Embassy, Bonn, 1955; Counsellor, Foreign Office, 1960–63; Under-Secretary at Cabinet Office, 1963–64; Senior Civilian Instructor at the Imperial Defence College 1964–66; Ambassador to Vietnam 1966–67; Under-Secretary at the Foreign Office, 1967–68; Chief of Administration, HM Diplomatic Service, 1968–70; Ambassador to Vienna, 1970–71; Co-ordinator of Intelligence, Cabinet Office, 1972–73. He was knighted in 1970 and other honours included: Cross of Valour (Poland) 1940; Order of White Lion (IV Class) (Czechoslovakia) 1945; Order of Jugoslav Banner (Hon.) 1984.

12 Public Record Office, Kew, Book HS4, File 31, Item 21a marked Secret, L2/M/P/3; hereafter to be known as PRO, followed by book and file reference.

13 In 1939, Harold Emery, on behalf of Section D, chose Julius Hanau to be head of their operations in Belgrade. It proved a shrewd choice. South African by birth, Hanau knew the country from the Salonica operations in the First World War. He then built a profitable business in Belgrade, including that of being agent for Vickers and obtaining in an imaginative manner contracts for them for two destroyers for the Yugoslav Navy. Writes Glen: 'He was thoroughly streetwise, an entertaining and amusing host with a vivid imagination and humour. We all owe a great deal to Julius Hanau.'

14 Hubert Miles Gladwyn Jebb, later Sir Gladwyn, 1st Baron Gladwyn: Private Secretary to the Permanent Undersecretary of State for Foreign Affairs 1937–40; Chief Executive Officer, Special Operations Executive 1940–42; Head of Reconstruction Department 1942; Counsellor at the Foreign Office 1943–46; Acting General-Secretary of the United Nations 1946; Assistant Undersecretary and United Nations Adviser 1946–47; United Kingdom representative at the United Nations 1950–54; Ambassador to France 1954–60.

15 Robert Anthony Eden, later Sir Anthony, 1st Earl of Avon (1897–1977): Conservative MP for Warwick and Leamington 1923–57; Parliamentary Private Secretary to Foreign Secretary (Sir Austen Chamberlain) 1926–29; Undersecretary of State for Foreign Affairs 1931–33; Lord Privy Seal 1933–35; Foreign Secretary 1935–38; Dominions Secretary 1939–40; Secretary of State for War 1940; Foreign Secretary 1940–45; Leader of the House of Commons 1942–45; Deputy Leader of the Opposition 1945–51; Foreign Secretary 1951–55; Prime Minister and Leader of the Conservative Party 1955–57.

16 Leo Marks was the brilliant young codemaker and breaker with the SOE and wrote of his experiences in his riveting and entertaining book,

Between Silk and Cyanide. His father was founder and owner of the famous bookshop at 84 Charing Cross Road, which was the subject of American writer Helen Hanff's book of the same name. Leo Marks himself earned legendary status as cryptographer and as a scriptwriter. His most famous work, *Peeping Tom*, became a cult classic of the cinema in the 1960s but he is also remembered for the famous poem '*The Life That I Have Is All That I Have, And The Life That I Have Is Yours*' which he gave to the agent Violette Szabo to use as her poem code when she was dropped by the SOE into occupied France.

17 Brigadier F.W. Nicholls, OBE: Director of Signals at the SOE.

6 YUGOSLAVIA, 1940: THAT BRAVE, UNLUCKY LAND

1 Julian Amery: son of politician Leo. In early 1940 took time out from Balliol to play whatever part he could in the war effort and was in Belgrade as Assistant Press Attaché at the British Legation. He was forced to leave the Balkans in October 1940 for 'stirring up trouble in Belgrade' but later returned to subversive work in Albania. From 1943–44 he acted as the SOE's Liaison Officer to the Albanian Resistance Movement. After the war he followed his father into politics. He was Conservative MP 1950–66 and 1969–92; Junior Minister 1957–60; Secretary of State for Air 1960–62; Minister of Aviation 1962–64; Public Building and Works 1970; Housing and Construction 1970–72; Minister of State at the Foreign and Commonwealth office 1972–74.

2 Colonel S.W. 'Bill' Bailey: another old Section D hand, a gifted linguist and a saboteur with aplomb, moving explosives around the country with calm assurance. In 1942 he was dropped back into occupied Yugoslavia as a British Liaison Officer with Mihailovic and his Cetniks.

3 In 1917 Commander Edward Ratcliffe Garth Russell Evans commanded HMS *Broke* which, together with HMS *Swift*, engaged and defeated six German destroyers, an action for which he was specially promoted to Captain for services in action and awarded the DSO. He was created First Baron Mountevans of Chelsea in 1945. In 1909, at the age of 28, Lieutenant Evans had joined Captain Scott's British Antarctic Expedition as second in command and was specially promoted for Antarctic service to Commander in 1912. He returned in command of the expedition after the death of Captain Scott in 1913.

4 PRO, MT71/2.

5 The Hon. Maurice Richard Bridgeman, later, the Hon. Sir Maurice Bridgeman: joined the Anglo Persian Oil Company in 1926 and was already attached to the Ministry of Economic Warfare as Petroleum Adviser when he was asked to help set up, and be chairman of, the Goeland Company. In 1942 he was temporarily loaned to the government of India as Petroleum Adviser and was Principal Assistant Secretary to the Petroleum Division of the Ministry of Fuel and power 1944–46; he was a Member of the Advisory Council on Middle East Trade 1958–63 and President of the

Middle East Association 1965–76. He was Chairman of British Petroleum 1960–69 and a member of the Industrial Reorganisation Corporation 1969–71.

6 Dennis Wright, later Sir Dennis: had a distinguished diplomatic career after the war and was at one time British Ambassador to Iran. Later he was a Director of Shell.

7 G.B. Marshall, who was always known as GB: later became chairman of Clarkson Holidays, when his paths again crossed with Glen who was for some time Chairman of the holding company.

8 Mining engineer and metallurgist Bill Hudson: introduced to covert warfare by Bill Bailey and became one of the most active and successful agents in Yugoslavia, being responsible for the demolition of at least one large ship in Split Harbour. He had worked in Yugoslavia since 1937 and in that time gained a working knowledge of the country, its politics and Serbo-Croat. In September 1941, just five months after the German invasion of Yugoslavia, Hudson was the first Liaison Officer to return to the country when he was landed from a submarine to link up with Mihailovic. Hudson had to survive one of the worst winters in Yugoslav history and did so thanks to his magnificent physique and his fitness as a former amateur boxer. As Glen observed, the emotional scars of that winter remained with him for the rest of his life.

9 John Bennett: a former Section D hand in Belgrade and brought back by the SOE under the codename D/H 20. Before the war he had stood as a Parliamentary Labour candidate against Neville Chamberlain, the Prime Minister at the outbreak of war.

10 Dr Milan Stoyadinovic, Yugoslav Prime Minister and Minister of Foreign Affairs 1935–38: President of the Yugoslav Radical Union 1935–39; founded the Serb Radical Party 1940; Interned 1940–41; handed over to the British authorities in March 1941 and interned at Mauritius. In his diary entry for 17 January 1939, Count Ciano records: 'There is no doubt about Stoyadinovich's solidarity with the Axis.' Stoyadinovic fell from grace with Prince Paul in February 1939 although Count Ciano made several references in his diary to a hope that he would one day be returned to power. In later conversation with the Prince Regent, Count Ciano said part of Stoyadinivoc's fall was due to his shady business dealings and that he had managed to accumulate great sums of money in foreign bank accounts.

11 Count Galeazzo Ciano (1903–44), Italian Foreign Minister 1936–43: Ciano, who took part in the Fascist March on Rome in 1922, held various diplomatic posts during the 1920s and virtually guaranteed his future career when he married dictator Benito Mussolini's daughter Edda in 1930. He became Italy's Foreign Minister in 1936 and while he advocated forging strong links with Fascist Germany, signing the Berlin-Rome Axis pact on Italy's behalf in October 1936, he changed his attitude after Germany initiated hostilities against Poland in 1939 – without consultation with Italy and in breach of the Axis agreement – and tried to persuade Mussolini to break off links with Hitler. However, Germany's early success in 1940 swayed Italy's leadership and Italy entered the war as Germany's ally in June 1940.

When Germany's offensive against Russia was halted and after America joined the war in December 1941, Ciano was convinced Italy needed to sue for a separate peace and this put him in conflict with his father-in-law. Ciano resigned in February 1943 and was exiled to the Vatican as Mussolini's ambassador. But he remained a member of the Fascist Grand Council and took part in the decision to depose Mussolini in mid-1943 and call on Marshal Badoglio to form a new government. But when Mussolini was restored to power, Ciano was imprisoned and then executed on the orders of his father-in-law.

12 *Ciano's Diary 1939–1943*, edited by and with an introduction by Malcolm Muggeridge (William Heinemann Ltd., 1947).

13 G.F. (George) Taylor (1902–79): an Australian, he was rated an outstanding member of Section D; he was later Chief of Staff at the Special Operations Executive 1940–42, first to Sir Frank Nelson and then to Sir Charles Hambro. In January 1941 he was sent to take over operations in Belgrade to prepare the way for a coup against the country's rulers; in 1943 he was appointed Special Emissary to the SOE Overseas Missions. Appointed CBE in 1944. Post-war, he had a distinguished career in international banking. He was an exceptional and widely-respected scholar.

14 General Draza Mihailovic (1893–1946): Yugoslav soldier who, with some brother officers, founded the Serbian Cetnik resistance group after the German invasion in April 1941. An ardent Royalist and Serbian nationalist, his post-war aims were different from the Partisans led by Moscow-trained Marshal Tito, and by November 1941 the two groups were in open conflict. Mihailovic received aid from Britain and the support of King Peter II's Government-in-exile in London, even after Mihailovic, anxious to avoid the enormous civilian and military casualties of the First World War, began cooperating with the Italian occupying forces against the mutual Communist foe. It was not until mid-1943 that Britain knew fully about the collaborative dealings of the Cetniks. Mihailovic was warned in November 1943 to take action against Axis forces and by May 1944 all British Missions in Cetnik territory had been recalled. Nevertheless, Cetnik groups continued to aid and support British and American aircrews shot down over their territory during various bombing campaigns. When Tito signed an agreement with King Peter's Prime Minister Subasic in June 1944, Milhailovic was removed from his post as War Minister in the exiled government and by September he had been forced to quit his HQ in Ravna Gora. After the capitulation of the Axis forces, Mihailovic remained hidden in the mountains until his capture on 13 March 1946. He was then tried as a collaborator and executed in July that year.

15 Tripartite Pact: On 27 September 1940, Germany, Japan and Italy signed an agreement by which the signatories undertook to recognise each other's expansionist claims in Europe and Asia and to come to each other's aid if attacked by a power not already involved in the war in Europe and the Pacific. This was generally accepted as an anti-American position. The contemporaneous political status of the USSR was explicitly confirmed by the Pact, although German foreign ministries subsequently persuaded

Hungary, Romania and Slovakia to join in 1940, to be followed by Bulgaria and Yugoslavia in 1941. A few days later, on 27 March, Yugoslavia rejected the Pact, resulting in the attack upon them on 6 April 1941. Following the breakup of Yugoslavia, Croatia, by then an Italian protectorate, joined the Axis.

7 BELGRADE, WINTER 1940/41

1 *One Man's War*, by Michael Mason, 1966.
2 Ibid.
3 Blackley was a former Tiffy (Engine Room Artificer) in a First World War destroyer who settled in Romania as a skilled engineer. Until Mason recruited him as his assistant, Blackley, who originated from Dunoon on the Clyde, had been one of Julius Hanau's part-time saboteurs.
4 *One Man's War*.
5 Mason doesn't mention the officer's name anywhere but he could well be the Sapper Major Davidson-Houston referred to in Maurice Pearton's paper and mentioned in Chapter 3.
6 Mason really hated Constanta. In one passage of *One Man's War* he writes: 'We went down to Constanta on the Black Sea. This is the place where they have a special venereal disease of their own. In the rest of the world there are four; Constanta has five.'
7 *One Man's War*.
8 Ibid.
9 Little Audrey was the nickname Mason gave to the local chief of the Gestapo, a man he claims to have constantly goaded, prompting Little Audrey to organise several attempts on Mason's life.
10 *One Man's War*.
11 Ibid.

8 BELGRADE MAKES ITS STAND: 27 MARCH 1941

1 Ian Pirie: also an old Section D hand, whose knowledge of and presence in Greece was invaluable not only to the SOE but to the Allies generally. He arrived in Greece in the guise of a specialist on air raid precautions for the British Community but was, in fact, No. 2 in the subversive cell which included various British Lloyd's agents and engineers.
2 Major General Robert (Bob) Laycock (1907–68): a colourful and distinguished Commando leader and British Chief of Combined Operations for the D-Day Invasion in June 1944. He first raised a Commando unit in 1940 and early in 1941 (the time being referred to here) he took three Commando units, including his own, to the Middle East for the main purpose of capturing Rhodes. This force, known as Layforce, was joined and strengthened by a locally-raised Middle East Commando force. While some elements of Layforce operated on the coast of Libya and took part in the

invasion of Syria in June 1941, Laycock took half his men to Crete after the German airborne attack there in May 1941 and they covered the British withdrawal to the south coast. But much of his force was decimated and was then disbanded. He raised a new force at Churchill's insistence for a raid on Rommel's suspected HQ in November 1941 but only Laycock and one other managed to return to safety. He later led another commando brigade for the invasion of Sicily in 1943 and on his return to Britain succeeded Mountbatten as Chief of Combined Operations. He remained in this post until 1947 and later became Governor of Malta.

3 Colonel 'Wild Bill' Donovan (1883–1959): a First World War veteran, New York lawyer Colonel William J. Donovan was President Roosevelt's choice to head the American 'black propaganda' outfit, the Office of the Co-ordinator of Information (COI) in July 1941, just a few months after the time referred to here by Sandy Glen. A year later in July 1942, the COI was succeeded by the Office of Strategic Services (OSS) and was organised more on the lines of the SOE, whose working operations had been closely studied by Donovan, who was again chosen to head the new structure. Donovan's wholehearted support of the SOE was decisive later in 1943 when another onslaught was launched by the Whitehall critics. Without his support, the SOE's preparations in France in support of the Normandy landings might never have taken place, in particular the Jedburgh Units, whose work with the French resistance was so productive. Nor, for that matter, would the Home Army in Norway, without the SOE's support, have been necessarily in position to make possible the peaceful surrender of the powerful Wehrmacht forces.

4 Tom Mapplebeck: as Assistant Air Attaché in Belgrade, played a crucial role in the 1941 *coup*, was a remarkable character right up until his death in 1990 at the age of 95. A fluent speaker of Serbo-Croat, he had refused to join MI(R) in Belgrade because he felt he would have to spy on old friends but nevertheless agreed to pass on any valuable information to the intelligence agencies. It helped, too, that his brother-in-law was Chief of Police in Zagreb, but he was murdered during the German invasion. He served in both world wars. When war broke out in 1914, Mapplebeck, the son of a Liverpool dentist, joined the 4th Battalion of the King's Liverpool Regiment and was wounded in the head at the second Battle of Ypres. On his recovery, he joined the Royal Flying Corps, with whom his brother had won one of the early DSOs of the war, but Tom was shot down over the Somme in November 1916 and spent the next two years as a prisoner of war in Germany. He first went to Yugoslavia as part of a British economic mission soon after the war and settled down as a commercial agent. After his links with the Yugoslavs ended in 1942, Mapplebeck rejoined the RAF, serving in Luxor, Baghdad, Jerusalem and Turkey. By the end of the war he was a Group Captain in charge of welfare for the whole Middle East. He stayed on in Cairo as an agent specialising in defence equipment but had his property confiscated during the Suez crisis and he settled in Beirut for the next 20 years. By the time he returned to Egypt in 1975, he was a legendary figure known for his scrupulous honesty, five marriages and a

certain English eccentricity. He was awarded the OBE in 1985, and on his return to Britain at the age of 92, continued to carry on business from his old people's home in London, in which he installed office equipment with telex and typewriter.

9 HITLER'S 'OPERATION PUNISHMENT' AND THE YUGOSLAV COLLAPSE, APRIL 1941

1 Hugh Seton-Watson: a Section D hand before the formation of the SOE. He served with them in Romania and Yugoslavia. After making his escape with Glen, he later returned to the Middle East and from November 1942 to June 1944 he was a member of the SOE's Yugoslav Country Section in Cairo. The name Seton-Watson was well-known throughout the Balkans because his father did so much to ensure Czechoslovakian independence after the First World War. After the Second World War, he became Professor of Russian History at London University's School of Slavonic and East European Studies.

10 INTERMISSION ELSEWHERE, BUT IN 1944 BACK TO THE DANUBE

1 Anthony Quayle, better known as Sir Anthony Quayle: the famous film star and theatre actor-producer, who also had a varied and distinguished war career, including a spell with the SOE.
2 Brigadier Fitzroy H.R. Maclean's mission to the Partisans from 1943–45 was at the direct request of Prime Minister Winston Churchill and was probably the most influential of all British military missions to Yugoslavia. He had a great rapport with Marshal Tito, who trusted him implicitly, and he won the respect and trust of all major Partisan figures. Djilas wrote of him: 'Above all, Brigadier Maclean impressed both the leadership and Partisans generally; a member of Parliament with his own "partisan" exploits in Africa, reserved but accommodating and with a political gift for words. We found it strange that, on ceremonial occasions, he wore the Scottish kilt. Yet he was not eccentric or amusing. Rather, he was extraordinarily brave. I myself was amazed, during an air raid on Drvar in February 1944, at the sight of his tall, bony frame moving about on the roads as if nothing was happening.' However, he demolished enemies at the Cairo HQ of the SOE with a highly critical report on its shortcomings. Although he was not the first to point these out to the various authorities, his position as a *confidant* of the Prime Minister lent his opinions considerable weight.
3 Commander Vladimir Wolfson: born in Odessa, as was the highly-regarded SIS (Secret Intelligence Service) operative Biffy Dunderdale, and both served as midshipmen in the Black Sea Fleet in 1917. Wolfson later became one of the real professionals in Naval Intelligence Division and in 1939 was appointed Assistant Naval Attaché in Turkey, with a wide remit.

190

After the war, he joined the British Overseas Airways Corporation and settled in Bishop's Stortford, Hertfordshire. In January 1954, Captain Wolfson was one of 35 passengers and crew who lost their lives when the BOAC Comet G-ALYP crashed into the Mediterranean off the island of Elba. Captain Wolfson had joined the Comet at Bangkok and the aircraft was on the last leg of its flight, from Rome to London, when it crashed. Captain Wolfson's son Mark was Conservative MP for Tonbridge until he lost his seat in the Labour landslide of 1997.

4 The Villa Emma in Naples was named after Lady Emma Hamilton and it was here that Admiral Horatio Nelson used to visit and relax with her.

5 This comment by Admiral Sir John Cunningham referred to Coastal Command's Arctic Operations in 1942. These involved flights of 24 hours or even longer by specially equipped Catalinas of 210 Squadron. Their purpose was to record regularly the limits of the sea ice, that year far to the south and, accordingly, restricting the distance of convoys from the Luftwaffe and U-boat attacks from north Norway. In addition, these sorties helped support and supply the Norwegian garrison holding the exposed and pivotal island of Spitsbergen. The operations were largely in German air space and for much of the time flying a mere 50 or 100 feet above the sea in W/T silence, subject not only to enemy attack but severe winds and heavy icing. Flight-Lieutenant Tim Healy carried out most of the sorties, being awarded an immediate DSO; his navigator, Flight-Lieutenant Schofield the DFC; and Glen, who was an observer on several of the flights as well as being one of the planners of the operation, his first DSC. These operations became a treasured part of Coastal Command's history. Their Air Officer C-in-C at that time was Air Chief Marshal Philippe Joubert de la Ferte and his Senior Air Staff Officer was Air Vice Marshal George Baker. Glen was privileged to become a friend of both, with future consequences in 1944 when Baker became SASO to Air Marshal Sir John Slessor in the new Mediterranean Allied Strategic Air Force.

6 Captain Roger Lewis: see Note 3, Chapter 16.

7 Public Record Office, Kew, Book HS5, File 196.

8 Jedburgh Missions were joint Anglo-French-American teams of not more than six, although they mostly comprised three-man groups dropped into France to aid resistance forces shortly before or in conjunction with the D-Day invasion of Normandy. They were there to provide paramilitary skills and bolster morale. They were to be dropped in uniform, again partly for morale and propaganda purposes but also in the hope that if they were captured by German combatant troops, as opposed to the Gestapo and Secret Police, they would be protected by the terms of the Geneva Convention.

9 Massingham was an SOE forward base for the Mediterranean theatre and among the most impressive of their achievements was the liberation of Corsica. After that they provided an invaluable service as a coordinating centre for operations during Operation Husky, the invasion of Sicily and later into Italy and France.

10 PRO, HS5/195.

11 JIC: The Joint Intelligence Committee.

12 Major Dolbey had distinguished himself in 1943 with a lone parachute drop into Rhodes to try and contact the Italian command there; he was unable to establish such contact but still managed to bring out some valuable intelligence.
13 PRO HS5/198.

11 CHINTZ AND SCRAMBLED EGGS

1 Partisans: the term Partisans, invariably with a capital P, is most closely associated with the small forces led by Marshal Tito against the Axis forces in Yugoslavia in the Second World War. In fact, the term was first used to describe Russian armed resistance groups engaged in espionage, sabotage and terrorism against Napoleonic supply lines in the 1812 campaign. Although dubbed by Tito the National Army of Liberation, the Partisans comprised compact, independent and self-sufficient groups. They originally numbered around 12,000 men and women and cleverly exploited their local knowledge of mountainous regions to thwart larger German forces. The Partisans had the distinction of resisting no fewer than seven major offensives by occupying armies as well as launching their own campaigns against them. They were forced back from their base at Uzice into the mountainous area of eastern Bosnia toward the end of 1941 but they slowly fought their way north towards the Croatian border and had the satisfaction of taking Bihac a year later. Early in 1943, the Partisans faced a combined attack by German and satellite forces and had to retreat across the Neretva River near Mostar by the end of May. They had time to regroup, especially after the Italian surrender in September 1943, which was followed by a lull in the fighting. The Partisans found themselves on the receiving end again when a renewed German onslaught, codenamed Operation Thunderbolt drove them back into the Bosnian hills. By then their fortunes were beginning to turn. Large numbers of volunteers added to their numbers and increased support from Britain in the shape of arms and supplies, and military missions put them in a position to take on Axis forces for control of Dalmatia. By the time Marshal Tolbukhin's 3rd Ukrainian Army reached the Yugoslav border near Turnu Severin early in September 1944, Partisan units were already forcing German troops into retreat in the central regions. It was a deservedly proud moment for Marshal Tito and his Partisans when, in November 1944, with Soviet forces, they liberated Belgrade.
2 Colonel F.W.D. (Bill) Deakin played a most decisive part in British-Yugoslav affairs from his leadership of the first British military Mission to the Partisan Supreme Staff HQ in Crno Jezero, to which he was parachuted on 28 May 1943, to the present day. His pre-war academic career at Wadham, Oxford, had led to a close relationship with Churchill in researching his book on Marlborough. Deakin joined SOE soon after its formation and was in the Cairo Office in 1942/1943 when doubts were growing as to the effectiveness of Mihailovic and the Cetniks, with equal concern given to

the little that was known of the Partisans. The opportunity during Churchill's visit to Cairo for these views to be discussed led to the decision that contact with Tito must be established ... a task first given, fortuitously, to Deakin, who was to perform it with outstanding skill, providing the groundwork so well exploited by him and Fitzroy Maclean in the months ahead. To Tito and his colleagues, this signalled the true beginning of Allied recognition, a record told brilliantly by Deakin in *The Embattled Mountain* (Oxford University Press 1971.) These events were only the beginning of Deakin's career. Appointed First Secretary, British Embassy, Belgrade, he widened his many friendships throughout Yugoslavia, which were to persist for many years. On his return to London, he played a major part in the founding of St Antony's College in Oxford, of which he was Warden from 1960 to 1968. This coincided with his long Chairmanship of the British Committee of The International Committee for the History of World War Two which, together with the Imperial War Museum, facilitated and stimulated research into wartime history of the Balkan lands. Now resident in France, Deakin retains the total trust and, indeed, affection of those who took part in those hard years.

3 Marshal Tito (1892–1980), real name Josep Broz: Tito was leader of the Yugoslav Communist Party and led the Partisans after the German attack on Russia in 1941. Tito had been a prisoner of war in Russia between 1915 and 1917 but then served with the Red Army until 1920. Imprisoned for his political views between 1928 and 1933, he then spent a year in Paris recruiting for the International Brigades in Republican Spain. He became leader of the then illegal Yugoslav Communist Party in 1937. Tito's early successes with the Partisans were compromised by complex and bloody internal conflict. After talks among the resistance organisations broke down in 1941, Tito was also fighting a violent civil war against the Cetniks and the Fascist Ustachi in Croatia. This rivalry between Partisans and Cetniks was well exploited by the Axis forces, who forced Tito's men back into the mountains. Although poorly equipped and funded, Tito held the Partisans together through determined political commitment and skilful military leadership. In November 1942, Tito formed the Anti-Fascist Council of National Assembly (AVNOJ) at Bihac on the Croatian border and in 1943 AVNOJ established a National Liberation Committee to act as a cabinet administration. From the middle of 1943, when it began to dawn on the authorities in London that Tito's Partisans were bearing the brunt of resistance fighting against the Axis, Britain began to supply Tito with arms, funds and considerable medical aid. Allied aid for the Partisans was formalised at the Teheran Conference in December 1943. Throughout 1944, Tito strengthened his military and political status and met with Stalin for the first time in August that year, while remaining nominally committed to working with the London-based government-in-exile under King Peter II. Pressure for unity in Yugoslavia and from the British forced the King to recognise AVNOJ in June and in November. This was a power-sharing agreement, heavily supported by Moscow, in which only 5 out of 28 cabinet posts were not held by Tito supporters. It effectively gave Tito control of

the new government. Post-war elections, which were boycotted by most of the smaller political groups, officially recognised the *de facto* control which Tito's Communist-dominated provisional government had already secured.

4 Cetniks: origins of the Cetnik Serbian guerilla units date back to action against the Turks. They then opposed German occupying forces during the First World War, incurring heavy losses. After the invasion of Yugoslavia by the Germans in April 1941, the Cetniks were activated under the leadership of General Draza Mihailovic, who recruited largely from the defeated Yugoslav army. The Cetniks were Serbian Nationalists, Royalists and anti-Communists; to them, Tito's Partisans represented as great a threat to their concept of a new Greater Serbia as the Germans. They continued to be supported by Britain – and supplied with equipment and arms via the SOE, until as late as May 1944 when all British missions to Cetnik-held territory were recalled. Nevertheless, many American and RAF pilots and aircrew shot down over Yugoslavia who fell into Cetnik-held territory reached safety thanks to Cetnik assistance. In the final phases of the war, the Cetniks were overrun and treated brutally by Soviet and Partisan forces and their leaders, including Draza Mihailovic, were executed.

5 Captain Jasper Rootham: a Special Operations Executive Liaison Officer who was parachuted into Yugoslavia with a New Zealander, Lieutenant E. 'Mickey' Hargreaves, as a British mission in May 1943 to join a previous British mission led by Major Erik Greenwood, and link up with Colonel Draza Mihailovic's Cetnik band. Captain Rootham wrote of his experiences in *Miss-Fire* (Chatto & Windus, 1946). He later became a Director of the Bank of England.

6 Major Erik Greenwood led a British mission into Yugoslavia on 18 April 1943, landing in the Homolje area in north-eastern Serbia. Greenwood, later joined by Captain Jasper Rootham, had a brief to attack enemy shipping on the Danube and to assess the possibilities of sabotaging the largest copper mine in Europe at Bor. Greenwood led an independent operation which temporarily disrupted river traffic in October 1943 but with the Bor mines heavily guarded, largely by White Russian troops under German command, local Cetnik commanders felt unable to support plans to attack them.

12 TITO'S PARTISANS

1 Dimitrije Ljotic and Milan Nedic: Ljotic was a Serbian Fascist who ran the Serbian Volunteer Corp, which fought both the Partisans and the Cetniks. He died in a car accident while fleeing Yugoslavia in 1945. Milan Nedic was a General in the pre-war Royal Army and was Minister of War. In 1941, he became Prime Minister of a puppet government in Serbia. He was captured by the Partisans at the end of the war and is said to have committed suicide during an investigation into his activities. Ljotic and Nedic were among the Germans' most enthusiastic and brutal collaborators. According to Milovan Djilas' fascinating book of the Partisans, *Wartime* (Secker & Warburg, 1977): 'so did the shooting of all adult males in

194

Kragujevec and Kraljevo, which the Germans carried out with the help of Nedic's people and Ljotic's fascist movement. It was believed at the time that some 5,000 were executed in Kragujevac and 1,700 in Kraljevo. These figures grew with time – by the thousands in both places – though the actual figures have never been confirmed.'

2 The Balkan Air Force formed the Casualty Air Evacuation Unit in May 1944 after information was received on 30 April 1944 that Marshal Tito had a total of around 10,000 Partisan casualties in need of urgent treatment and for whom no hospital facilities existed. A report dated 18 June 1945 and signed by Air Marshal Sir Harold Whittingham, KCB, KBE, KHP, Director General of Medical Services, says: 'The mobility of the guerrilla troops was being impeded by these casualties. The alternative to transporting them with his field forces was to leave them behind to the mercy of the Germans. This latter commodity, unlike the "gentle dew from heaven", dropped with intent to kill' (PRO, Kew, AIR49, File 399). Sir Harold recalled that a detachment of 31 Mobile Field Hospital, with experience of air evacuation, was sited at the airfield in Bari in short notice and they showed a 'more than average amount of keenness for the work'. The first evacuation, carried out on 8 May 1944, comprised 52 Yugoslav casualties brought out at night on an improvised airstrip. 'From this small beginning', wrote Sir Harold in April 1945, 'the CAEU was evolved and to date the number of casualties with which it has dealt has been 50,000 (approximately). This figure includes British casualties from Northern Italy as well as Yugoslavs.' The Casualty Air Evacuation Unit was the only one of its kind in the Mediterranean theatre and on 2 June 1945 Air Vice Marshal T.J. Kelly, the Principal Medical Officer, reported: 'It will be observed from the analysis of patients evacuated that they are of 26 nationalities, enough to make a satisfactory League of Nations, but it was necessary from time to time to keep some apart from others, lest their enthusiasm for the Allied cause, or their own, should lead to further casualties. This small unit of one officer (Flight-Lieutenant F.S. Shepherd) and some 12 NCOs and airmen, supplemented by Yugoslav or other labour, has done remarkably fine work in a very quiet and efficient manner' (ibid).

3 Milovan Djilas: served with Tito's Partisans and led his own force in his native Montenegro. He was involved in fighting the Germans from the time of the People's Uprising in May 1941. After the war he wrote many books including the excellent *Wartime* in which he described the struggle against the Axis powers through personal insight and involvement.

4 Marshal Fyodor Tolbukhin (1894–1949): Soviet commander of the 57th Army which figured prominently in the encirclement of the German Sixth Army inside Stalingrad in early 1943. In 1944 Tolbukhin was appointed to command the 4th Ukrainian Front for the drive to recapture the Crimea. Promoted to Marshal, he subsequently directed operations in the Ukraine, Romania, Austria and Hungary. In 1945–46 Tolbukhin was Supreme Commander of Soviet forces in Bulgaria and Romania.

5 NKVD: the following information is taken from *The Macmillan Dictionary of the Second World War* (1995). 'Narodnyi Kommissariat Vnutrennykh

Del. – Soviet Secret Police and counter-intelligence organisation created from OGPU (Unified State Political Administration) in July 1934 under Hendrik Yagoda, its multifarious functions before the war included control of the militia (regular police), concentration camps and maintenance of a huge intelligence network and subversive operations abroad. With the outbreak of war, NKVD's activities expanded (now under the leadership of Lavrenti Beria) to include counter-intelligence operations, conducting political surveillance of military units and searching for deserters and "draft dodgers". The NKVD also conducted massive purges of foreign populations considered hostile to the Soviet state. In eastern Poland, Bessarabia and the Baltic states (Estonia, Latvia and Lithuania) hundreds of thousands of people were executed or deported to Siberia. After the German invasion had begun in 1941, NKVD squads carried out mass executions of political prisoners and were also allocated to fighting units to prevent unauthorised desertions on the Front and to try deserters at special NKVD tribunals. As the tide on the Eastern Front turned against the invaders, many of the NKVD's most brutal operations were conducted against war criminals and collaborators.'

6 The Dniester and Dnieper river crossings were hard fought as the retreating Germans held up the advancing Red Army and inflicted many casualties.

13 WEST MEETS EAST: SEPTEMBER, 1944

1 Admiral Sergei G. Gorshkov (1910–88) was commander of the Russian naval formations in the Black Sea Squadron from 1931 to 1944 and he also commanded the Azov (an inland sea bordered by Crimea in the west and the Caucasus in east) Military Flotilla, which took part in the defence of the Crimea and the Caucasus in the Battle of Stalingrad. In 1956, Stalin's successor, Nikita Khrushchev, appointed Gorshkov C-in-C of the Red Navy and he later radically reshaped Soviet naval strategy, creating the great post-war Soviet fleet.

14 THE RED ARMY

1 *Stalingrad*, by Anthony Beevor (Penguin Books, 1999).
2 General Oxley was head of the British element of the Allied Control Commission on the Danube which visited Romania in September 1944.
3 W.E. Houston-Boswall, CMG, MC, one-time Political Advisor to the SOE Council.

15 THE DOLPHIN MISSION

1 PRO, Kew, Book HS5, File 195. Navratil and his family had, in fact,

settled in the Hakin district of Milford Haven in Pembrokeshire, south-west Wales and put down roots there that survived for some time after the war. They lived with another East European family there, the Poppers, who were to become well-known musically. In later years, one of Navratil's daughters, Ludmilla, was a leading member of the world-famous Manchester-based Halle Orchestra.

2 Ibid.

3 PRO, HS5/196. The Danube Sub-Committee was formed to monitor progress of all operations concerning the Danube and was represented by all the major participants: the Balkan Air Force (205 Group), the 15th United States Army Air Force, British Military Missions to JANL (the SOE code for the Yugoslavian Liberation Army or Partisans), Force 133 (the SOE Mission for Greece and Bulgaria), Force 399 (the SOE Mission for Yugoslavia), FOLEM (Flag Officer Levant and Eastern Mediterranean), FOTALI (Flag Officer Taranto, Adriatic and Liaison Italy), and the C-in-C Mediterranean, Admiral Sir John Cunningham.

4 PRO, HS5/198.

5 Here, and in his general conclusions about the Dolphin Mission, Captain Franks refers to lack of information about the effects of mining on the river but, as we have already heard, Glen was often fed information about the disruption as he travelled with the Partisans and a welter of eye-witness reports and aerial reconnaissance photographs about the damage caused reached MAAF HQ and the C-in-C Mediterranean. So, we may draw the conclusion that, as the first two objectives of Dolphin were obsolete almost before they left Bari, Captain Franks was seeking to justify Dolphin being sent at all. As it turned out, they did elicit an enormous amount of river intelligence and in this Dolphin certainly achieved their third objective.

6 PRO, HS5/198.

7 PRO, HS5/197.

8 PRO, HS5/198.

9 Paragraph (a) referred to the original sabotage and counter-scorch aims of Dolphin.

10 PRO, HS5/198.

11 PRO, HS5/200.

16 ALLIED AIR AND NAVAL BUILD-UP

1 See Note 5, Chapter 1.

2 The Official history of HMS *Vernon* was compiled by a dedicated group of naval officers under the inspired direction of Rear Admiral Nico Poland. Of those who contributed to this remarkable tome, involving every kind of problem, two contributions stand out: those of Captain White, RN, and Rear Admiral Sir Morgan Morgan-Giles, DSO, GM.

3 Captain Roger Lewis, DSO, was a key member of the small group given, by Winston Churchill himself, the task of defusing the mines laid by the Germans to cause havoc on the English east coast and the Thames

estuary almost immediately after war was declared. This group was comprised initially mostly of young RNVR officers, many of them barristers, such as Lieutenant Ashe Lincoln, QC, who later wrote of his experiences in an absorbing book, *Secret Naval Investigator*. The mine defusers worked in pairs linked over some 200 yards by telephone so each detailed move was recorded in case the next move proved fatal. Often working upside down in cold, dark water, their patience and cool nerve was legendary. Roger Lewis was one of the most expert of that team and Glen deems it an especial privilege that long after the war he met him again in old age in the Cotswolds: 'this quiet, brave rather lonely man to whom we owe so much'.

17 THE ATTACK ON AND DEFENCE OF PLOESTI, 1944

1 General Carl Spaatz (1891–1974): America's Chief of the Air Staff when Japan attacked Pearl Harbor in December 1941, precipitating the United States entry into the Second World War. He was an official observer in London during the Battle of Britain and returned there in June 1942 to take command of America's 8th Air Force, which flew daytime bombing missions as part of the strategic bombing offensive. From January 1943 his command was extended to, first, the 12th Air Force operating in the Desert war and then to command of the north-west African Air Forces which supported the Allied offensives in Tunisia, Sicily and Italy. He was promoted to Lieutenant-General in March 1943 and became, briefly, Deputy Commanding General, Mediterranean Allied Air Forces before returning to Britain in January 1944 to coordinate the England-based 8th Air Force and the Italy-based 15th Air Force under the aegis of the new United States Strategic Air Forces in Europe. Despite differences of opinion with Air Chief Marshal Sir Trafford Leigh-Mallory, Air C-in-C of the Allied Expeditionary Force and Air Chief Marshal Sir Arthur W. Tedder, Deputy C-in-C to the Allied Expeditionary Force over the strategic role of the Allied air forces for the D-Day invasion, he is credited with playing an important part in the success of the air offensives against German communications and installations in the second half of 1944, including stepping up the attacks on synthetic and refined oil plants. After collecting his fourth star, Spaatz was transferred to Guam to command the United States Strategic Air Forces Pacific (8th and 29th Air Forces) and he directed the final stages of the bombing offensive against Japan that culminated in the atomic missions to Hiroshima and Nagasaki.

18 ALLIED MINING OF THE DANUBE

1 *Sperrbrecher*: literal translation is 'barrage-breaker'.
2 Taken from *From Darkness to Light* by Patrick Macdonald (Images Publishing Ltd., 1994).

3 GEE was the most widely-used radio-navigational aid of the war with thousands of Allied aircraft and Royal Navy vessels equipped with it. Not the least of its advantages for Allied aircrews was the fact that, as no transmission was required from the user, radio silence could be maintained at all times – an important asset when travelling over enemy territory. Because of this, it could not be swamped by the number of simultaneous users. This was to be an enormous advantage on D-Day, when it was employed on a huge scale. The following is taken from *Radar: A Wartime Miracle* by Colin Latham and Anne Stobbs (Sutton Publishing Ltd., 1996): 'Credit for the concept is due to R.J. Dippy, of Bawdsey Research Station. Although the idea was considered shortly before the war, it was not followed up then due to the pressure of essential early-warning radar work. However, when it became painfully clear that Bomber Command desperately needed a significant improvement over its traditional methods of astral navigation and dead-reckoning, it was developed as a high-priority project. Service trials began in the early part of 1941 and it was used extensively on operations from the Spring of 1942 onwards, despite some eventual German jamming.'

19 AFTERMATH

1 Lieutenant-Colonel Gardyne de Chastelain, a member of Britain's pre-war colony in Romania and a highly successful and forceful businessman, became an early Head of the SOE's Istanbul section. He spent some time in early 1942 trawling Canada for refugees from Europe who could speak Balkan languages, and returned with a list of Croats, Slovenes, Slovaks, Bulgarians, Czechs and others, many of whom were later recruited either to work in London or join Balkan operations. When King Michael overthrew the government of Ion Antonescu in August 1944 it was de Chastelain whom he asked to go to Istanbul to announce Romania's switch to the Allies. He is the father of General John de Chastelain, who was appointed to head the inspection body checking IRA weapons under the Anglo-Irish Good Friday Agreement.

2 When British diplomats (and undercover agents attached to the British Legation) left Romania in February 1941, one wireless set was left behind for tenuous contact and this was for some time stored in the home of Prince Barbu Stirby who was then able to maintain some contact with his son-in-law, Colonel Eddie Boxshall, who ran the SOE's Romanian desk in London. Boxshall, an old SIS hand, was rated a first-class intelligence officer, who also represented Vickers in the Balkans before the war and was extremely well connected. He was the natural choice to run the SOE's Romanian desk. When the SOE was wound up after the war, Boxshall returned to SIS in charge of Eastern European Affairs.

3 Juliu (sometimes Iuliu) Maniu was Head of the Romanian Peasant Party, whom the SOE and other British agents tried to cultivate, as they had Yugoslavia's Serbian Peasant Party and others. Maniu, however, was known, and treated, as a necessary but difficult contact.

LIST OF OPERATIONS

DOLPHIN MISSION:

An SOE-organised operation mounted in September 1944 originally designed for intelligence gathering and counter-scorch and sabotage operations around the Danube and to disrupt river traffic by suborning Danube pilots and crews. It was part of *Operation Dancer* (see below).

HALVERSON PROJECT:

The first long-range assault on the Ploesti oil fields involving 13 B-24 Liberators flown from El Fayid in Egypt on 12 June 1942. Heroic as the venture was, its results were limited, if not minimal, and alerted the Germans to the fact that Ploesti was no longer immune from attack by air.

OPERATION BARBAROSSA:

Hitler's attack on Russia on Sunday, 22 June 1941; not the least of its consequences was that it galvanised a previously indifferent Communist Party in Yugoslavia to mount opposition to the Axis under Marshal Tito and his Partisans.

OPERATION DANCER:

A series of co-ordinated measures intended to disrupt Danube shipping and transport organisation. The above-mentioned *Dolphin Mission* was an SOE contribution to this operation.

OPERATION FRANTIC:

The first use by the American Air Force of Russian bases in the summer of 1944. This enabled aircrews of the 15th AAF to attack oil and communications targets while flying from their bases in Italy across Romania and Yugoslavia and then repeat the punishment on the return journey

OPERATION GARDENING:

The codename for the aerial mining of the Danube by 205 Group of the Royal Air Force between April and October 1944 using mines designed by experts from HMS *Vernon*. The mining areas were referred to as 'gardening beds' and the mines themselves as 'vegetables'.

OPERATION MARK TWAIN:

Propaganda campaign mounted by the Special Operations Executive in support of the scheme to subvert Danube river captains and their crew, 1944.

OPERATION OVERLORD:

The Allied D-Day invasion of Normandy on 6 June 1944.

OPERATION POINTBLANK:

The concentrated bombing campaign 'to bring about the progressive destruction and dislocation of the German military, industrial and economic system and the undermining of the German people to a point where the capacity for armed resistance is fatally weakened'. It was under this directive, which came into full operation early in 1944, that the assaults on Ploesti and the Danube were made.

OPERATION PUNISHMENT:

The German invasion of Yugoslavia on 6 April 1941 ordered by a furious Hitler after the abrupt change in policy towards Germany caused by the *coup d'état* led by General Dusan Simovic on 27 March, only two days after the Government of Prince Paul had guaranteed Axis troops passage across Yugoslavia for the invasion of Greece.

OPERATION RUBBLE:

A daring operation planned by the Admiralty, Ministry of Economic Warfare and MI(R) in Sweden – the successful cutting out in Gothenburg, by Commander Sir George Binney, DSO, RNVR, and the sailing to the UK of four fast Norwegian cargo liners loaded with precious ball bearings. This operation is used as an example of how such an operation can be mounted successfully compared with the ill-fated Danube venture involving the SS *Mardinian*.

201

OPERATION TIDAL WAVE:

The courageous but costly low-level attack by 177 B-24 Liberators of the 8th USAAF on the Ploesti oil fields on 1 August 1943.

TWILFIT MISSION:

An SOE-organised operation planned to coincide with D-Day (*Operation Overlord*) under which British naval and army officers were infiltrated into Partisan brigades in Yugoslavia to help cause maximum disruption and to gather vital intelligence.

SELECT BIBLIOGRAPHY

This list contains only some of the many publications dealing with the subjects covered in this book.

Amery, Julian: *Sons of the Eagle: A Study in Guerrilla Warfare* (Macmillan, 1948)

Andric, Ivo: *Bridge over the Drina* (Harvill, 1995)

Astley, Joan and Wilkinson, Peter: *The Life of Gubbins* (Pen and Sword)

Auty, P. & Clogg, R. (Eds): *British Policy Towards Wartime Resistance in Yugoslavia and Greece* (Macmillan, 1975)

Beevor, Anthony: *Stalingrad* (Penguin Books, 1999; first published by Viking, 1998)

Beevor, Jack: *SOE, Recollections and Reflections 1940–1945* (The Bodley Head Ltd., 1981)

Beloff, Nora: *Tito's Flawed Legacy* (Gollancz, 1985)

Bennett, Dr Ralph: *Behind the Battle* (Sinclair Stevenson, 1994)

Bennett, Dr Ralph: *Ultra and Mediterranean Strategy 1941/1944* (Hamish Hamilton, 1989)

Bergen, Jean-Francar: *Dans L'ombre de Tito: Entretiens avec Le General Vladko Velabit* (Statkine Sodifer, Geneva, 2000)

Brissaud, Andre: *Canaris* (first published in France, 1970; English translation Weidenfeld & Nicolson Ltd., 1973; translated and introduction by Ian Colvin)

Ciano's Diary 1939–1943 (the Diary of Count Galleazzo Ciano) Edited and with an Introduction by Malcolm Muggeridge (William Heinemann Ltd., 1947)

Clissold, Steven: *Yugoslavia and the USSR* (Oxford University Press, 1975)

Deakin, F.W.D.: *The Embattled Mountain* (Oxford University Press, 1971)

Dear, I.C.B. & Foot, M.R.D. (gen. & consult eds): *The Oxford Companion to the Second World War* (Oxford University Press, 1995)

Dedijer, V.: *With Tito Through the War: Partisan Diary 1941–1944*, translated by Alex Brown (Alexander Hamilton, 1951)

Djilas, Milovan: *Wartime*, translated by Michael B. Petrovich (Secker & Warburg, 1977

Foot, M.R.D.: *SOE, The Special Operations Executive 1940–1946* (Pimlico, 1999)

Footman, David: *Balkan Holiday* (Heinemann, 1935)

Fraser, David: *Alanbrooke* (HarperCollins, 1982)

Glen, Alexander: *Footholds Against a Whirlwind* (Hutchinson, 1975)

Glenny, Misha: *The Balkans 1804–1999 Nationalism, War and the Great Powers* (Granta Books, 1999)

Halley, James J.: *The Squadrons of the Royal Air Force* (Air-Britain Publications)

Heathcote, Dudley: *My Wanderings in the Balkans* (Hutchinson, 1925)

Howarth, Patrick: *Undercover: The Men and Women of the S.O.E.* (Arrow Books, 1990)

Howarth, Stephen: *A Century in Oil, the Shell Transport and Trading Company, 1899–1999* (Weidenfeld & Nicolson, 1997)

Ismay, Lord: *The Memoirs of General the Lord Ismay* (Heinemann, 1960)

Jones, W: *Twelve Months With Tito's Partisans* (Bedford, 1946)

Knezjevic, Radoje: *The 27th March, 1941* (Misic Printing Co, Windsor, Ontario, 1979)

Latham, Colin & Stobbs, Anne: *Radar: A Wartime Miracle* (Sutton Publishing Limited, 1996)

Lees, Michael: *SOE Executed* (Kimber, 1996)

Leigh-Fermor, Patrick: *Between the Woods and the Waters* (John Murray, 1986)

Macdonald, Patrick: *Through Darkness to Light* (Images Publishing (Malvern) Ltd., 1994)

MacKenzie, Prof. W.J.M.: *The Secret History of SOE: The Special Operations Executive 1940–1945* (St Ermin's Press, in association with Little, Brown and Company, 2000)

Maclean, Fitzroy: *Disputed Barricade: The Life and Times of Josip Broz-Tito, Marshal of Yugoslavia* (Jonathan Cape, 1957)

Maclean, Fitzroy: *Eastern Approaches* (Jonathan Cape, 1949)

Maclean, Lady Veronica: *Past Forgetting, a Memoir of Heroes, Adventure and Love* (Headline Books, 2002)

Macmillan: *The Macmillan Family Encyclopaedia*

Macksey, Kenneth: *Military Errors of World War Two* (Cassell Military Classics)

Marks, Leo: *Between Silk and Cyanide, The Story of S.O.E.'s Code War* (HarperCollins, 1998)

Martin, David: *The War of Disinformation* (Harcourt Brace Jovanovich, 1990)

Mason, Michael: *One Man's War* (Michael Mason, 1966)

Masters, Anthony: *Literary Agents, The Novelist as a Spy* (Basil Blackwell Ltd., 1987)

Meehan, Patricia, *A Strange Enemy People: Germans under the British 1945–50* (Peter Owen, 2001)

Minshall, Merlin: *Guilt-Edged* (Panther Books, 1977)

Nicolson, Nigel (Ed.): *Harold Nicolson, The War Years Diaries & Letters 1939–1945* (Atheneum, 1967)

Ogden, Alan: *Romania Revisited* (Centre for Romanian Studies, 2000)

Pimlott, Ben: *Hugh Dalton* (Jonathan Cape Ltd., 1985)

Pimlott, Ben (Ed.): *The Political Diary of Hugh Dalton, 1918–1940; 1945–1960* (Jonathan Cape Ltd, 1986)

Pimlott, Ben (Ed.): *The Second World War Diary of Hugh Dalton, 1940–45* (Jonathan Cape Ltd., 1986)

Ranfurly, Lady: *To War with Whitaker: The Wartime Diaries of the Countess of Ranfurly* (Mandarin Paperbacks 1995)

Ready, J. Lee: *World War Two, Nation by Nation* (Arms and Armour Press, 1995)

Reed, John: *The War in Eastern Europe* (Schreiber NYC, 1966)

Ridley, Mark, *Tito* (Constable, 1994)

Roberts, Andrew: *'The Holy Fox' A Biography of Lord Halifax* (Weidenfeld & Nicolson, 1991)

Rootham, J.: *Missfire: The Chronicle of a British Mission to Mihailovich, 1943–1944* (Chatto & Windus, 1946)

Runciman, Stephen: *A Traveller's Alphabet* (Thames & Hudson, 1991)

Schofield, Ernest and Conyers Nesbitt, Roy: *Arctic Airmen* (Kimber, 1987)

Seton-Watson, R.W.: *History of the Romanians* (Cambridge University, 1934)

Shtemenko, General S.M.: *The Last Six Months* (William Kimber & Co. Ltd., 1978)

Sweet-Escott, Bickham: *Baker Street Irregulars* (Methuen, 1965)

Trepton, Kurt: *The History of Romania* (Centre for Romanian Studies, 1997)

Walked, David: *Death at my Heels* (Chapman & Hall, 1942)

Waldock, Countess Rosie: *Athenee Palace* (Constable, 1941)

West, Nigel: *Secret War, The Story of SOE, Britain's Wartime Sabotage Organisation* (Hodder & Stoughton, 1992)

West, Rebecca: *Black Lamb and Grey Falcon* (Macmillan, first published 1941)

Wheal, Elizabeth-Anne and Pope, Stephen: *Macmillan Dictionary of The Second World War* (Macmillan, 1995)

Young, Peter, Brigadier (Ed.): *Almanac of World War II* (Hamlyn, 1981)

SPECIALIST PUBLICATIONS

Cantwell, John D.: *The Second World War, A Guide to Documents in the Public Record Office* (HMSO 1993)

Fowler, Simon, Elliott, Peter, Conyers Nesbitt, Roy & Goutter, Christina: *RAF Records in the PRO* (PRO Publications, 1994)

PAPERS

Naval Staff History: *British Mining Operations 1939–1945* (Ministry of Defence, 1973)

Pearton, Dr Maurice: *SOE in Romania*, presented at a Conference on The Special Operations Executive at the Imperial War Museum 27–29 October, 1998

INDEX

207

209

Romanians, population in Yugoslavia 6
Rootham, Captain Jasper 78, 194
Rosetti (Greek minister) 43
Royal Air Force
  205 Group 3, 107, 114, 116–18, 140,
    146
    aircraft 165–8
    attacks on Ploesti 123
    losses 127
    mine laying operations 3, 128–40
    Operations Record Book 159–64
  Bomber Command 124
  cooperation with Royal Navy 116
Royal Navy
  cooperation with RAF 116
  mine sweeping unit 71
Runciman, Steven 36
Russians
  3rd Ukrainian Army 82, 89, 96–7, 119
  contact with Allies 86–7, 107
  and Eastern Europe countries 148–9
  Red Army 75, 82–92, 95–100

sabotage of Danube shipping 3, 32, 60–6,
  73
sabotage of rail traffic 36, 40
sabotage of oil wells 26–7
Sanderson, Ivan 4
Saseno U-boat base 4
Schofield, Flight-Lieutenant 191
Secret Intelligence Service 11
  and Foreign Office 13
  and Naval Intelligence 12–13
  sabotage of oil wells 26–7
  Section D 12–13, 30, 36
Serbia 7, 9, 43–45, 79, 154
  Yugoslavia *coup d'état* 59–61
Serbian Democratic Party 41, 44
Serbian Peasant Party 41, 43, 49, 59
Serbs
  and Croats 80, 149, 154
  history 35, 154
  political parties 41
  population in Yugoslavia 6
Seton-Watson, Hugh 63, 147, 190
Shaw, Lieutenant 128, 160
Shone, Terence (later Sir Terence) 34
Sicily liberated 69
Siguranta 15, 19
Sima, Horia 23
Simovic, General 60
Simpson, Air Commodore J.H.T. 140, 165

SIS *see* Secret Intelligence Service
Slessor, Air Marshal Sir John 3, 72, 114,
  165, 175
Slovenes, population 6–7
Slovenia 9, 154
SOE *see* Special Operations Executive
Sofia 95
South African Air Force 118, 137, 140–2
Spaatz, General Carl 124, 198
Special Operations Executive 12, 30–33,
  73, 147
  Bari 71, 74, 101–2, 104
  Cairo 74, 83, 101
  Danube Sabotage Progress Report
    101
  relations with Glen 73–4
  in Yugoslavia 40, 42, 59
Spitsbergen 69
Sporborg, Colonel Harry N. 31, 183
SS 29
Stalingrad 97
Stefanescu, Captain 27
Stirby, Prince Barbu 147, 199
Stirling, Colonel Frank 45
Stoyadinovic, Dr Milan 41, 186
subversive operations in the Balkans
  12–21
Sucharnikov, Colonel 87, 89, 97
Sulina 20, 39

Talbot Rice, Lieutenant Colonel 73
Taylor, George 42, 58, 187
Termode 18–19
Thomas, Flt. Lt. Norman W. 131
Tito, Marshal 44, 78, 80, 193
  post war 148–54
Titulescu, Nicolas 24
Tobescu, Aurel 25
Tolbukhin, Marshal Fyodor 82, 89, 95,
  119, 195
Tripartite Pact 46, 58, 187–8
Tudjman 152
Tupanjanin 42, 59, 63, 65–6
Turkey 17
Turks, population in Romania 10
Turner, Mark 38
Turner, Sergeant 74–8, 84, 87, 98, 138
Turnu Severin 52–3, 89, 91, 99, 109
  attacks on 123
Turpin, Ralph 83, 87–9, 98, 101–5,
  108–12
Twilfit Mission 84, 101, 202

CZECHOSLOVA
(occupied)

Munich

Passat

GERMANY

Linz

Vienna

Bratislava
Komarno

R. Danube

B

AUSTRIA
(occupied)

HUNGA
(occupied)

Ljubljana

Ba

Mohacs

Venice

Trieste

Zagreb

Vukovar

N

R. Sava

Rimini

Belgra

JUGOSLAV

Ancona

THE ADRIATIC

Split

Sarajev

ITALY

Dubrovnik
Kotor

Foggia

Bari

0   100   200

Kilometres